a sketch of
VENETIAN HISTORY

Library and Archives Canada Cataloguing in Publication

Title: A sketch of Venetian history / written and illustrated by Sarah Pierroz.

Names: Pierroz, Sarah, author, illustrator.

Identifiers: Canadiana (print) 20210203579 | Canadiana (ebook) 20210203595 | ISBN 9781771615846 (softcover) | ISBN 9781771615853 (PDF) | ISBN 9781771615860 (EPUB) | ISBN 9781771615877 (Kindle)

Subjects: LCSH: Venice (Italy)—History—Pictorial works. | LCSH: Venice (Italy)— Pictorial works. | LCSH: Venice (Italy)—Guidebooks.

Classification: LCC DG676 .P54 2021 | DDC 945/.31100222—dc23

Published by Mosaic Press, Oakville, Ontario, Canada, 2020.

MOSAIC PRESS, Publishers
www.Mosaic-Press.com
Copyright © Sarah Pierroz

All rights reserved. Without limiting the rights under copyright reserved here, no part of this publication may be reproduced, stored in or introduced into any retrieval system, or transmitted in any form or by any means—electronic, mechanical, by photocopy, recording or otherwise—without the prior written permission and consent of both the copyright owners and the Publisher of this book.
All materials in this book are published on a non-exclusive basis.

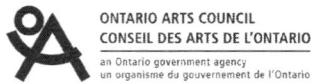

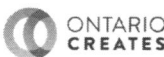

MOSAIC PRESS
1252 Speers Road, Units 1 & 2, Oakville, Ontario, L6L 5N9
(905) 825-2130 • info@mosaic-press.com • www.mosaic-press.com

"And Polo said: 'Every time I describe a city
I am saying something about Venice'."

-Italo Calvino, Invisible Cities

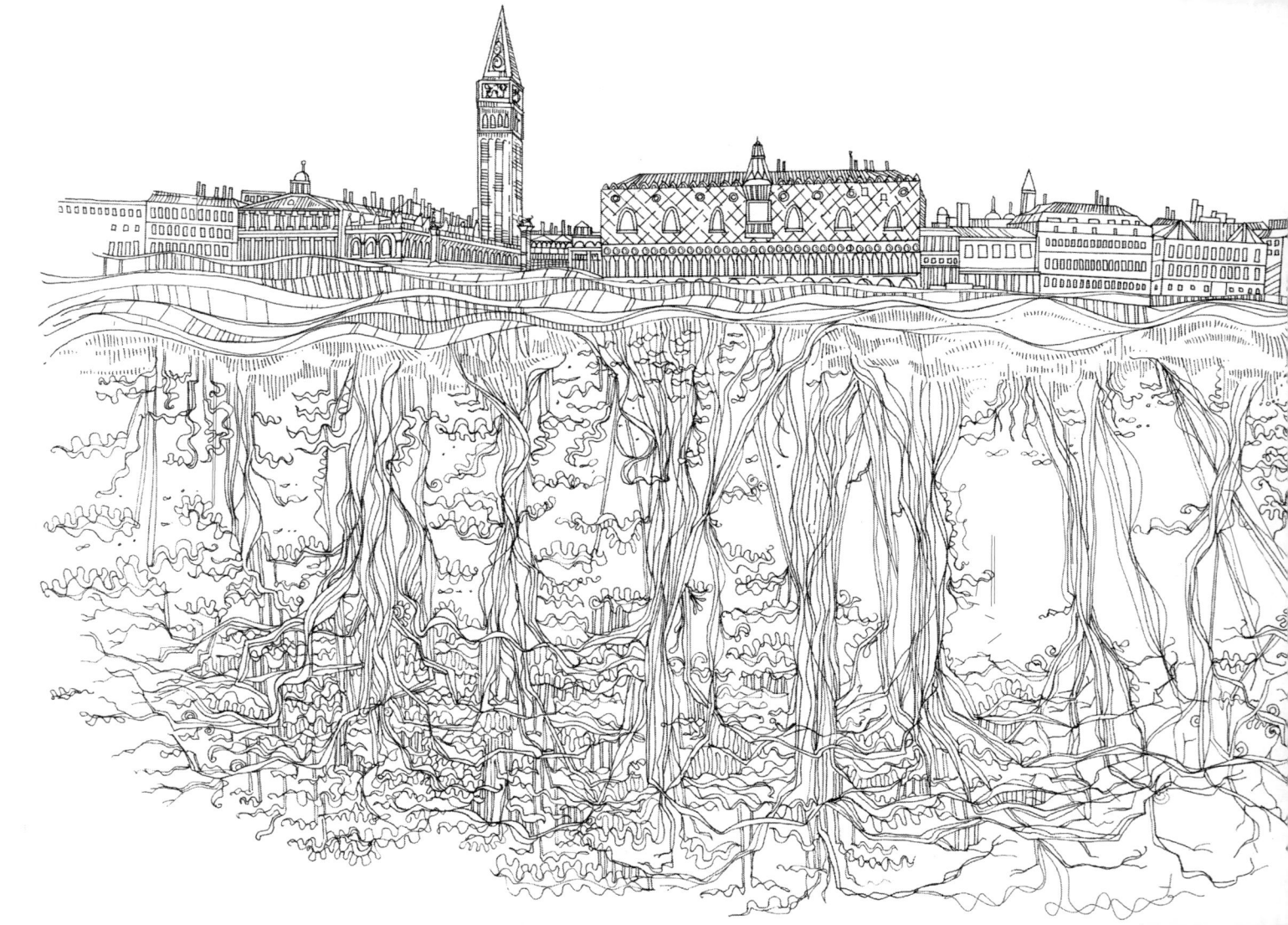

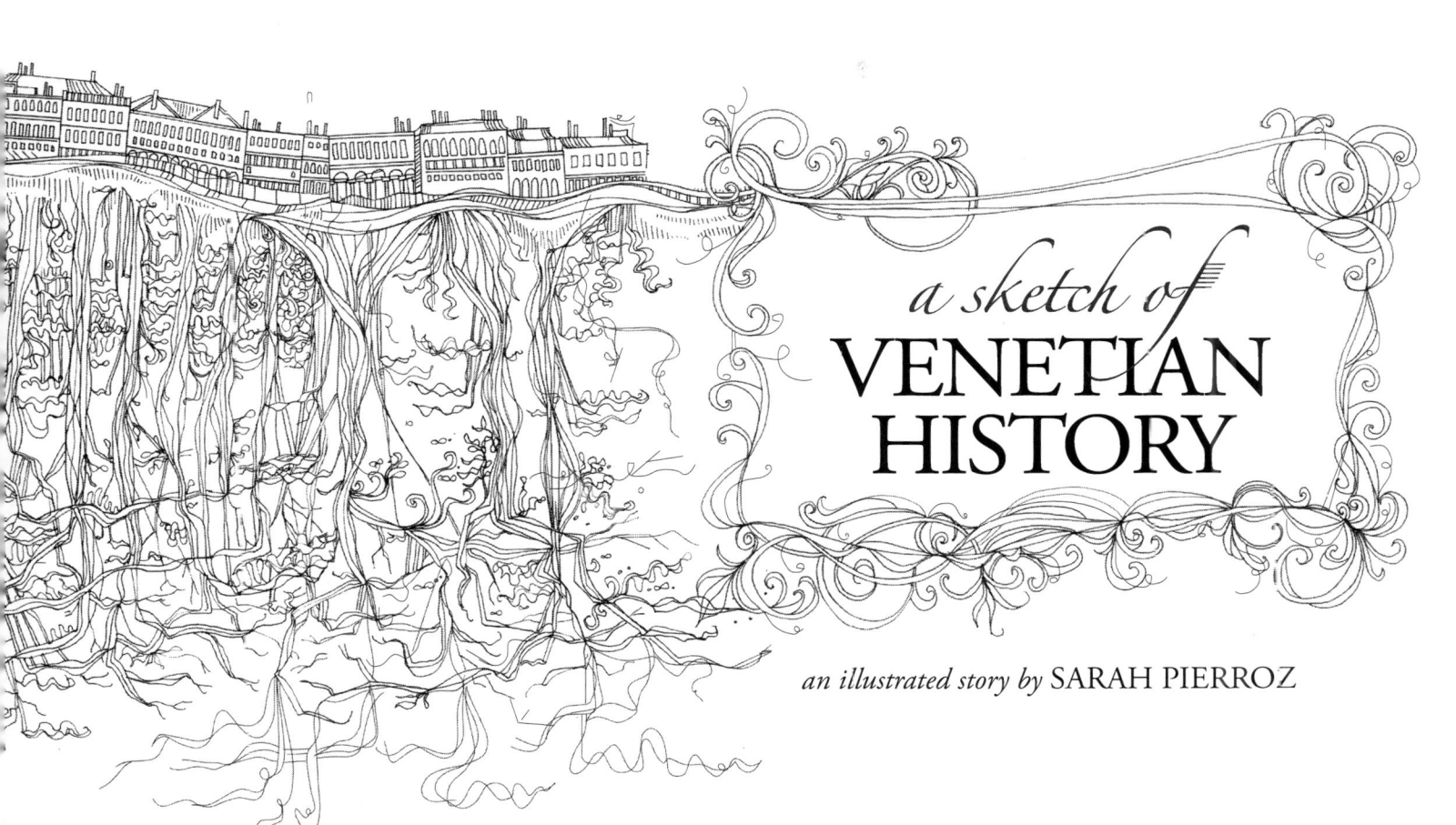

a sketch of VENETIAN HISTORY

an illustrated story by SARAH PIERROZ

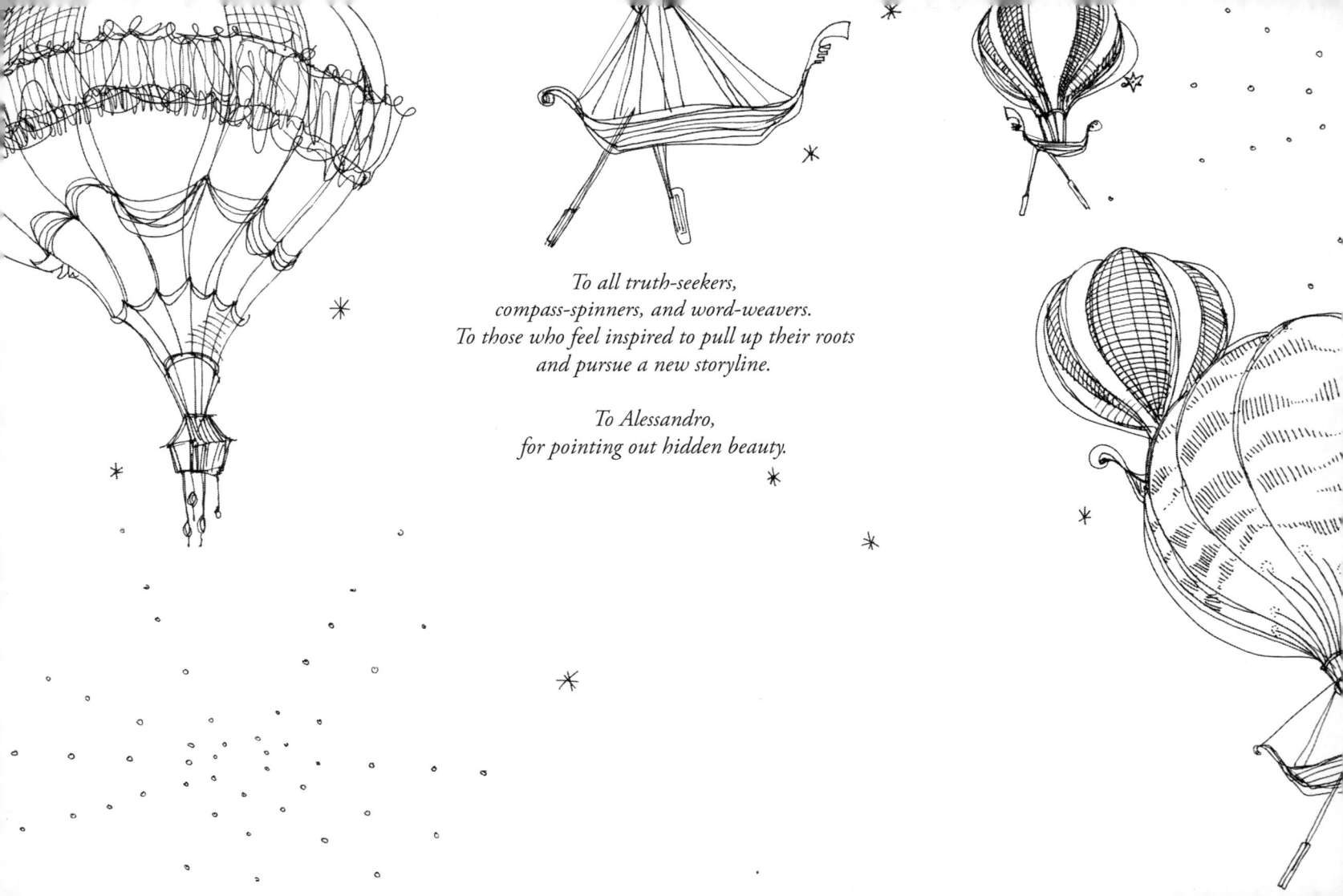

*To all truth-seekers,
compass-spinners, and word-weavers.
To those who feel inspired to pull up their roots
and pursue a new storyline.*

*To Alessandro,
for pointing out hidden beauty.*

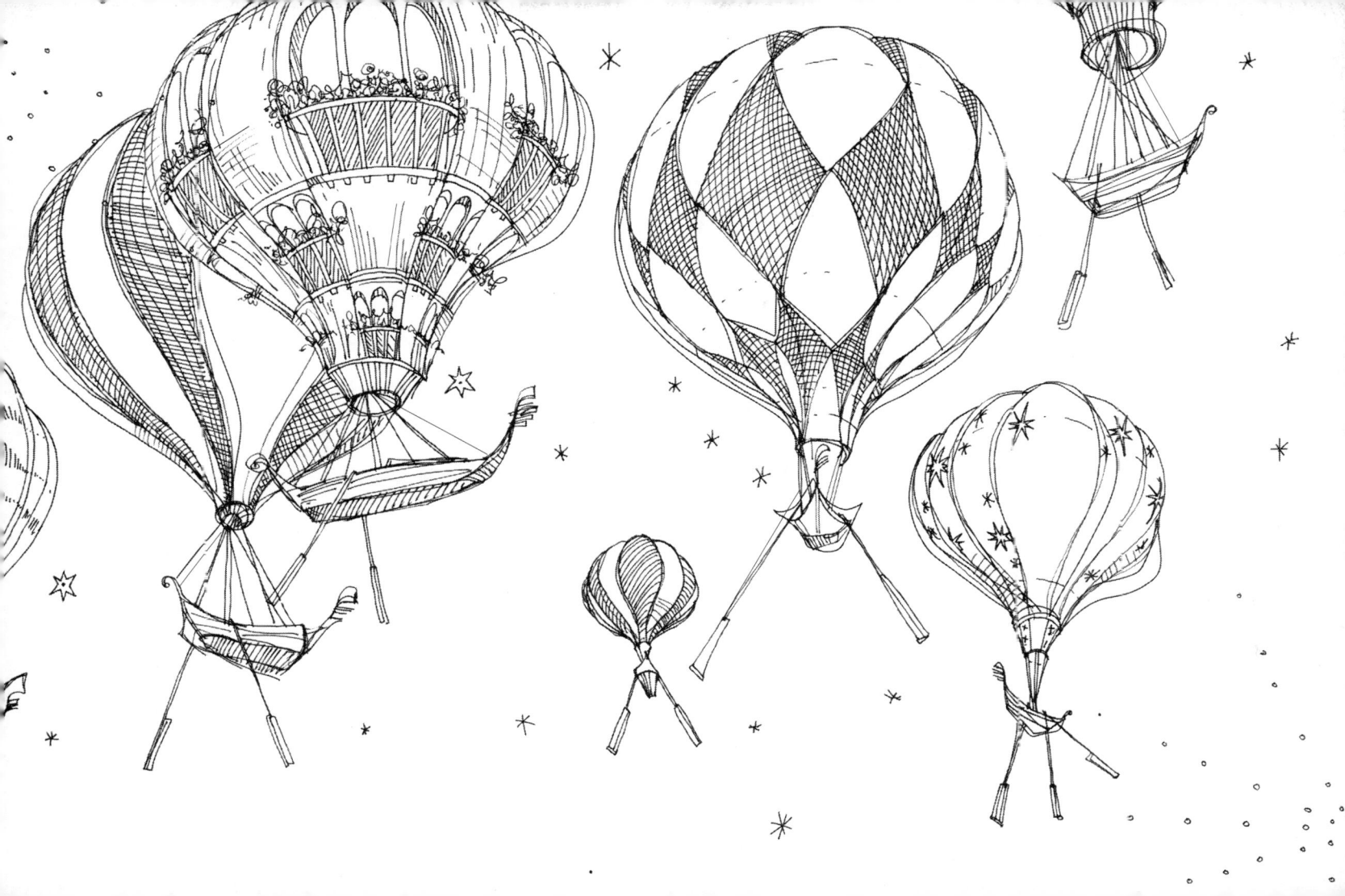

benvenuti a venezia. ("welcome to venice.")

She is Mesmerizing, non? Or is Stunning the word? Charming? Her beauty is inescapable. Standing here, perched in the middle of a vast sea, presenting a delight at every corner, you know you are truly somewhere different.

In Venice, even the ordinary can be unbearably beautiful. Either by twisting footpaths or a leisurely boat ride, you have all the freedom to explore this intricate maze. Whether we are indulging at a *gelaterie* or nursing a warm *macchiato* next to a Renaissance masterpiece; stealing a kiss in a perfect, photogenic nook; admiring a balcony bursting with flowers, pouring over a building sewn together with hanging laundry; or enjoying some other equally charming, unexpected, aesthetic moment, Venice has the power to completely captivate us.

It is easy to overlook the reality behind her cracked and slanted buildings, to forget that she is precariously balanced on top of a slippery base of silt and sand. In fact, this city should have crumbled back into the water years ago. Yet, she prevails. We must remember that the sea has ultimate reign here.

When we notice the wild waters swirling and pushing against every edge of this city, we come to realize that Venice is battling a force greater than the human spirit. Any sense of permanence here is deceiving. She is always changing. She is always moving forward.

It is worth the effort to tread a little slower and consider what came before. If we learn a few of her stories, dig deeper into her history, and try to imagine her many invisible aspects, we start to see the many layers of her enchantment and learn from her past. Then we may fall in love with Venice again and again, each time more profoundly.

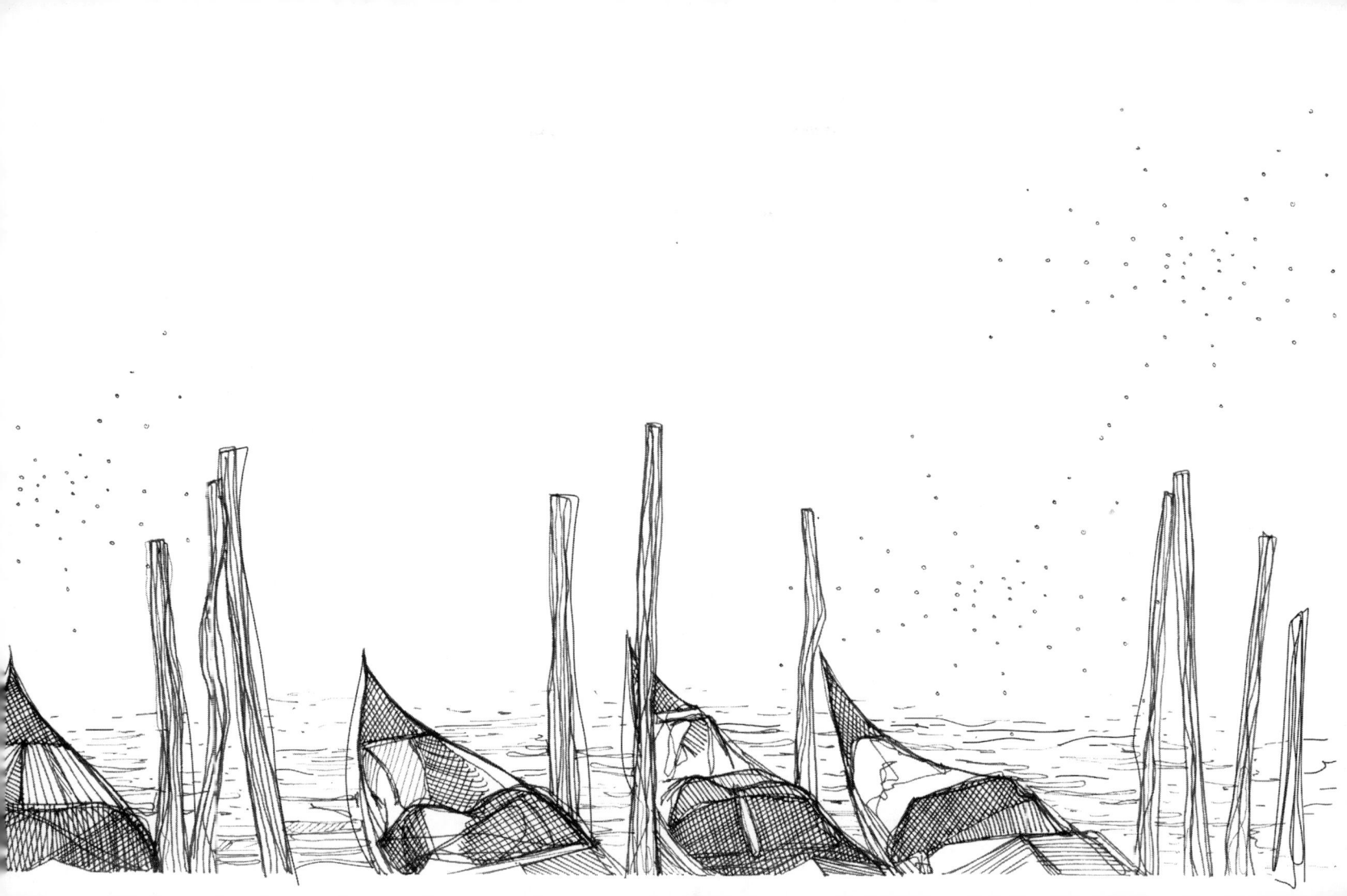

chapters

0 ········· Introduction
1 ········· Starting Point
2 ········· Expansion
3 ········· Struggles
4 ········· Exchanges
5 ········· Implosion
6 ········· Perseverance

timeline	4000 - 1000 B.C.E	5th - 9th Century	9th - 13th Century
	introduction.	**starting point.**	**expansion.**
	• Lagoon formation • Early wildlife • Fishermen & salt miners	• Barbarian invasions • Early architectural structures & foundations • Saltworks & mainland trade • Torcello, Pepin invasions & malaria threats • St. Mark's bones & *basilica*	• Early Rialto & *Piazza* • Expanding salt trade, Byzantinum-Venetian partners, the Golden Book • *Arsenale*, Dante • Crusades & four bronze horses • Spice monopoly, Marco Polo, Far East exploration • Republic maturation

14th - 16th Century	15th - 16th Century	17th - 18th Century	19th Century - Present
struggles.	exchanges.	implosion.	perseverance.
• The Plague, Wars with Genoa • Age of Discovery: Zen Brothers, Dias, Columbus, Cabot, Vespucci, Verrazzano • League of Cambrai • Inquisition, Reformation, *Concilio di Trento*, Sarpi • Moneylenders, the *Ghetto* • Marrani, Battle of Lepanto	• Venetian Renaissance: printing press, Manutius, Sansovino, & Palladio • Liberal learning: University of Padua, Anatomy & Vesalius • Great cosmopolitan, Guilds, glass makers & artisans • The Golden Age, Oil painting, the Venetian School, Mainland nobles & Country estates • Galileo & the spyglass	• Decadence: casinos, courtesans, Casanova, Grand Tour, Canaletto • Extravagant Baroque: theatre, opera, music, *Commedia dell'Arte*, Vivaldi • *Carnevale*: festivities, masks & indulgence • Age of Reason: fashion, cafes, revolution, Rousseau, Voltaire • Napoleon, Manin, French occupation • Austrian rule, Industrialization, *spritz*	• Mainland identity, partisans, Cavour, Kingdom of Italy • The Romantics, Byron, Turner, Whistler • Modernism vs. preservation, Ruskin, Campanile collapse • War, Futurism, Fascism • *Acqua alta*: flooding, tourism, sustainability • Ecological concerns, *MOSE* • Perseverance, *sempre dritto*

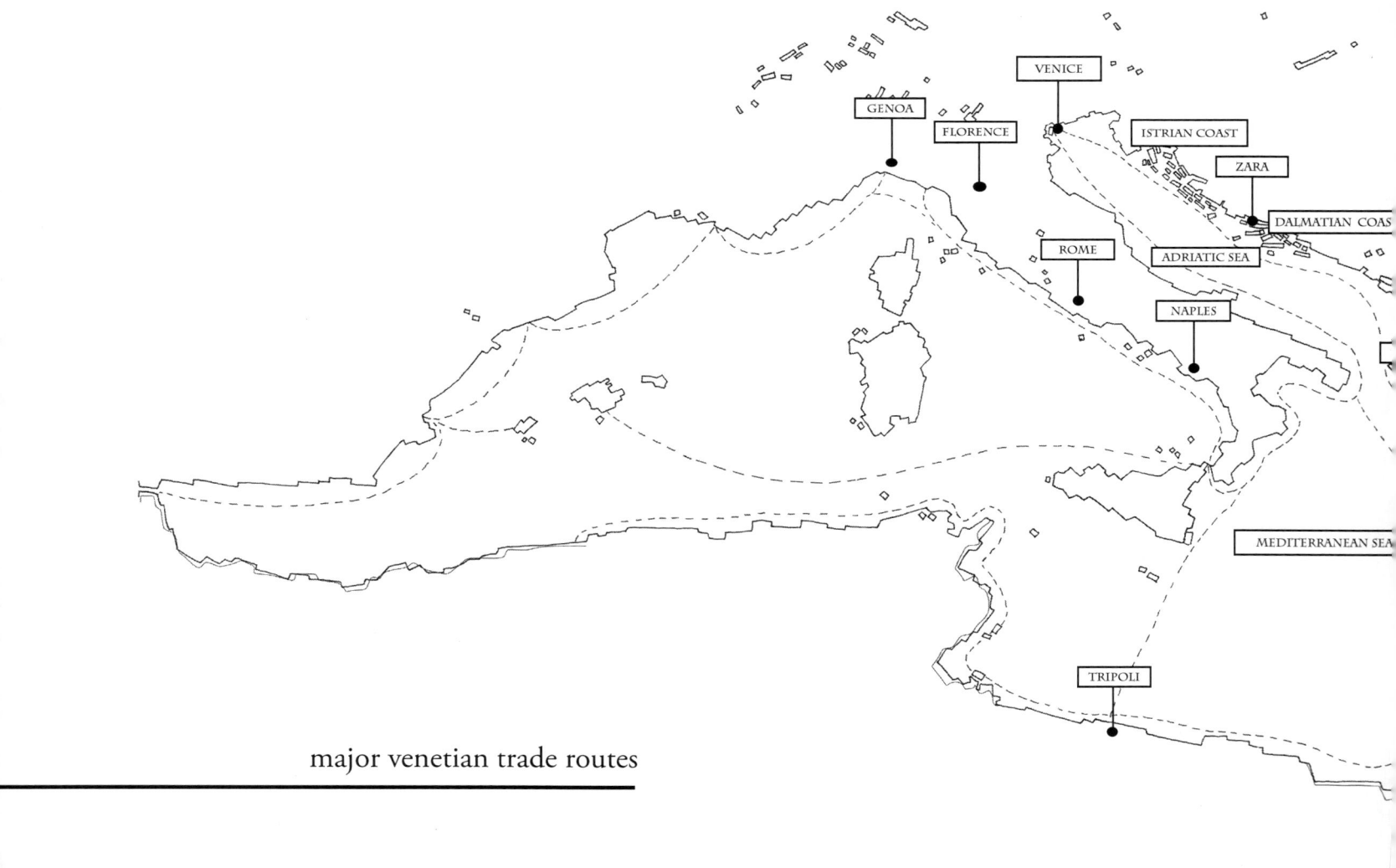

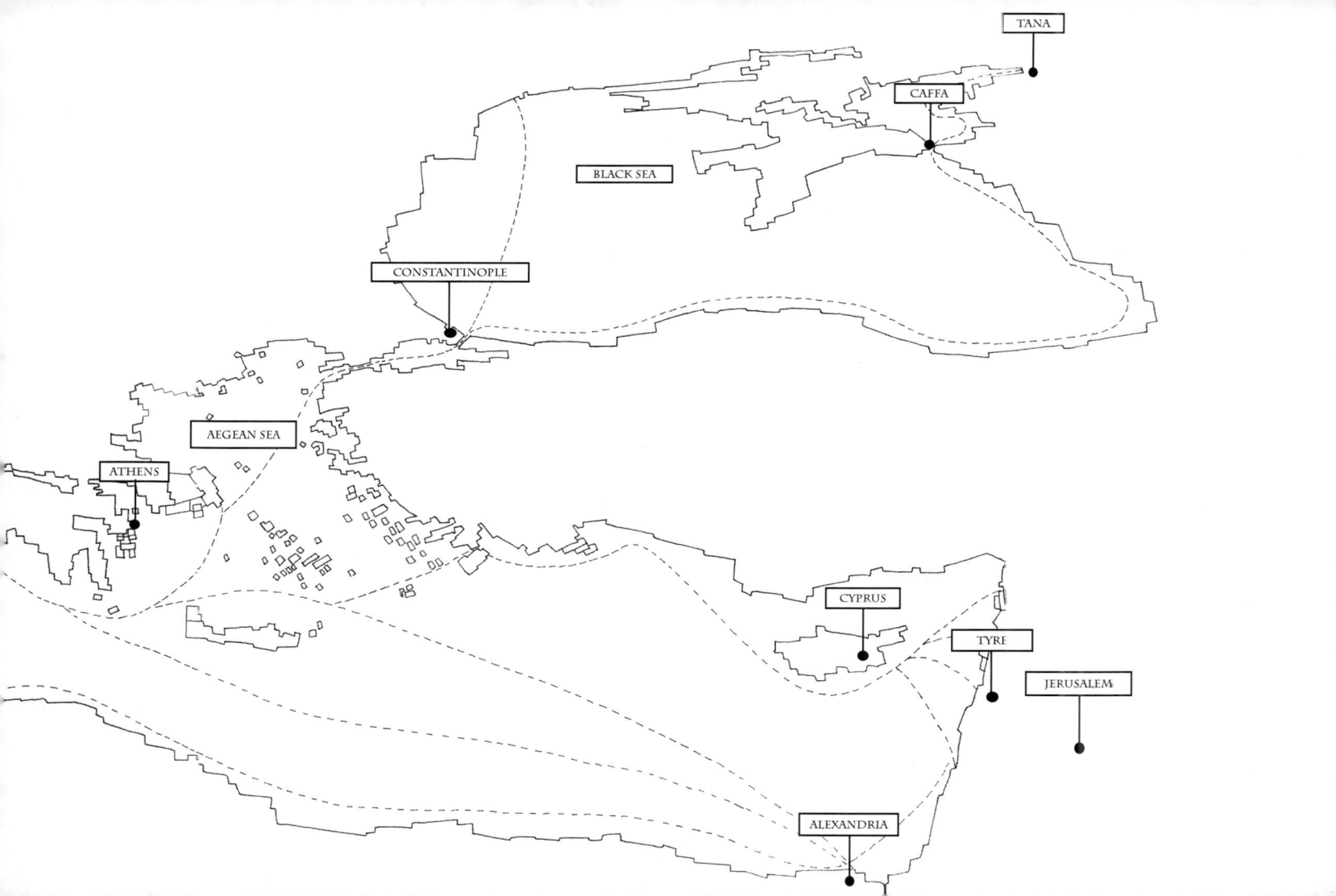

introduction: c'era una volta

(4000 - 1000 B.C.E)

c'era una volta…("once upon a time…")

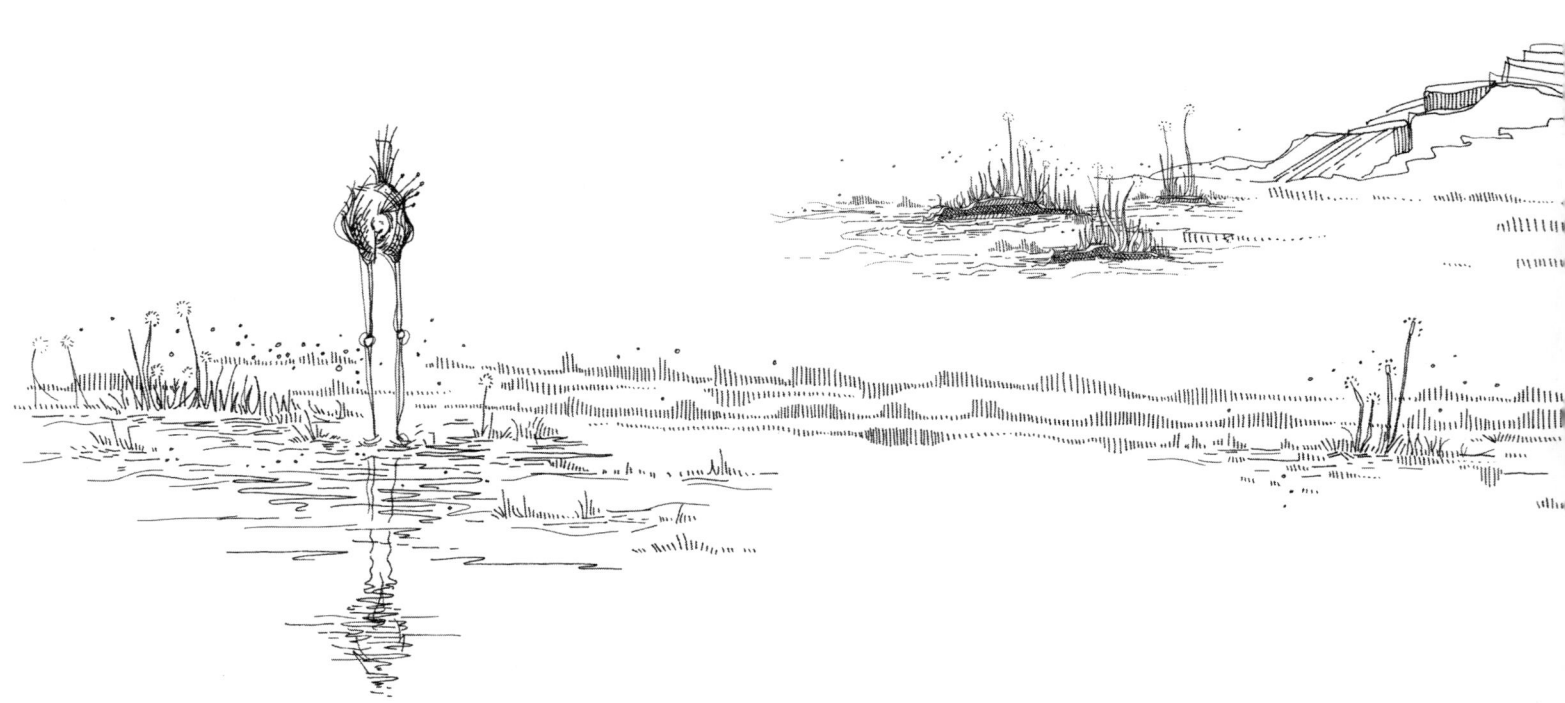

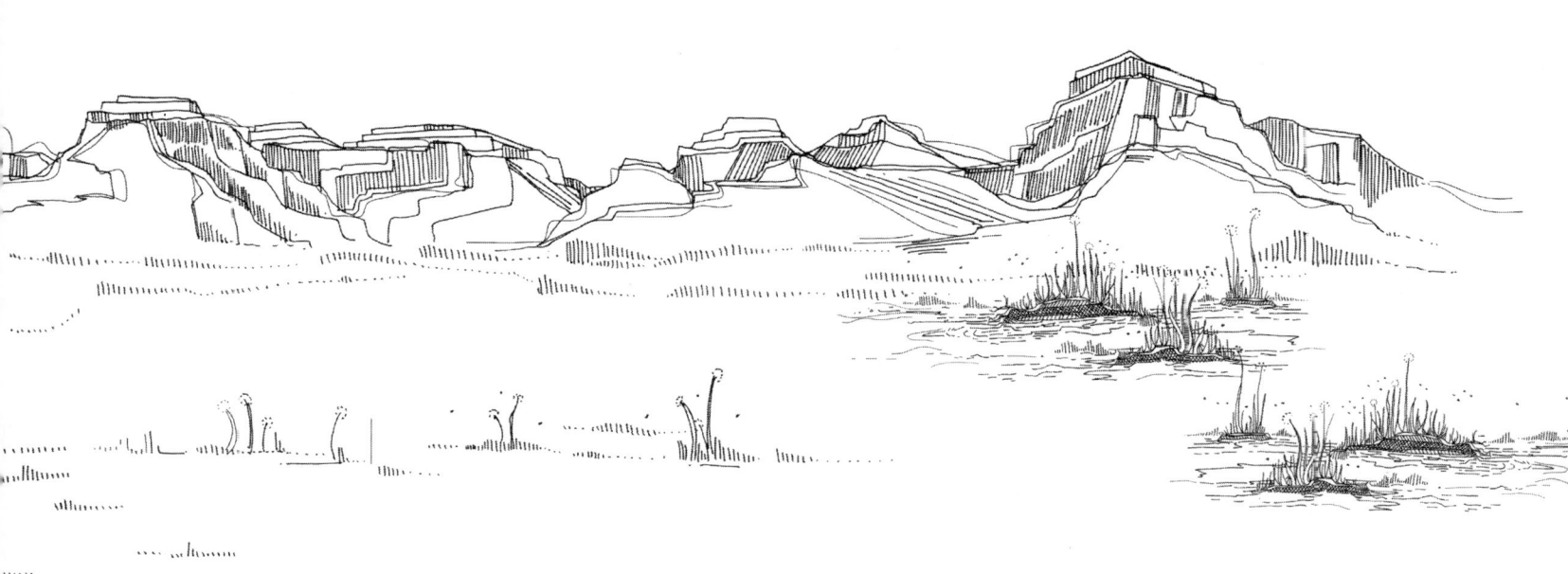

there was a mountain and many rivers...

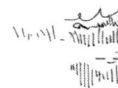

Close your eyes and imagine a large, flat body of water ebbing and flowing into a shallow mudbank. There is not much here, apart from a few empty islands, the hollowing sense of a nearby, yet muffled, sea, some tall reeds and blades of grass piercing into the sky, and snow-capped mountains silently peaking in the distance. From a distance, these scattered islands appear more like the smooth backs of resting whales, rather than any sort of firm ground to build upon.

This lagoon was formed over 6,000 years ago, where the mouths the Piave, Sile, and Brenta rivers came out to meet the flow of half a dozen others in the north-western corner of the Adriatic. Fresh water rushed down from the Alps and the Apennines, and along the way, relentlessly grounded the mountainous rock into a fine silt that was tossed out into the large, salty sea.

Over years, estuaries pushed, pulled, and piled up the debris to form long, thin lines of islands, called *lidi*. They came to shield and protect the lagoon from the vast, open sea. All the while, the sediment continued to pour in. It shifted with the currents, creating a mercurial mix of wide floors and deep, elusive channels.

Too shallow to hold deep sapphire Mediterranean blues, or bright, emerald green like the Adriatic, the lagoon usually presents a vibrant turquoise hue. Each drop of water steals shimmers and glistens in the light of the sun and of the moon, both equally splendid displays.

Overall, the lagoon is at the mercy of the moon; it directs her tides to rise and fall, and wash over her islands. It keeps her waters shifting and moving, so much so, that everything stays in a quiet, constant state of flux.

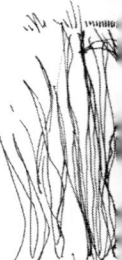

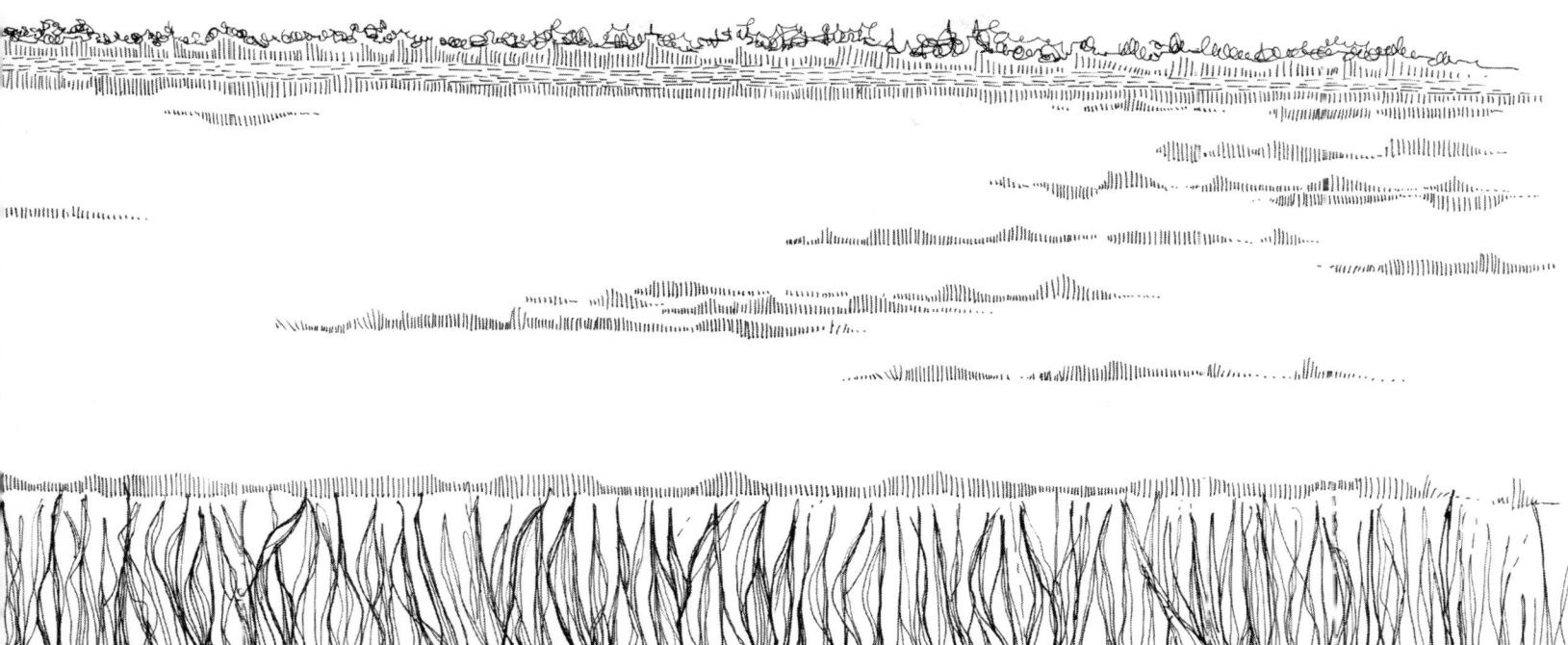

...and a lagoon with a few inhabitants...

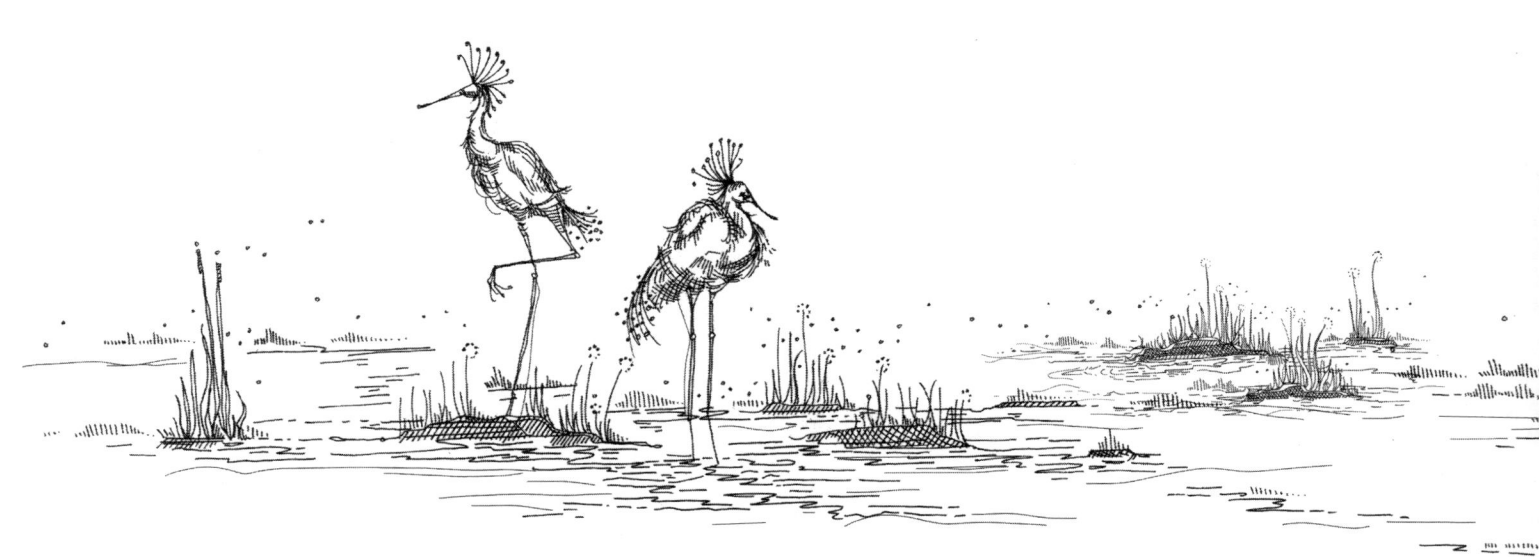

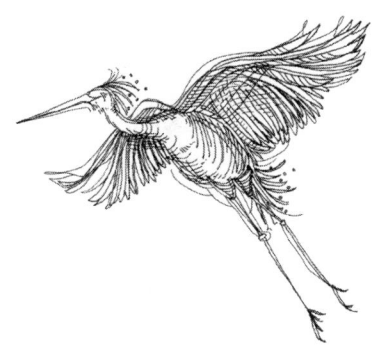

Upon first impression, the lagoon must have appeared completely inhospitable, especially when the surrounding seas thundered against her shoals.

Every now and then she was visited by a swarm of feverishly buzzing mosquitoes, some wriggling crabs, prawns, the odd octopus, a large school of migrating fish, some eels coming in with the tide, or a few aquatic birds finding nesting sites on the scrubby mudflats. Cranes and wild ducks would effortlessly careen in on expansive wings to snatch their next meal or float on her calmed waters for a rest. The waterbirds would bow and tilt their tall crowns of feathers in every possible direction as they shook their catch past their perfectly adept bills, deep down into their throats.

The wildlife here experienced a sparse, yet rich, uninhibited existence. Even after the first human settlers crept in, the wildlife remained unharmed, tucked away, and safe within the secluded lagoon.

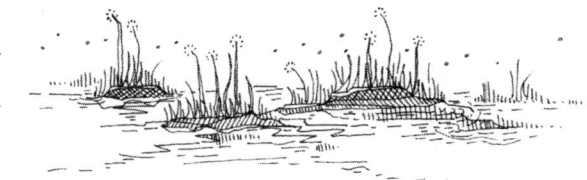

...then, a few passing visitors...

From as early as three thousand years ago, more lively communities began to gather along the coastline. Populations scattered along the north-eastern edge of Italy, and built up the shores of present day Slovenia and Croatia. Yet, the distant lagoon remained largely isolated.

From time to time a few fishermen, bird fowlers and salt miners ventured into the lagoon's difficult shallows and sludge. In specially designed, flat-bottomed boats and barges, they navigated her iridescent waters, leaving ephemeral imprints. They memorized the lagoon's vast network of uneven channels and marked her deep, elusive trenches with long, wooden poles.

By closely observing the lagoon's nature and temperament, they knew to return home before the wind swept in with the afternoon tide and chopped and churned the waters in a treacherous, heaving mass.

Only the most skilled navigators, braved her daunting waters. Early in the morning, they cast their nets, chased migrating birds, or dragged and scraped the bottom of her salty ponds. These few were rewarded with brimming baskets for their families to share, store away, or trade with others on mainland, or *terra firma*. For the most part, the lagoon maintained a mostly anonymous, sedate existence, far removed from the mainland bustle.

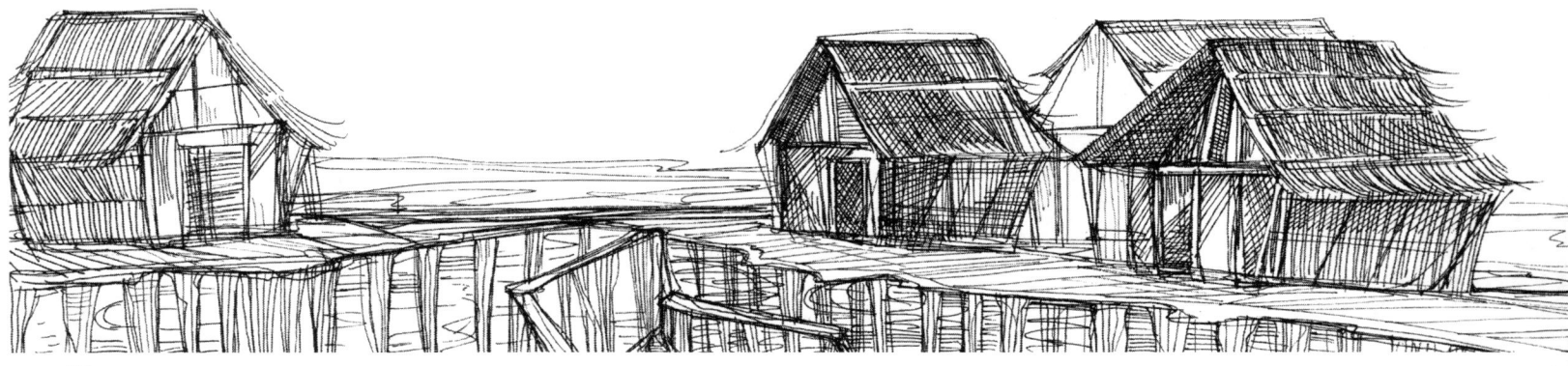

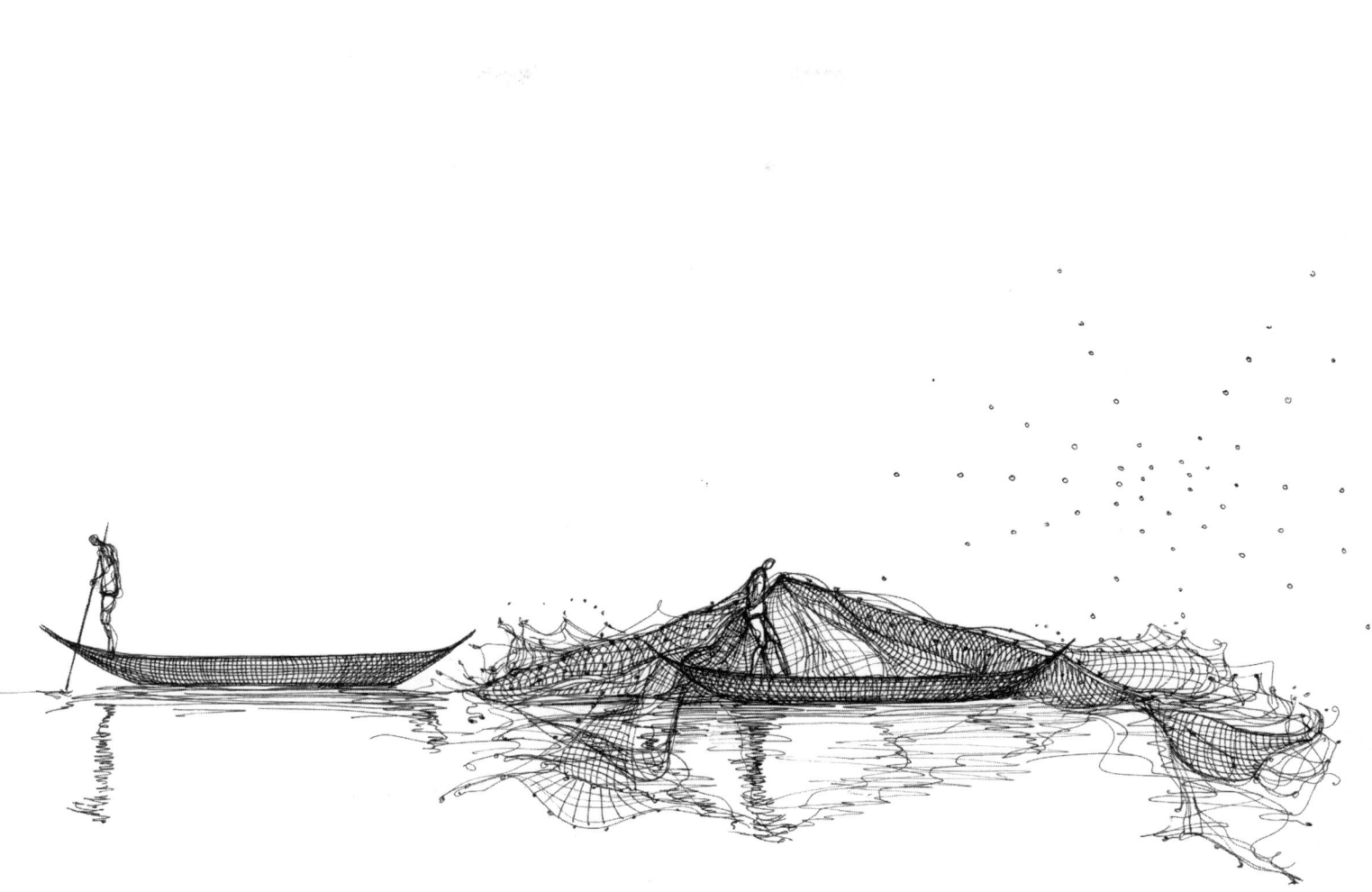

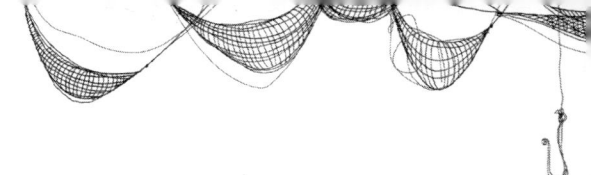

...and an impossible dream of hope.

In the second century B.C.E., as the *Veneti* populations came under Roman rule, the Emperor Augustus formally distinguished their region as *Venetia*. Their province extended from the Alps to the Adriatic Sea, and from Istria down to the Oglio river. The lively city centres of Padua, Altino, and Grado soon emerged, and Aquileia was set as the region's capital.

The *Veneti* were mostly merchants who traded salt, honey and cheese. They were so skilled in the sea that they could reach markets in ports as far away as Greece. With increased trade and resources, their cities adopted characteristic Roman structures. Whilst elaborate forums, temples, bath houses, amphitheaters, and basilicas organized their communal spaces, the *Veneti* populations also stratified and came to express Roman political and social systems. Meanwhile, the peripheral waters of these developing coastal cities remained marginal, functioning at most as a distant port.

With no solid ground, no freshwater stores, no fertile land, and no building materials, there was little reason for anyone to journey to this particular lagoon at all. It certainly seemed a place of impossible beginnings. And yet, this shallow stretch of sea became the birthplace of Venice. From here, from the very mud, like life itself, a thriving, dominating, elaborate empire emerged, reigned, celebrated and came to a tragic collapse. It may challenge the beautiful limits of your imagination to contemplate how so much ingenuity could have emerged from so little.

Out of elemental simplicity, this backwater became a destination for incomparable opportunities, excessive abundance and flooding creativity. By the sixteenth century, a tourist guide had already acclaimed that the name *Venezia* must have derived from the Latin *veni etiam*, which professes to all to "come back again to see this beautiful place".

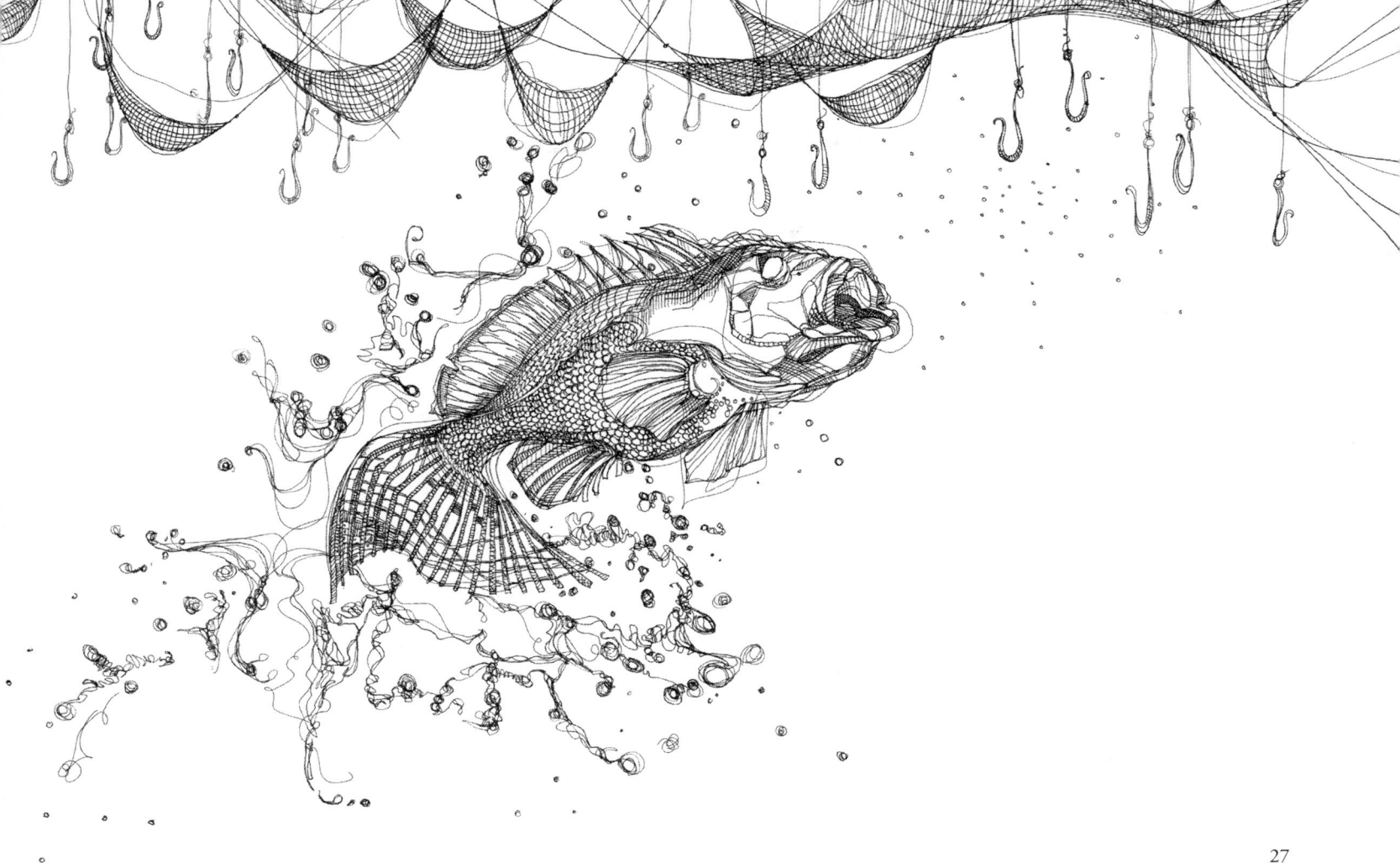

part one: starting point

(5th century - 9th century)

the barbarian invasion hideaway.

The lagoon remained relatively undisturbed for thousands of years, but in the fifth century everything changed. The Roman Empire was beginning to collapse and more than one hundred thousand dissatisfied, nomadic barbarians squirming on its edges were willing to rise up against it.

These *barbi*, or "foreigners", like the Visogoths from the distant Germanic forests, and the Huns from the Far East, under the leadership of the notorious Attila, fearlessly marched over the Alps and into the sunny lands of Italy. They were unquestionably master horsemen and skilled warriors. They fought with unabashed violence and sent a tangible tremor of fear down through the Italian peninsula.

However, being from landlocked areas in Central Europe and Asia, few barbarians knew how to swim or handle a boat, and most feared the sea's far-reaching waters.

Many stealthy Roman populations strung along the northeastern shores of the mainland fled into the lagoon. They waited in its sheltered waters until each gruesome raid stormed by. They ruthlessly pushed southward and tried to claim Rome, the centre of the universe at that time. After each wave of attack, the overwrought lagoon refugees would return home to resume their quotidian way of life.

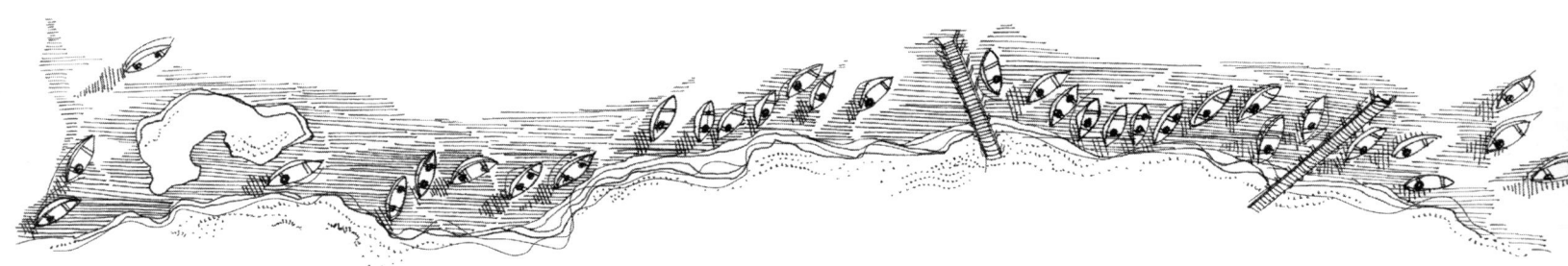

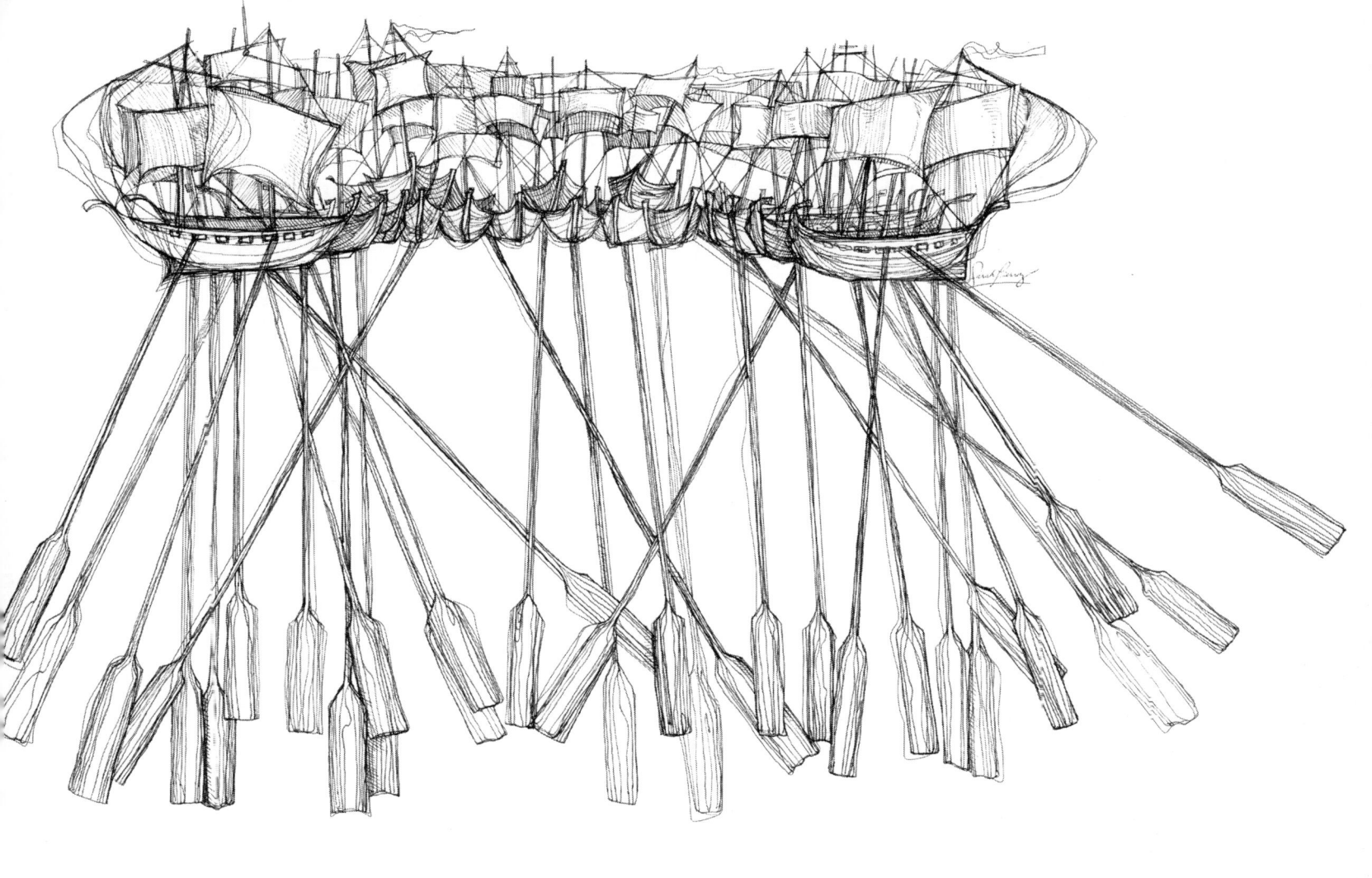

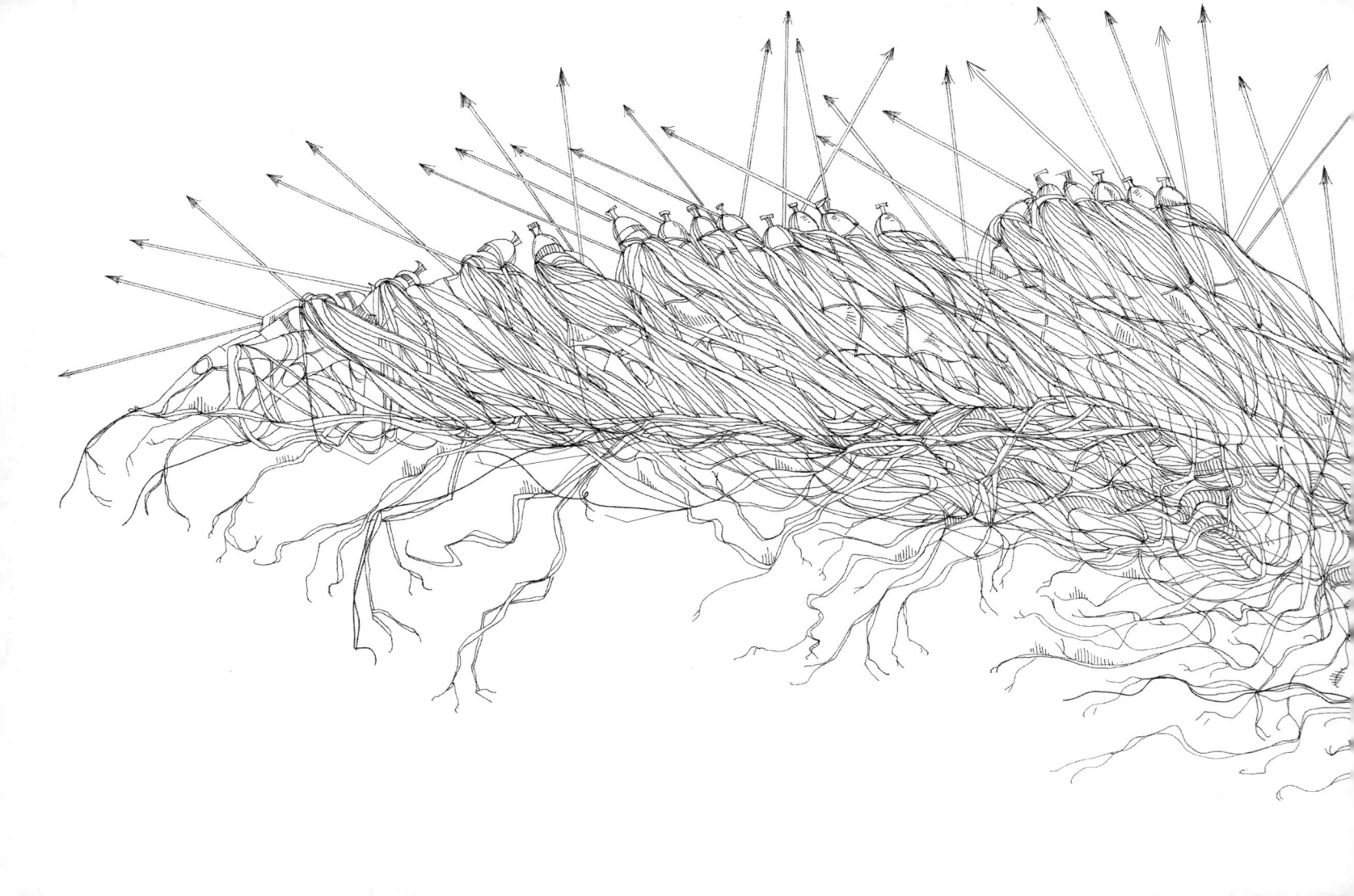

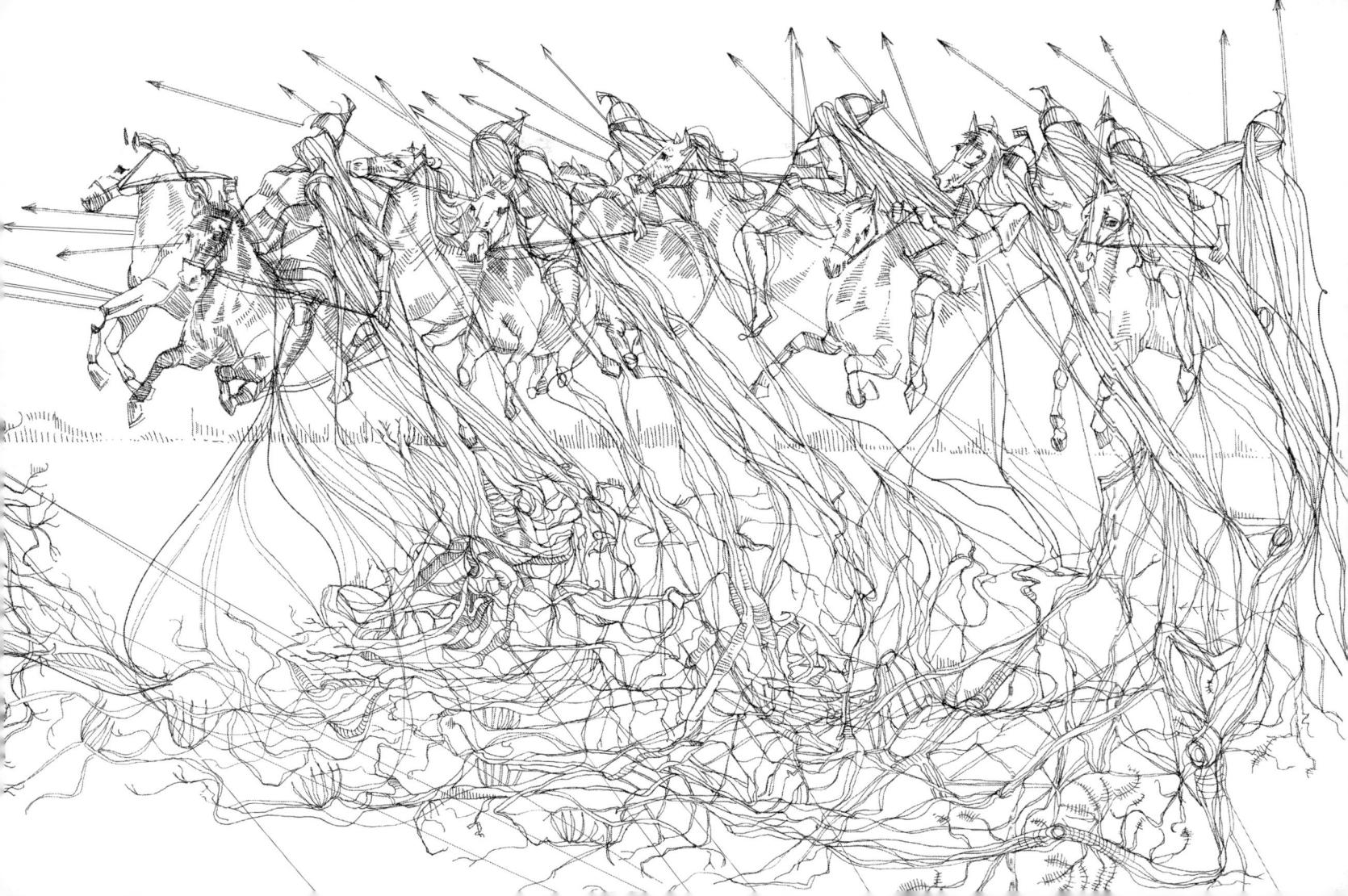

the floating city.

The protective waters of the lagoon proved especially essential in the sixth century against the ruthless *longobarde*, or "long beard" barbarian incursions. Unlike the previous attacks, this particular tribe did not continue on down to Rome. Instead, they forcefully rooted in northeast Italy and stayed for over two hundred years; the "Lombardy" region still holds their name.

The *longobarde's* riotous settlement on the *terra firma* left many casualties stranded in the far away lagoon. They had to fortify their hideaway and permanently assemble on the waters. As the bloodshed worsened on the mainland, more and more Roman descendents migrated to the lagoon, where they watched pieces of their beloved civilization collapse. Eventually, after the many waves of invasions marauding further south, Rome succumbed to the barbarians, and later the Franks.

After the western Roman Empire fell, its eastern brother, the Byzantine Empire inherited its surviving fragments, such as the capital, coastal city of Ravenna. However, its heart was in the other corner of the Mediterranean, in the faraway city of Constantinople. The Byzantine Emperor appointed a governor, or *exarch*, to oversee his estranged, western outpost. But it was mostly left as a lonely kin, an increasingly autonomous afterthought.

In as early as 466 C.E., representatives of the lagoon's small, separate communities worked out a loose self-governing system, which vested their powers in tribunes. Even without a strong sense of identity, survival was everyone's focus. They all sought to strengthen their trade and maximize their defenses. Above all, they kept far away from dragging conflicts with the *longobarde* and feudalism on the mainland, and moved towards forming an independent republic.

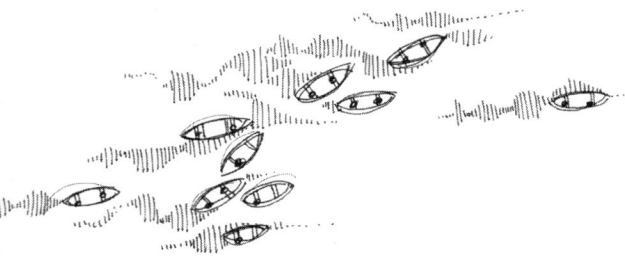
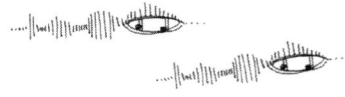

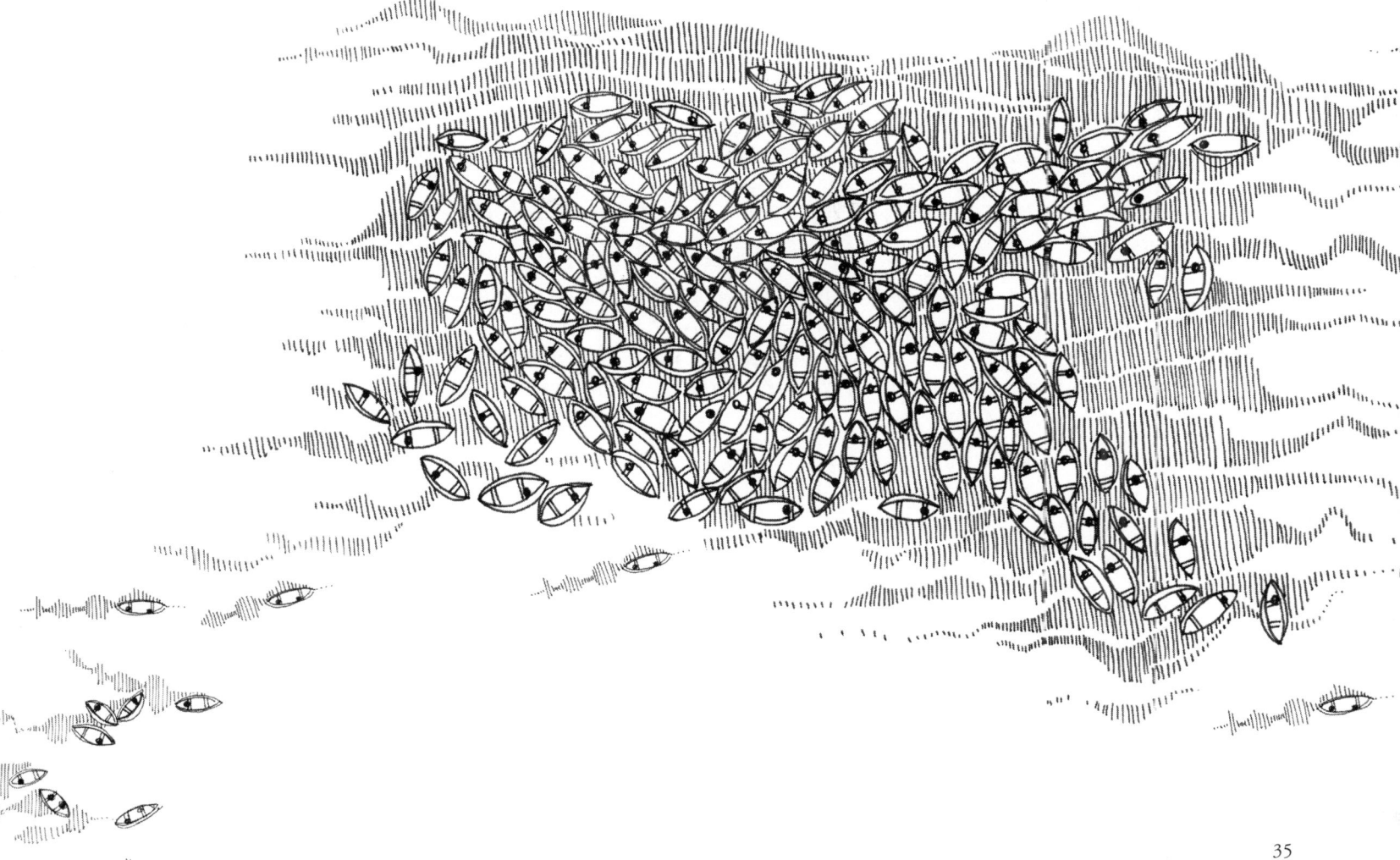

early shelters and structures.

The lagoon offered its populace a protection which was more secure than any medieval city wall. For some time, it served well as their only defence against the *barbi* and other surrounding powers, who were put off by the sea.

Beyond safety, the remote area provided few raw materials to its refugees: fish, mud and salty water. They had little option but to embrace a maritime life. Yet, these rudimentary beginnings proved to be enough for these desperately resilient people.

In the tradition of the region's fishermen, the early Venetians quickly constructed huts, with thatched roofs, shored up by bundles of pliant reeds and willow, on any semblance of land. These *casoni* resembled old, worn birds' nests, perched high above the lagoon's ever-changing waters and beds of seaweed. Like seabirds, they sought steady footing, equally divided between the sea and the land. Maintaining this fundamentally fragile balance would challenge the lagoon dwellers for the remainder of their residence in the sea.

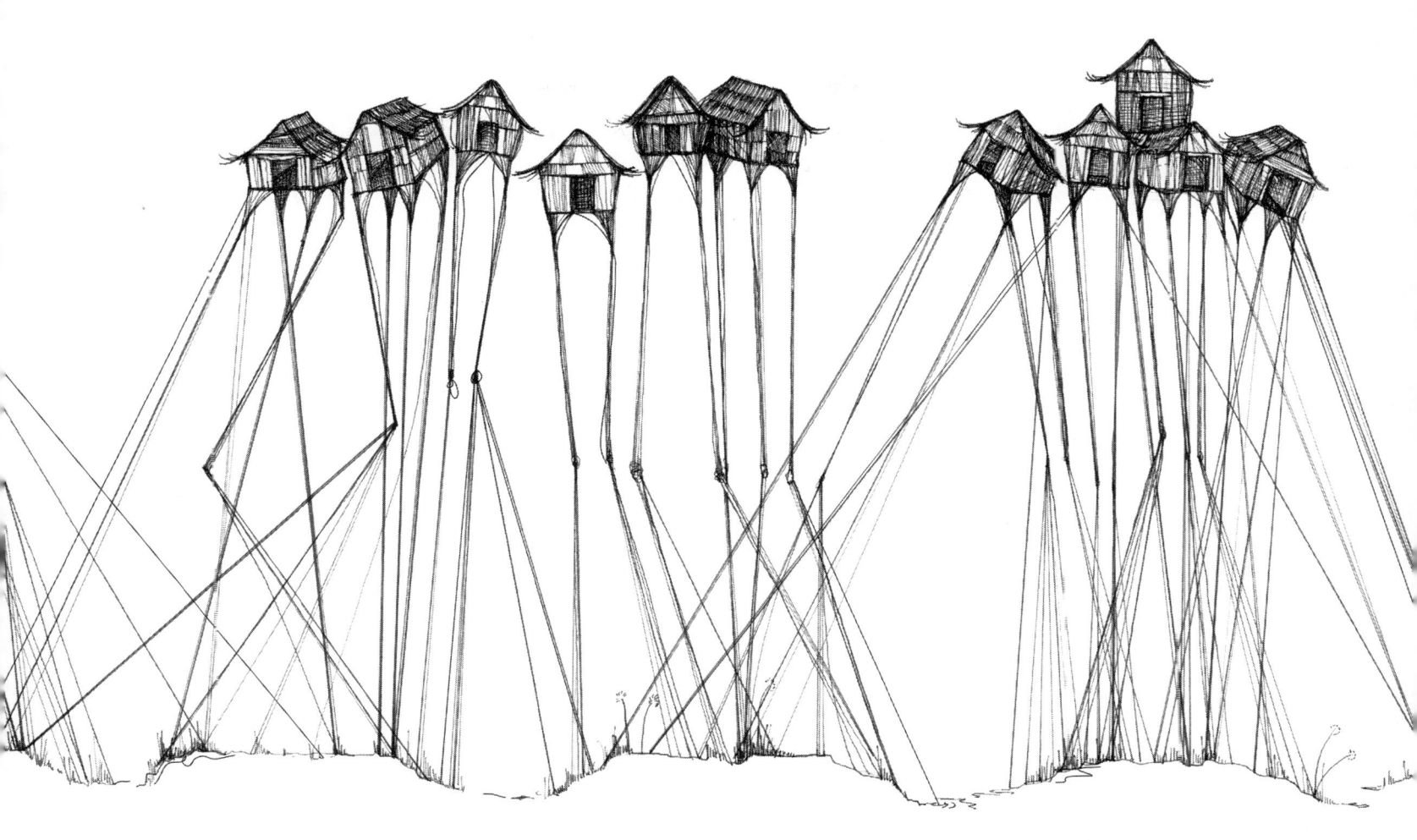

reinforced foundations.

During these tumultuous beginnings, resources were sparse, the sea was rough, and storms raged. The settlers built boats and shelters and laboriously lashed and shackled the lagoon's shifting physique to form a more stable, permanent base. But their efforts were continuous threatened. Catastrophic flooding alone in 589 C.E. significantly changed river courses and could have ended this story then and there; some luck was certainly on their side.

They pushed on. Canals were dug out and made wider and the lagoon's feeding rivers were strategically diverted in order to stabilize the flow of water. The intrepid engineers also carved canal pathways, vaulted bridges into place, and designed flat-bottomed barges, like the *gondola*, to ease their water transport.

River trade was quickly established to meet their immense hardwood needs. Hundreds of thousands of strong, water-resistant trees were felled from forests far away in the mainland, near the crests of the Dolomites. Oaks and alders were hauled along rugged donkey paths, dropped in nearby glacial rivers, floated down to the coast, and then rowed back to the lagoon.

Painstakingly, the mucky land was pressed and drained, then strengthened and buttressed. Millions of long, heavy wooden poles were sharpened into pointed spikes and driven deep into the mud with a large anvil and hammer along her edges. Tightly, side by side, the trees braced and supported her terrain. It was as if any semblance of land was squeezed into a tiny, fitted, wooden corset, and then pulled taut to define her emerging silhouette.

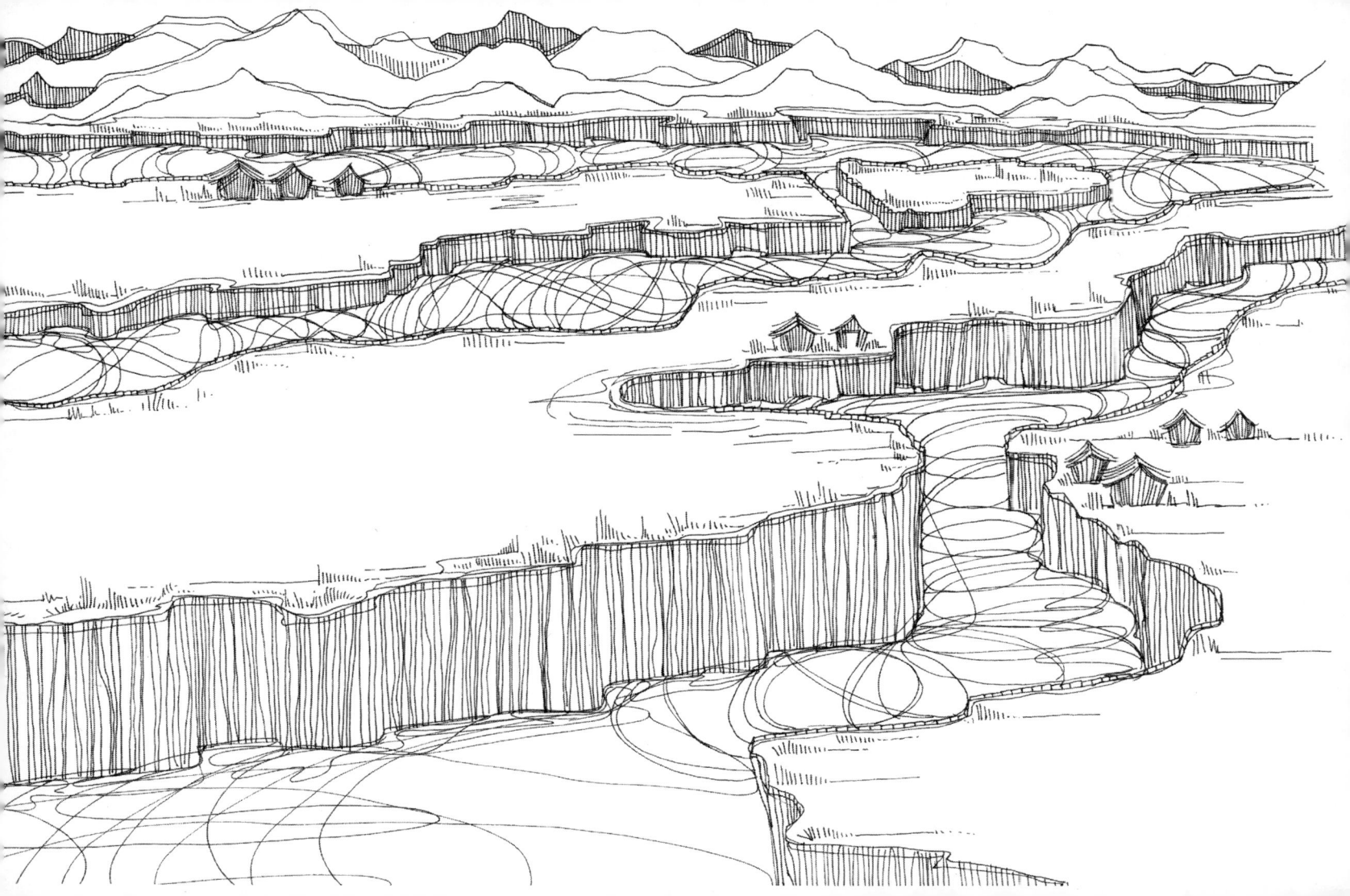

the underwater forest.

As the Venetian builders gained ground, they continued to fell the seemingly inexhaustible pines on the mainland. For centuries, they drained, expanded, and reinforced the lagoon's water-logged islands. Hundreds of thousands of tree piles were hammered head-down into each pliable island, deep down into its dark, airless muck. In time, without exposure to oxygen, these buried, stilted trunks became petrified and turned as hard as stone.

Layer by layer, more materials were added on top of this vast upside-down forest. First, giant, long wood beams were place over the vertical piles, as if on a bed of nails. Then, flat slabs of Istrian stone were dug up from the coast added as well. This white, marble-like limestone was made from the shells and spines ancient sea creatures. It was soon framed with stronger, grey-coloured volcanic rock; adept to constant flooding and salt exposure, it formed the city's tough backbone.

This growing skeleton anchored her shifting foundations, and outlined the city's emerging piscine shape. It fixed her position in the lagoon, like a fish caught on a line, but never fully reeled in.

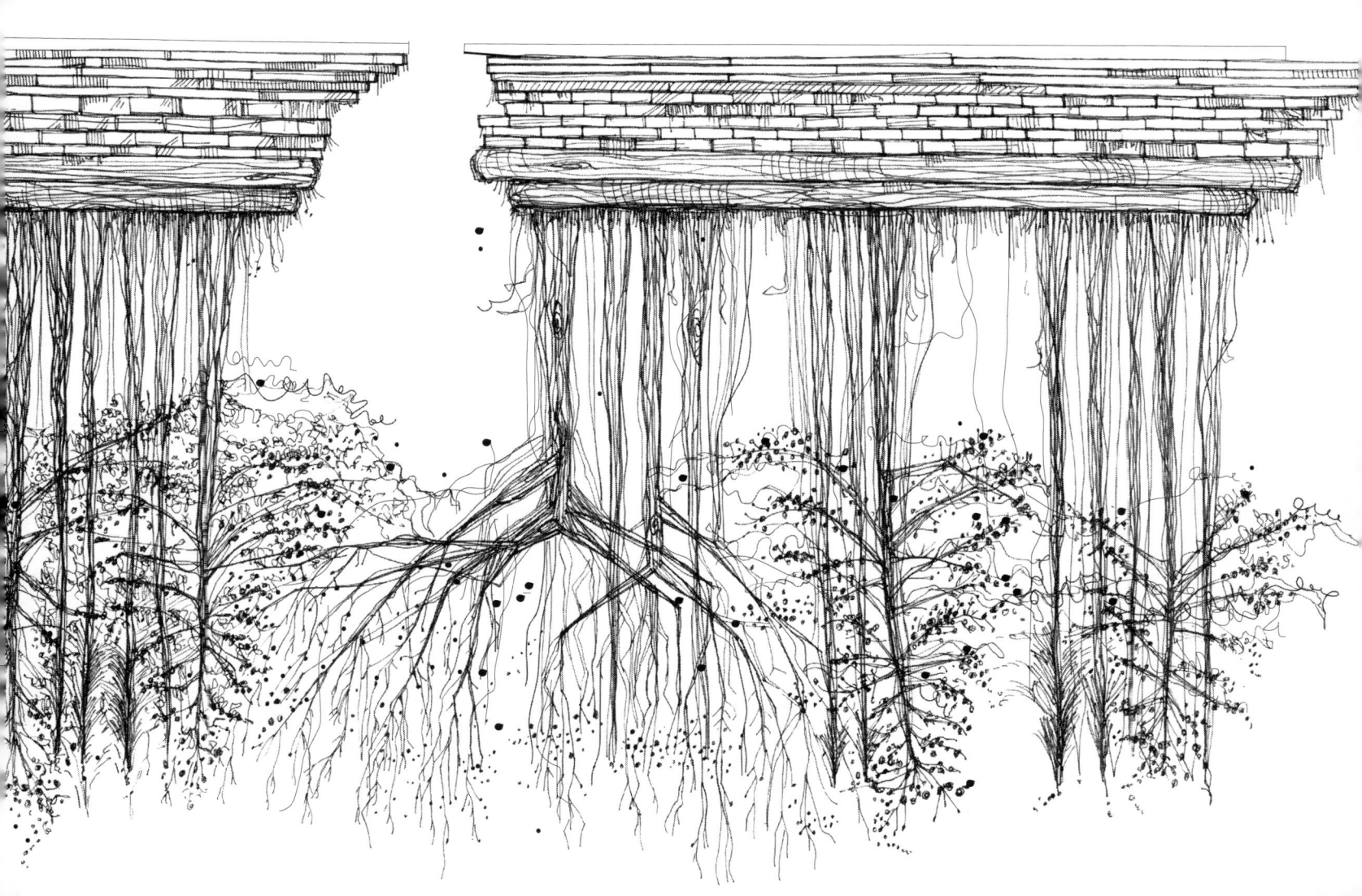

sprouting marble gardens.

Although the base of Venice has remained the same over time, the original scene above was strikingly different from today's imposing stone elegance. It was once full of lush gardens, benevolent orchards, ripe vineyards and green pastures. It was a place where sheep and cattle grazed, pigs wandered freely, and where horses leisurely trod through vineyards in the thousands. As the Venetian population grew, their agricultural lands were converted into residential spaces, and most animals were shipped to islands on the outskirts, or back to the mainland.

By the sixteenth century, the lagoon's settlers had become prosperous traders. Their first buildings, made of simple reeds and straw, were replaced by expensive blocks of brick, tile and stone.

Only the most important buildings were dressed in marble. In an array of diverse Gothic, Roman, and Byzantine styles, elaborate leaves and flora, and exotic wildlife, emerged from her walls and columns. Detailed figures and motifs from the sea, such as crabs, dolphins, shells and a myriad of ancient crustaceans, were carved into her façades. The city began to mirror an imaginary facet worthy of Neptune's own underwater palace.

In time, her veined, marble buildings over this improbable floating world, hardened and grew resistant to the salty air. It was as if the lagoon was an alchemist who transformed wood to stone underneath her waters, and coaxed a vast, marble garden to sprout above.

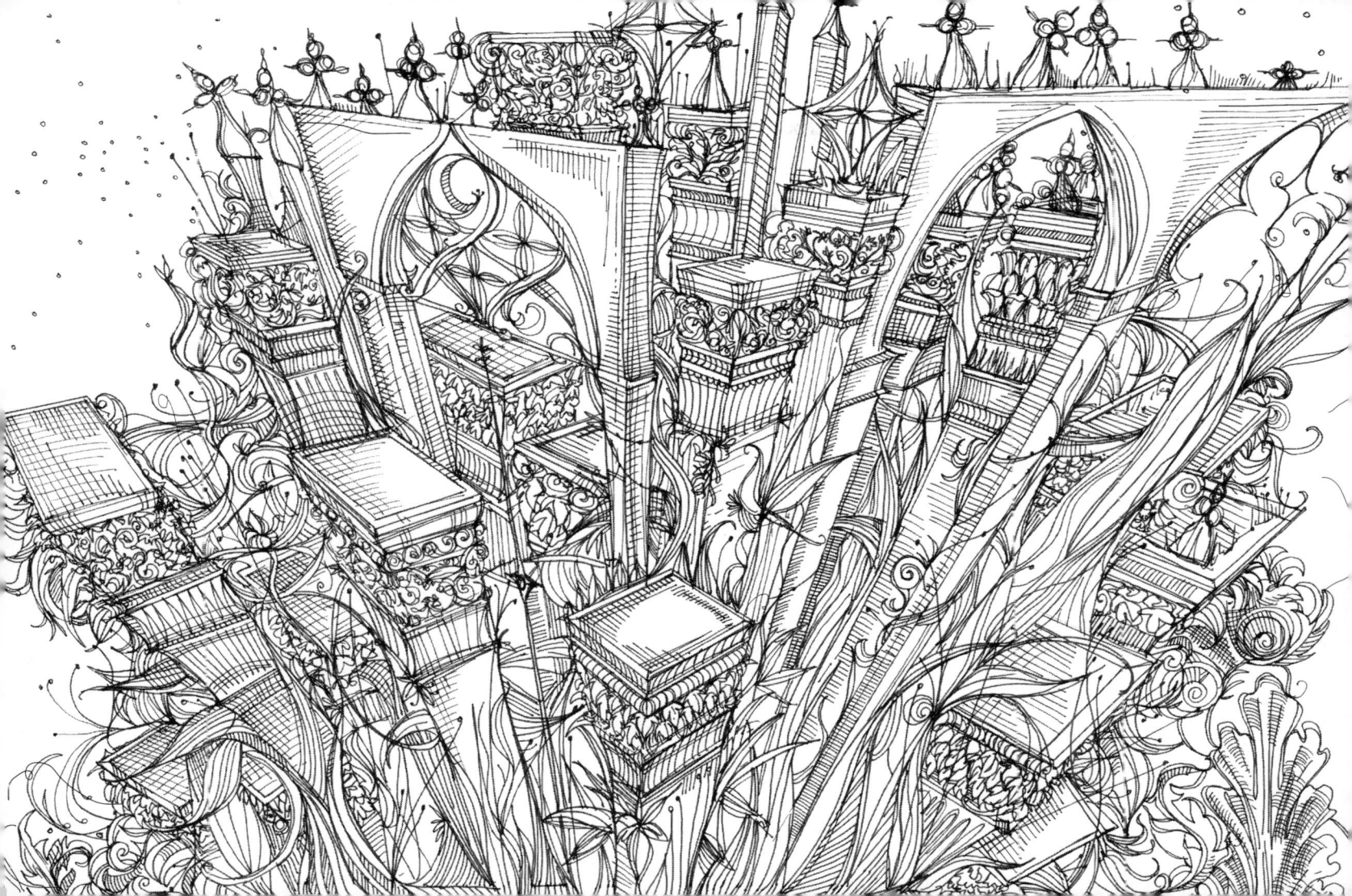

unearthing salt.

The swampy marsh offered few obvious riches. Yet, the low rainfall and hot, dry Mediterranean climate compelled its shallow basins to present invaluably large salt crystals. At this time salt was valued as highly as gold for its ability to preserve food items. Left untouched, fish, meat, vegetables, and butter quickly went rancid. Bacteria and fungus alone could quickly destroy an entire catch or harvest. Salt was a crucial buffer in the cycle between feast and famine and could prevent communities from facing starvation. In fact, Roman soldiers were commonly paid in handfuls of salt, earning their *salarium,* or "salary".

The ambitious lagoon inhabitants embraced a founding proverb: *coltivar el mare e lasser star la terra*, which means "cultivate the sea and leave the land to itself". They determinedly gouged and extracted the lagoon's white gold. In time, more extensive and complex saltworks were built. They created sophisticated dykes, and locks, and moveable doors, to direct the lagoon's briny water through a series of shallower bays, where it could evaporate and form substantial saline rocks. By the middle of the sixth century, countless Venetian barges frequented the rivers of northern Italy to trade with the mainlanders. From this one precious, pale product they amassed enough capital to meet their immediate need for wood, oil and grain.

They jealously protected their vital cornerstone and did not hesitate to extinguish any encroaching competitors. Even when their own stocks could not meet growing demands, and they had to import salt from as far as Cyprus, their original, local saltworks were always heavily guarded and almost superstitiously venerated.

With a stronger fleet and navy, the Byzantine Emperors more frequently called upon the Venetians for assistance in battle. In return for their loyalty, Byzantinum offered exceptional contacts and exclusive trading privileges. Thus, her commerce and sea power became inevitably intertwined.

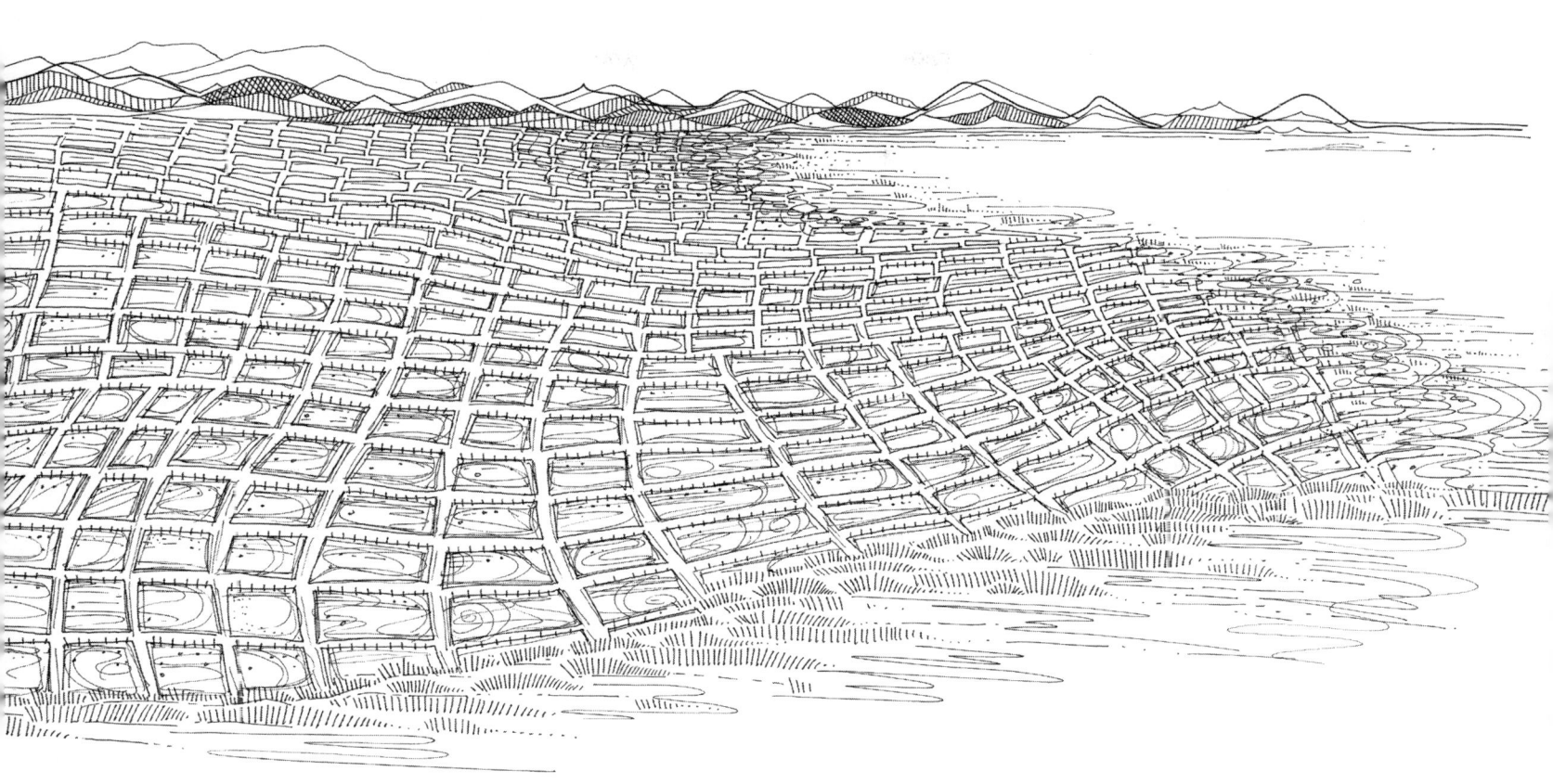

stealing the mainland.

From time to time, the amphibious lagoon dwellers would return to the mainland to scavenge any usable scraps from their old stomping grounds. Piece by piece, stone by stone, they stole back their existence, and feathered their new floating nests. They retrieved pavement from old Roman roads, stacks of bricks, clay pots, doors, chimneys, sculptures, and any other artefacts that they could glide away with. Even heavy busts of Hercules and bronze casts of Achilles were snatched and remounted in the lagoon.

At first, much effort went into the largest of the lagoon's islands, Torcello, which lies eight kilometers to the north of Venice today. While the early Venetian settlers were struggling to survive, they were also ambitious enough to create great beauty. By 639 C.E. a stone cathedral on the mainland had been completely dismantled and crudely, reconstructed on Torcello. The basilica of *Santa Maria Assunta* was filled with sparkling mosaics and imagery from the East, and made fit to host a bishop's see, as well as the throne of Attila the Hun.

In time, the lagoon inhabitant reorganized and expressed the various rights, functions and more complex social roles reminiscent of their Roman origins. Chief among them stood the leading members of the ecclesiastical hierarchy, alongside representatives of lagoon's tribune. The early Venetians benefitted from their cultural and commercial ties with Constantinople, which had stayed amicable throughout their development.

Torcello island served as Venice's first viable trading port, and connected the European West to the Islamic and Byzantine areas in the East. Highly desired commodities continually passed through Venetian ports, such as leathers, spices, skins, iron, lumber, and richly dyed goods from distant lands. Although it was banned, the slave trade was also bringing in a large amount of profit for Venetians. However, her increased commercial assets was not without consequence; it made her more vulnerable to lustful eyes on the mainland wanting access to the world markets.

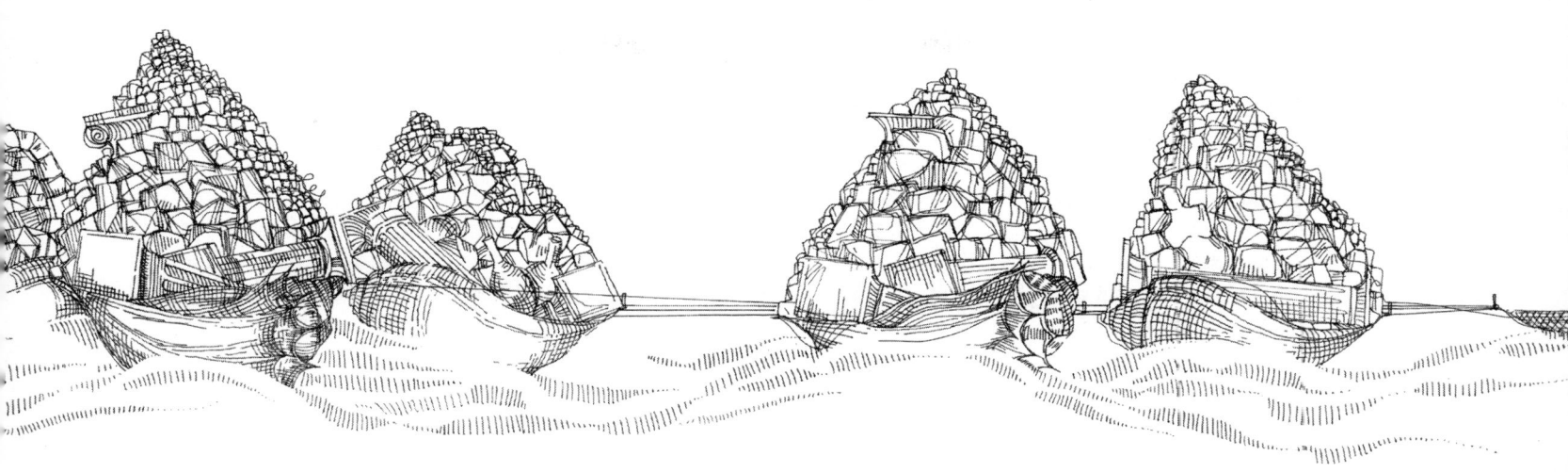

lagoon infestations.

By 810 C.E. the lagoon's mercurial waters were irrevocably challenged for the first time; Pope Leo III, agreed to support the Franks, under the rule of Charlemagne, in their quest to oust the *longobarde* from the Italian mainland. Sweeping in on a tide of conquest, the Franks wanted every scrap of Byzantine territory, including its often overlooked, but steadily growing, holding in the lagoon.

The troops of Charlemagne's son, King Pipin, were the first to invade the early Venetians. Legend has it that Pipin's troops were directed deep into the lagoon's deceptive shallows following an old Venetian woman's instruction, *sempre dritto*, or to "continue always forward," and became instantly grounded in its treacherous topography.

Impossible to advance, from across the waters, the Franks fought determinedly. They naively thought that time was on their side and that they could starve the Venetians out of their island refuge.

Their traditional tactics proved futile; The Venetians still had access to their vast trade routes and grain stores, and confidently launched heaps of bread at their enemy. Conversely, the Venetians used the tactic of time to their own advantage. They waited for the summer heat to stir the lagoon's swampy, malarial waters and ravage their intruders with disease. After one season, the Frank troops had become so depleted and humiliated, that the Venetians could force them to withdraw with such simple weaponry as arrows, rocks, and a few heaps of boiling pitch.

It was during this battle that the inhabitants of the lagoon united as a single force. For the first time, they fought for their freedom together as *Venetians*. And finally, after a series of treaties between Charlemagne and the Pope, Venice was ratified as a truly independent niche in the medieval Western world. The Venetians began to elect their own *doge*, and continued to secure their autonomy for over one thousand years afterwards.

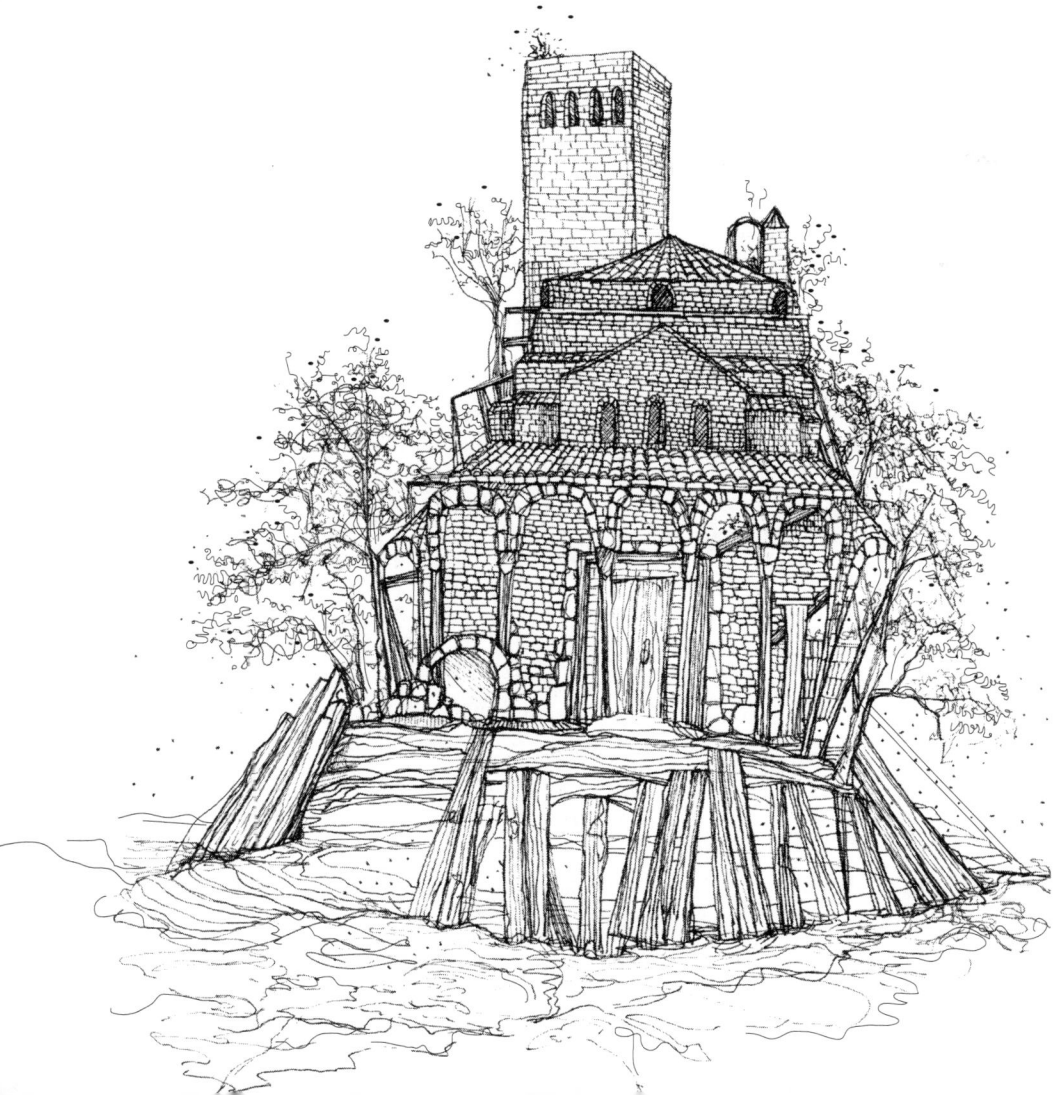

At times, the swampy lagoon also blighted her own inhabitants. By the twelfth century, the canals of Torcello silted up and bred unbearable malaria. Trade boats could no longer access its ports. Many evacuated to islands of Amminana and Constanziaca, but these landforms were swallowed up by the sea just a century later. While, most moved to the lagoon's larger islands, such as Burano, Murano and San Giorgio.

The more inspired journeyed even further into the lagoon, to the untouched *rivo alto,* or "high banks" area. In this dangerously favoured position, with treacherous shoals and shallows, it was near to impossible for unexpected strangers attack. The early Venetians transformed its one hundred and eighteen detached islands into a unified entity. Here, they formed the beginning of the major city as we know it today.

founding bones: st. mark's basilica and treasury.

In the wake of their triumph, the early Venetians grew hungry for power and independence. But during the Middle Ages, when politics and religion were inescapably tangled, they fell short; Saint Theodore, who was originally named to sanctify the lagoon, lacked the clout to match their political ambition. Consequently, in 829 C.E., two cunning Venetian merchants stole the bones of Saint Mark from his tomb in Alexandria. They smuggled them away from Muslim ports underneath flabby layers of offensive, decomposing pork. Celebrations filled the lagoon when the relics were presented to the *doge*. With this direct link to Christ, Venice could now rival a power as strong as Rome, and its cult of Saint Peter.

The winged lion of Saint Mark became the upstart empire's insignia. Fierce stone and marble lions guarded her most important buildings and golden lions were printed onto bright red banners to adorn her growing domain and naval fleets. In time, they constructed an astounding Byzantine-style basilica, with five grand domes resting on five great arches, to proudly house their precious assets.

Over centuries, the exterior of *Basilica di San Marco* became encrusted with the most expensive prizes of Venetian conquests. Innumerable columns, precious marble, ornaments, reliefs, and carvings, most older than the building itself, were affixed to its coralloid exterior, while thousands of square kilometers of mosaics came to depict dazzling, religious imagery inside. Her lavish treasury was filled with gold and exquisite jewels. It also housed countless venerated items as the purported finger of Mary Magdalene and one of Saint George's many "discovered" arms. Every addition to the sacred hoard brought in profits from the many pilgrims awaiting passage at her ports the Holy Land.

The stage was set for her rise in power. Just outside of the basilica, Saint Theodore, astride a crocodile, and the winged lion of Saint Mark were raised on the city's two highest columns; they marked the floodgate where Venice furiously opened to the world. These pillars also framed where traitors to the Republic were unhesitatingly executed. With a deep-seated confidence, the lionized Venice appeared as a force worthy of contention.

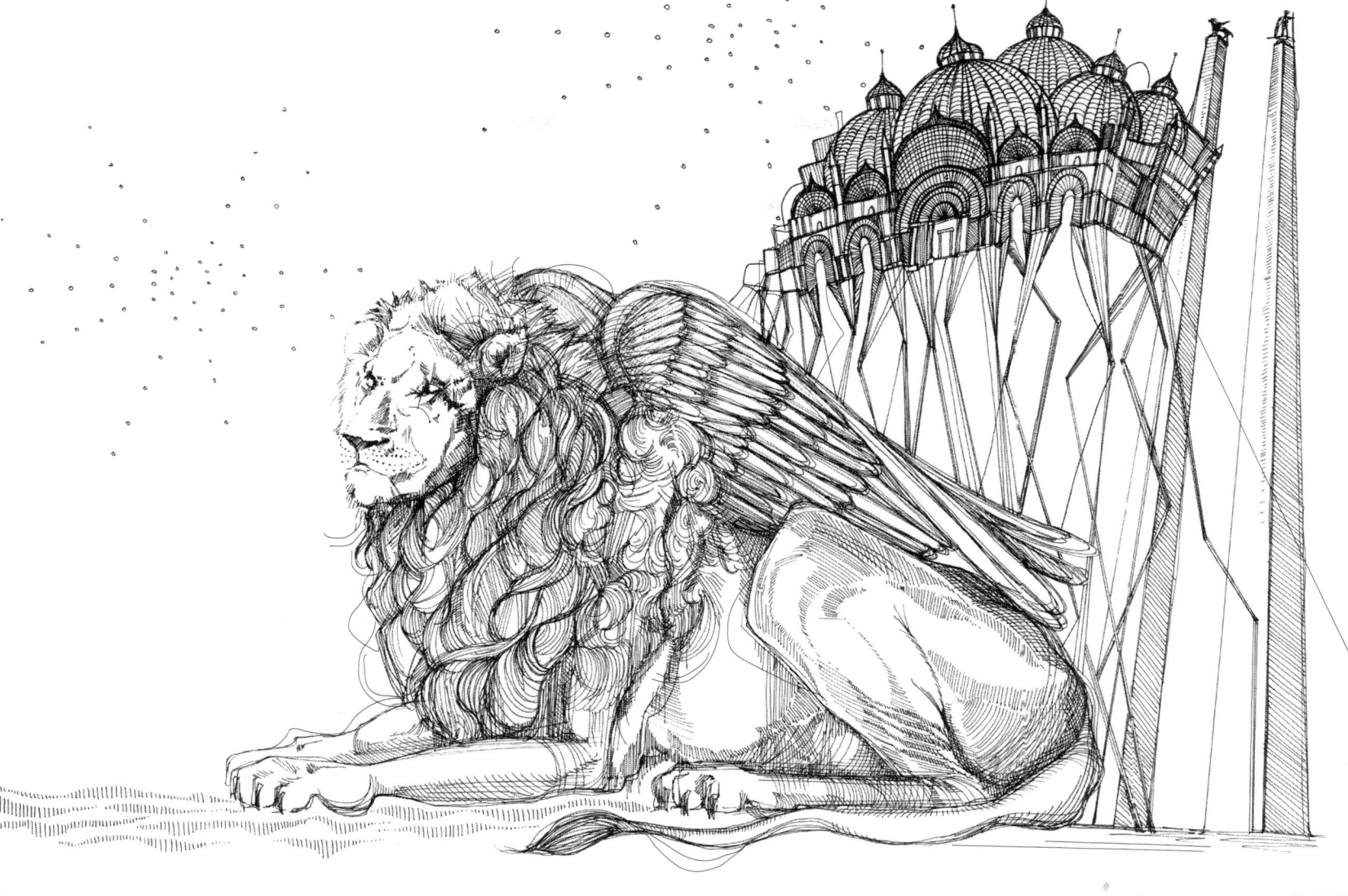

part two: expansion

(9th century - 13th century)

early life on the rialto.

By the ninth century, worrisome raids still continued on the mainland. The early Venetians heavily fortified their hideaway in the *rivo alto,* or "Rialto" area. They constructed lookout towers, high, protective walls and even ran a massive, iron chain across the Grand Canal to control ships traveling through their waters. Political and aristocratic powers moved close to the Ducal Palace and *Basilica di San Marco* to be better protected.

With a seemingly endless amount of goods arriving at Venetian ports, trade and manufacturing became the city's specialty. Merchants constructed more docks, showrooms and warehouses in the pulsing Rialto area to house their wonders from around the world. Smaller, dedicated sections of labour concentrated in nearby, winding alleyways.

Visitors could easily find the specialized businesses by locating their corresponding streets names, like the *calle della frezzeria,* "path of arrow makers", the *calle del remer,* "path of oar makers"; even the *calle degli assassini* was clearly marked. Great crowds flooded to the Rialto discuss politics, gather news from the East, exchange currencies, invest, consult revised maps, restock supplies and embark on new journeys. By the thirteenth century, the first permanent wooden bridge to cross the Grand Canal was constructed here, further linking it to the city's founding political centre in the lower lying *San Marco's* basin.

With her two main centres established, the city's fry-like shape began to emerge. Around the year 1175 C.E., Venice was already divided into her six buzzing neighbourhoods or *sestieri,* which still distinguish the city to this day: *San Marco, Castello, Cannaregio, Dorsoduro, Santa Croce,* and *San Polo*. Each district is thought to be represented by the slits on the decal of each equally ancient gondola; The *ferro* design, or the lopsided, *s*-shaped metallic prong, still trumpets proudly throughout every canal in the city, driven by tradesmen who have passed their boats from father to son through the generations.

With so much vibrant activity evolving, Venetians had to quickly organize themselves into an extremely efficient and well ordered system, one which carefully considered and thoroughly documented every detail of trade and daily life.

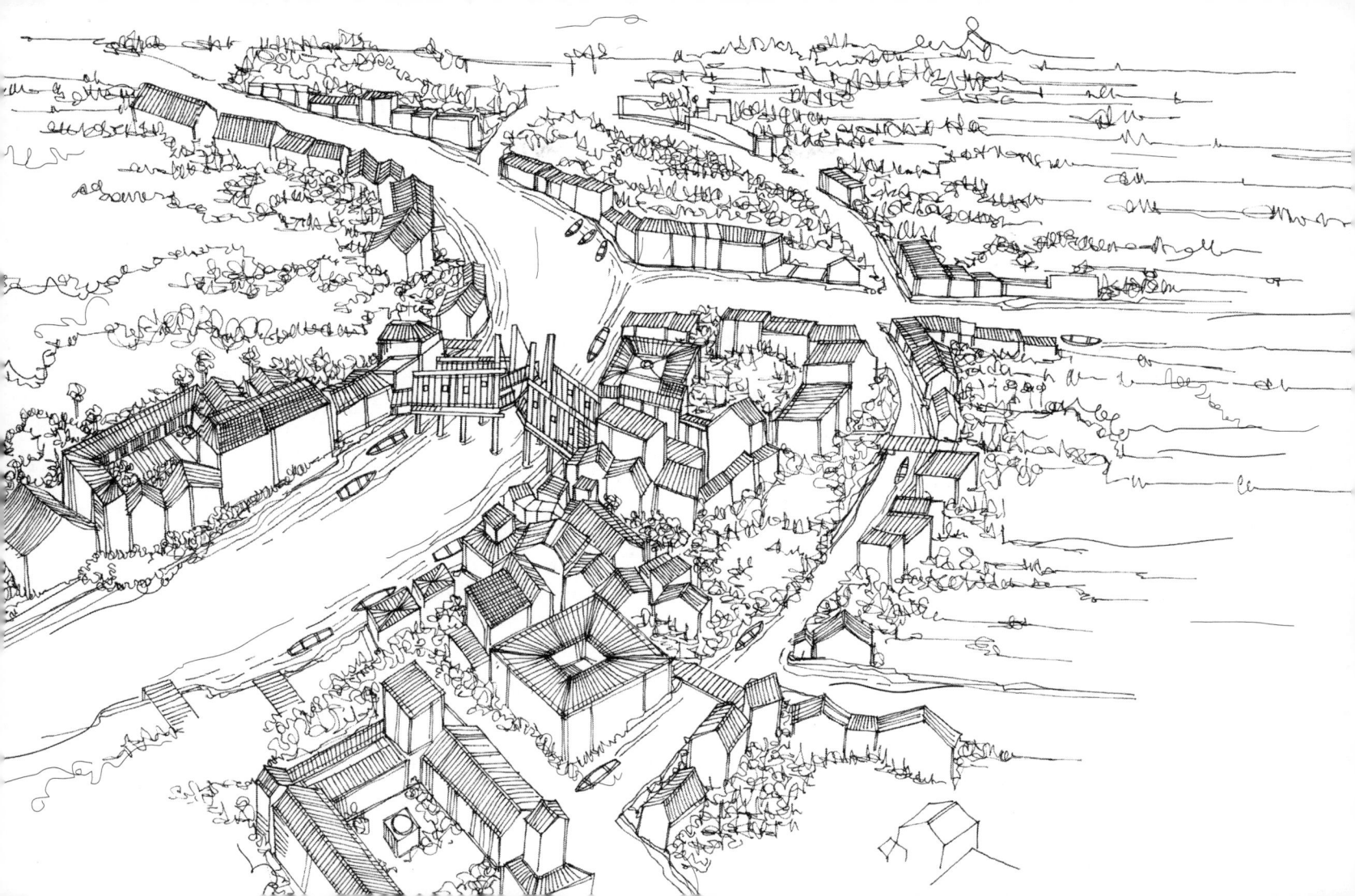

the campo and catching rain.

Within this bustling city, large residential communities naturally clutched together. Groups of families huddled in residences up to five stories high and set up their shops below. In each small neighbourhood, or *campo*, residents of every age and background shared their resources, thereby increasing their level of social health and personal safety. However, a large degree of one's privacy was exchanged for these mutual benefits.

Each *campo* had its own church, a bell tower or *campanile*, and a common, square courtyard, which is also called a *campo*. Centre to every neighbourhood was the most vital communal structure of all - a large, white well. In a city surrounded by kilometers of salt water. This basin was typically kept under lock and key to secure its store of scarce, drinking water.

Below their heavy grates, each well inconspicuously stretched down deep, past laid clay foundation, to access the lagoon's reservoirs of fresh, flowing water. At the same time, the wells opened to the skies above; they swallowed rainwater through their tiny slits carved in surrounding pavement stones. Each precious drop was filtered through sand, which filled their enormous cistern bellies. Here, water was kept safe and carefully rationed out each day.

Yet, despite these measures, high tides contaminated the city's water reserves with little warning from time to time. Drinkable water would have to be rowed into the lagoon until new stores could be replenished. Every development within the lagoon's waters continually reminded its inhabitants of the same lesson - that every effort will at some point fall to entropy; nothing is, in fact, stable. Nothing is permanent.

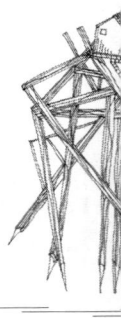

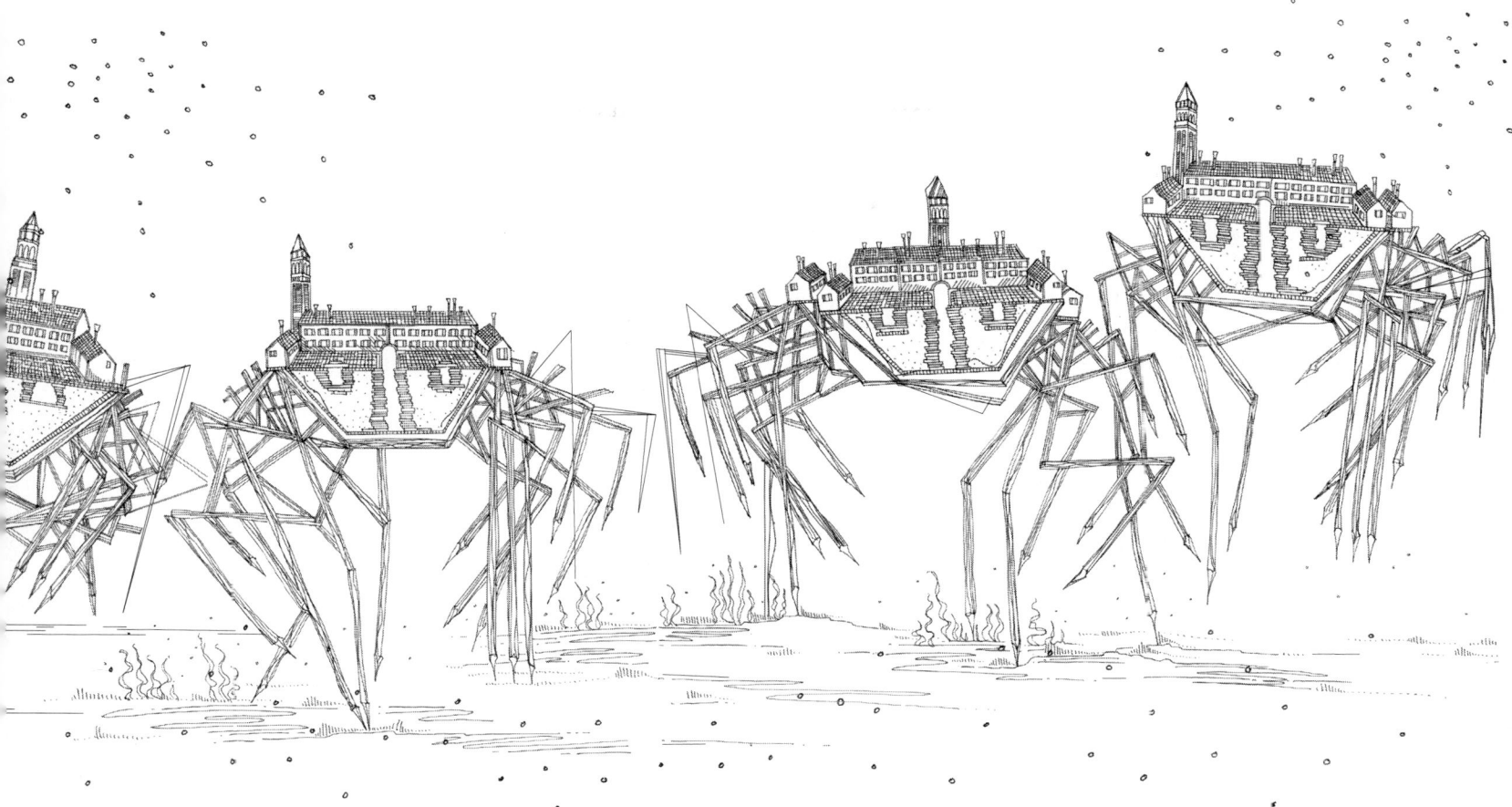

currents of power & the golden book.

Strong in their resiliency, yet founded on unpredictable waters, Venetians preserved their autonomy and outdistanced their Byzantine rulers during their formative years. They prioritized commercial gain over political loyalties, and formed a remarkably stable government, which lasted over a millennium without civil war.

The Venetians developed a number of measures to prevent their *doge* from becoming a hereditary ruler, with unlimited power, and stayed on course of a true republic. For example, if the title of *doge* became concentrated in any one lineage, or if he dared to place his own interests before the state, he was easily banished, cast away to a monastery, unexpectedly stabbed. Over time, the personal power of the *doge* diffused and sovereignty moved down to a rising noble class, the *maggior consiglio*. Unlike the powerful in her neighbouring monarchies, as France, England and Germany, who gained status by blood alone, only the most skilled merchants and naval commanders were invited to join Venetian aristocracy and have their names inscribed in the *Libro d'Oro*.

The specialized *maggior consiglio* developed many financial and legal innovations to support aspiring entrepreneurs in Venice: the first state bank, the *Banco Giro*, was opened by Venetians in the twelfth century, which pioneered modern banking practices; corporate forms, such as the *colleganza*, which was an early form of a company, were also created to finance single trade expeditions and limit liability for trading partners. In contrast to many other fleets, Venetian oarsmen were not slaves, but highly motivated merchants; by rowing a vessel one could make substantial personal profit trading goods at port stops. But, they had to heavily guard their expensive cargo against pirates who notoriously swarmed their expanding trade routes.

By emulating Mars, the god of war, and Neptune, the god of the sea, Venetians forged one of the most expansive maritime empires throughout all of history. While remaining tenaciously focused on conquest by sea, they moved forward with the hope that their strides would even outlast the marble statues of these gods, which still guard the entrance to the Ducal Palace.

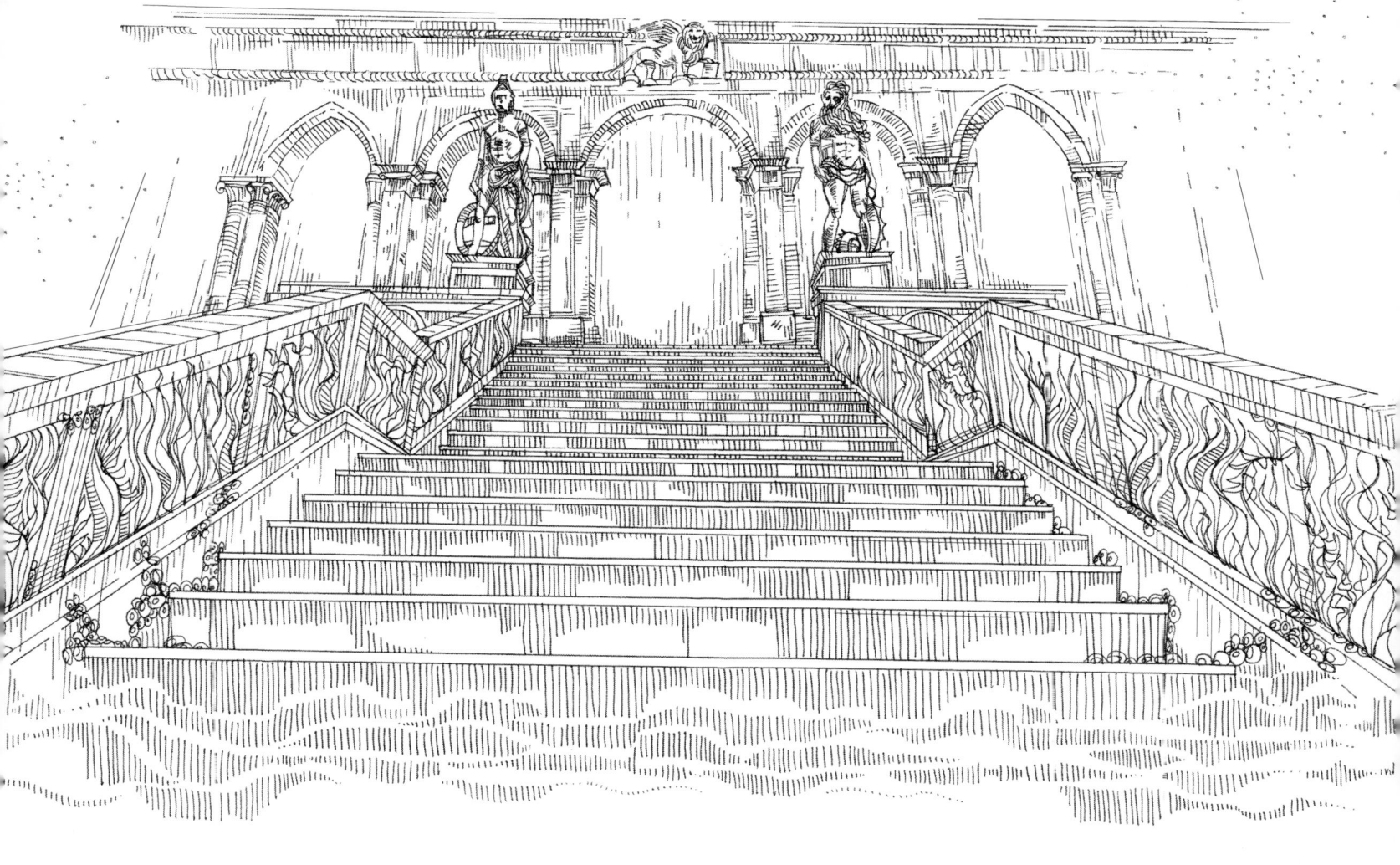

salt trade diversification.

Even though salt was the original base of Venetian trade, her own saltworks were fundamentally flawed; they were vulnerable to floods, storms, and changing currents. As a result, Venetians built more saltworks along the Adriatic, and coarsely attacked nearby rivals. Any ship embarking from her ports had to return with the stash of her white gold. Yet, by the ninth century, the Venetians discovered that it was more lucrative to trade salt rather than produce it, and confidently pushed their commercial ascendancy further across the Mediterranean.

The Venetians immediately reinvested all gains into shipbuilding. They sent out diplomats and pushed to create the most competitive fleets of the day. They had to keep a close eye on the waters; the Saracen fleets from Sicily would creep close to their shores from the south, while the Slav expansion and pirates along the Dalmatia coast could sever their access to the Adriatic from above. Yet, each year, she grew stronger. While the Venetians enjoyed a more democratic social system, where each citizen could try to improve their circumstances by using the bounty and freedoms of the sea, the people on the mainland were locked into a more rigid feudal regime, where a few rich lords and clergymen held all the power, while the serfs worked the land for a harsh and meager existence. In Venice, one's wealth came to indicate one's skill and character, as only the most brave and talented sailors and merchants returned home with substantial profits.

Venetian trade was founded on a golden principle which allowed it to be controlled and easily monitored: all goods traded by Venetians could only travel on Venetian ships and be sold at her ports. They designed unique cargo ships, which were large, rounded, and walnut-like, and regularly transported lucrative spices from the East. Venice quickly became the preeminent emporium of trade in Europe. Every detail of Venetian trade routes, schedules, markets and cargo were recorded, scrutinized, and maximized for efficiency. Necessary innovations, such as maritime insurance and refined banking systems, also safeguarded her crucial pillar of trade. Overall, her tenacious focus, and almost obsessive attention to detail, set a inviolable base for maritime domination.

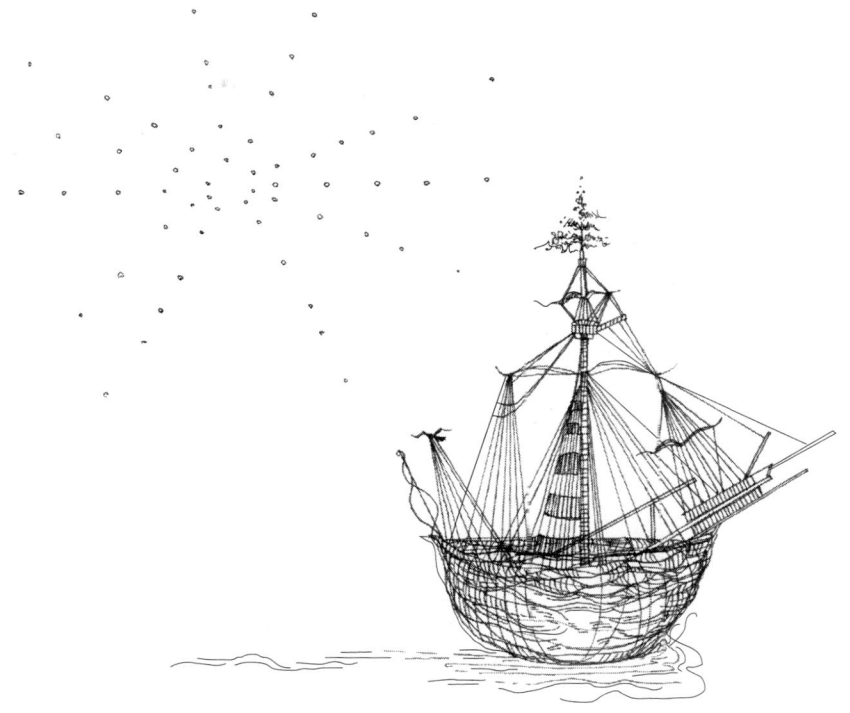

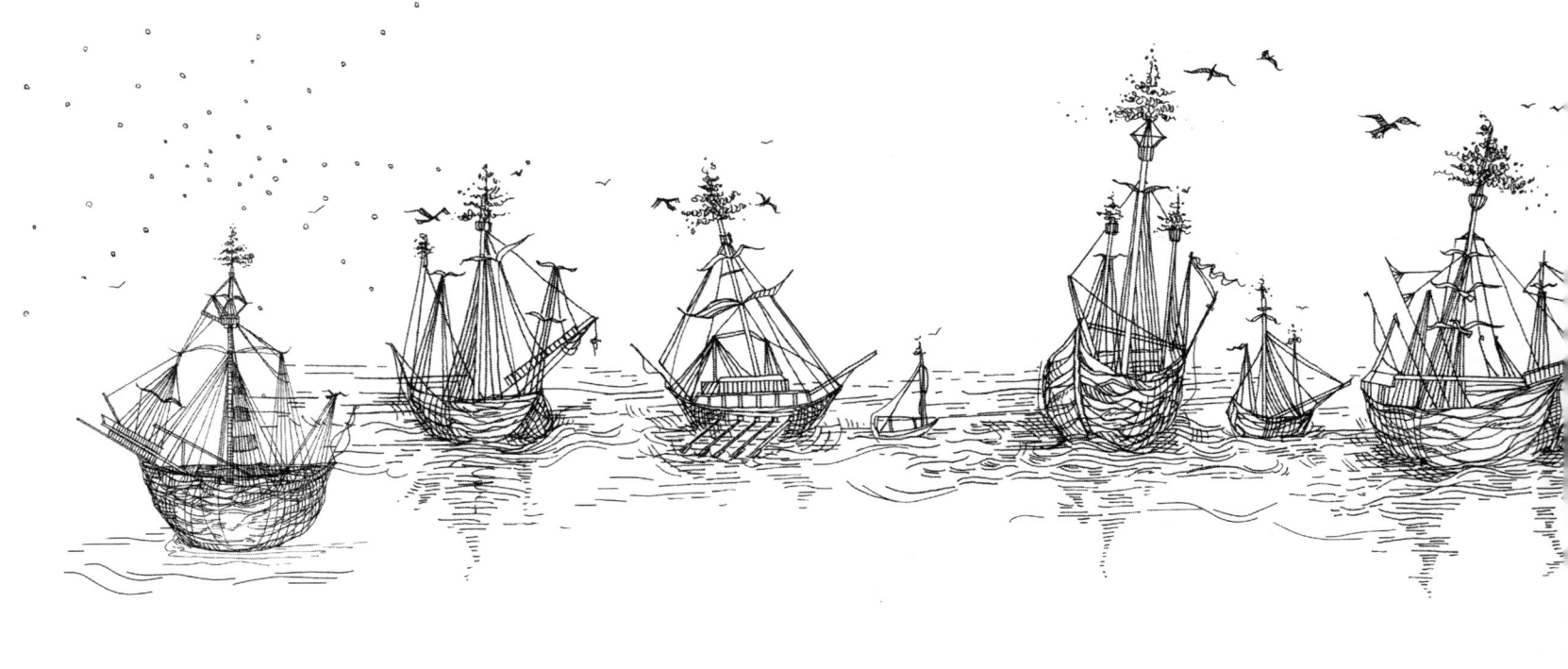

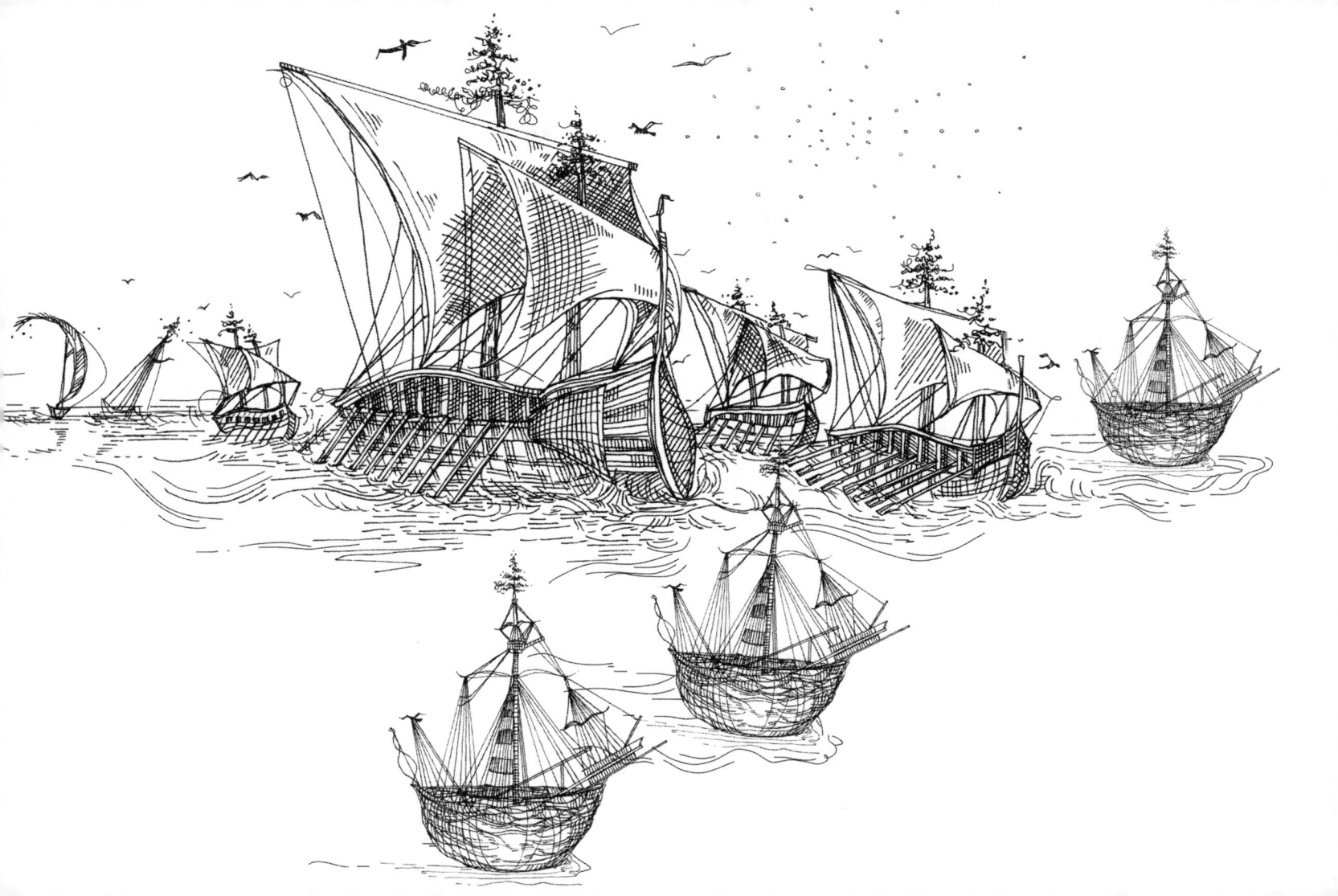

byzantinum-venetian partnership.

Venice was perfectly situated to mediate trade between the East and the West; unlike many others, Venetians could sail the daunting seas to access distant ports in Constantinople and Alexandria. Her salt-bearing ships ventured further and further and found more exotic cargo, like brilliant jewels, fragrant spices, incense, cotton and fine silks.

To better support convoys on their longer sea journeys, Venetians utilized a number of strategic, mainland bases in Byzantine territory along the Dalmatian and Istrian coasts to store food rations and supplies. They used cunning naval tactics to assist the Emperor with conflicts in his faraway territories. For example, in the eleventh century, when the Normans, supported by the Pope, encroached along the Adriatic coast, near the south of Italy, the Byzantines called upon the Venetian fleet for aid.

With little warning, the Venetians blocked the Norman fleets in their ports. They then lashed their ships together and hoisted up smaller, manned dinghies to the tops of their masts. From their artificial, higher ground, the Venetians threw down heaps of lime and soap and heavy rocks to blind and slip and sink their enemies. To top their efforts, they blew fire through submerged pipes and burnt down any remaining vessels. Such battles earned the Venetians their reputation as a formidable foe, one which was to be dearly reckoned with.

In 1082 C.E., the Emperor awarded the Venetians his esteemed gold seal for their pugnacious efforts. He also gave them tax exemptions and special trading privileges, more than any of her Italian rivals. They became the first foreigners to build in Constantinople, and became a major player in its local economy.

The Venetians continued to foster their relationship with Byzantinum. They notably stepped into the Norman-Byzantine war, to help win back the strategically vital island of Corfu, and gain even more favours. The keen diplomats also helped to negotiate a long awaited peace accord between the Pope and Emperor in 1177 C.E, which was signed in the lagoon's very own *San Marco's Basilica*.

As their trade network expanded, Venetians annihilated any pirates and pesky enemies in their way and lauded their commitment to the sea. To formally symbolize this relationship, *dogi* began to ceremoniously throw gold rings into the lagoon's waters, in a ritual called *la Sensa*. Between roaring waves, Venetians vibrantly celebrated their amassed wealth provided by the sea; with pomp they deepened their union with the surrounding, wild waters.

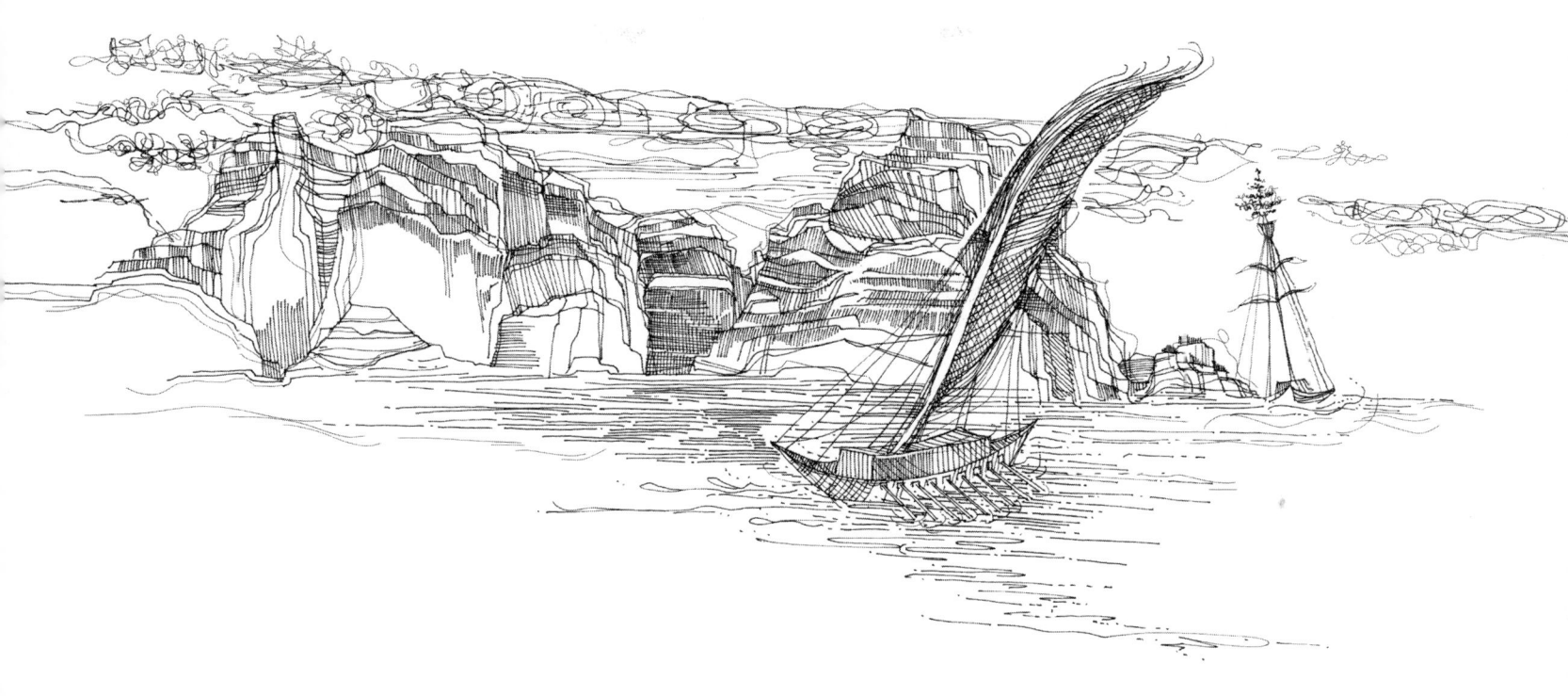

the arsenale: secret shipyard production.

At the heart of Venice's maritime supremacy was its *Arsenale*. Located in the *Castello* area, this massive shipyard was established in 1104 C.E.. It was the first and largest known factory assembly line to exist in the Middle Ages.

Inexhaustible effort and resources were put into constructing and maintaining every aspect of her naval fleet and trade convoys. Long and narrow, these flat-bottomed, oar-powered *galere* were the lifeblood of all Venetian conquests. Every aspect of its unprecedented production was organized into specialized areas, such as: carpentry; tarring; fabricating sails, ropes, anchors, and weaponry; and preserving rations. The *Arsenale's* power of production was exceptional; its secrets were more carefully guarded than the city of Venice herself.

At its height the *Arsenale* employed over 16,000 workers. They produced hundreds of thousands of warships, placing a tangible and inexpressible fear into anyone who witnessed it in action. They could construct and completely outfit a vessel in a single day, a feat which would take months elsewhere in Europe. Kings and rulers were strategically invited to witness their intimidating efficiency. The unfathomable concentration of sweaty labourers slaving amongst endless vats of boiling pitch even came to inspire Dante for some of his *Inferno's* darkest images. His three verses have since been carved on stone outside the *Arsenale's* original entrance:

"Quale nell'Arzana de'Viniziani, bolle l'inverno la tenace pece, a rimpalmar li legni lor non sani..."
(As in the Arsenal of the Venetians, In wintertime they boil the viscous pitch...) (Inf. C. XXI. VERSI VII-VX)

Tragically, Dante's visit to Venice is believed to be the unintentional cause of his own death; the poet contracted malaria near the Valli di Comacchio, and died in Ravenna in 1321 C.E..

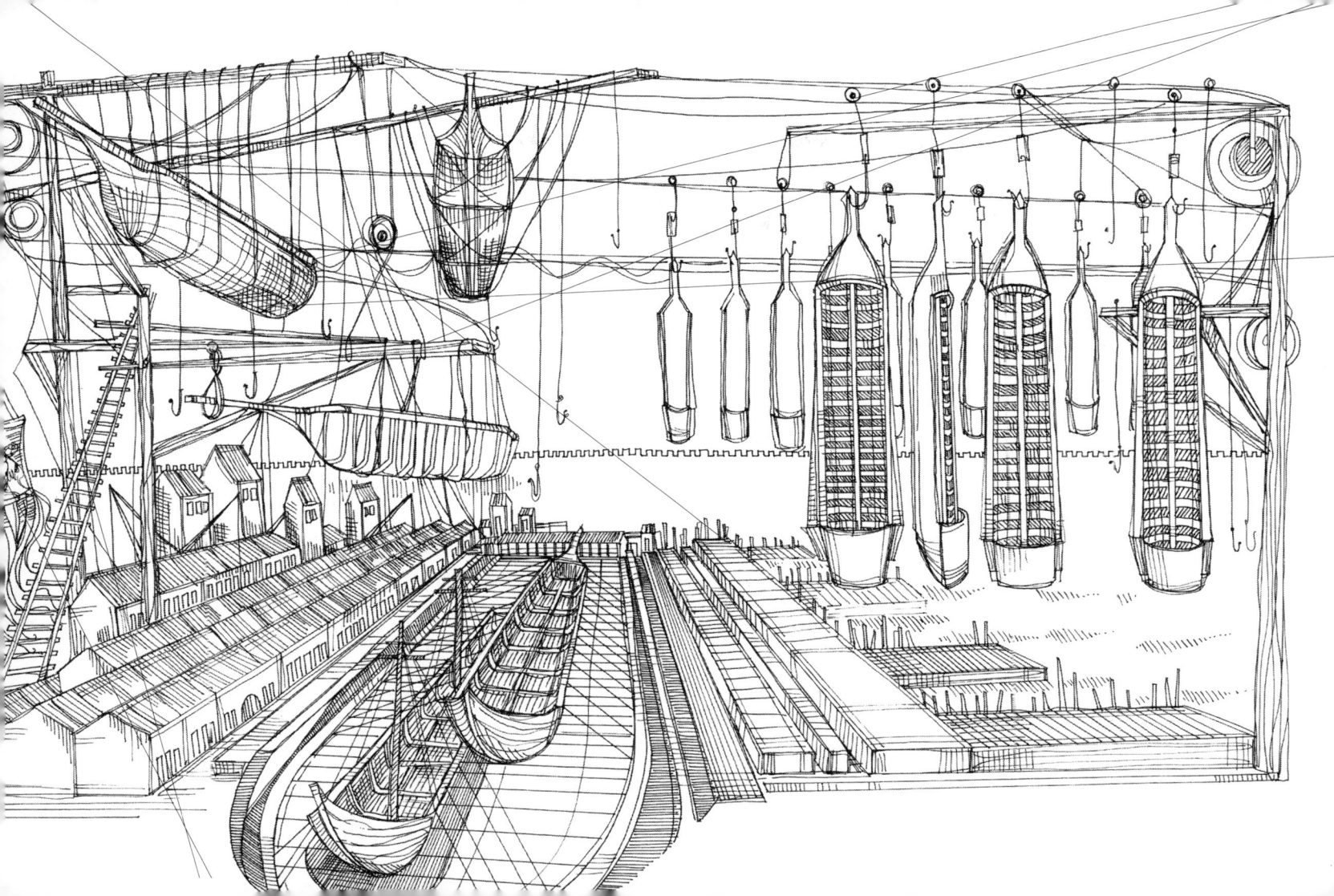

cultivating power.

In spite of having strong forces on the sea, Venetian traders on land had little protection. For example, in 1171 C.E. at the height of the Republic's profits in Constantinople, the Byzantine government grew weary of their growing power and influence within their city walls. They abruptly arrested, imprisoned, and seized the possessions of over 10,000 Venetians merchants living in their respective quarter of Constantinople.

When news that their major trading partner was holding Venetians hostage, there was public outcry in the lagoon for ruthless retaliation. However, the Plague had just hit Venice, and throttled any action. The *doge* eventually led an expedition to Constantinople to try to resolve the crisis, but it failed to have any major impact.

During this saga, a notable merchant, Enrico Dandolo, was taken prisoner, tortured and returned to the lagoon blind. Yet, he never abandoned the case of the Republic; he served as an ambassador to Constantinople. After twelve years of negotiations, a treaty was finally reached, but Dandolo held on to his distrust and patiently waited for the chance to have his real revenge.

Years later, when Dandolo was elected *doge*, even as an old man without sight, he set into motion one of the most devastating attacks on Constantinople in all of its history.

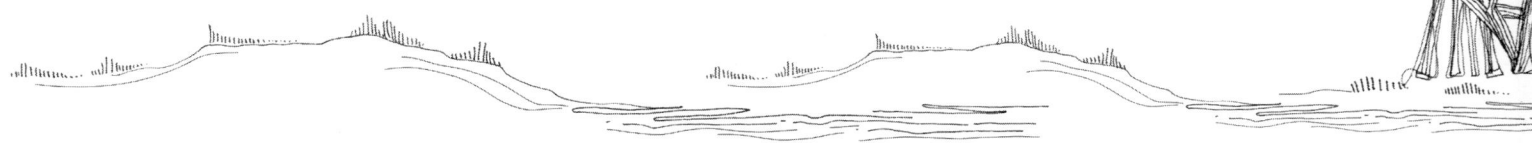

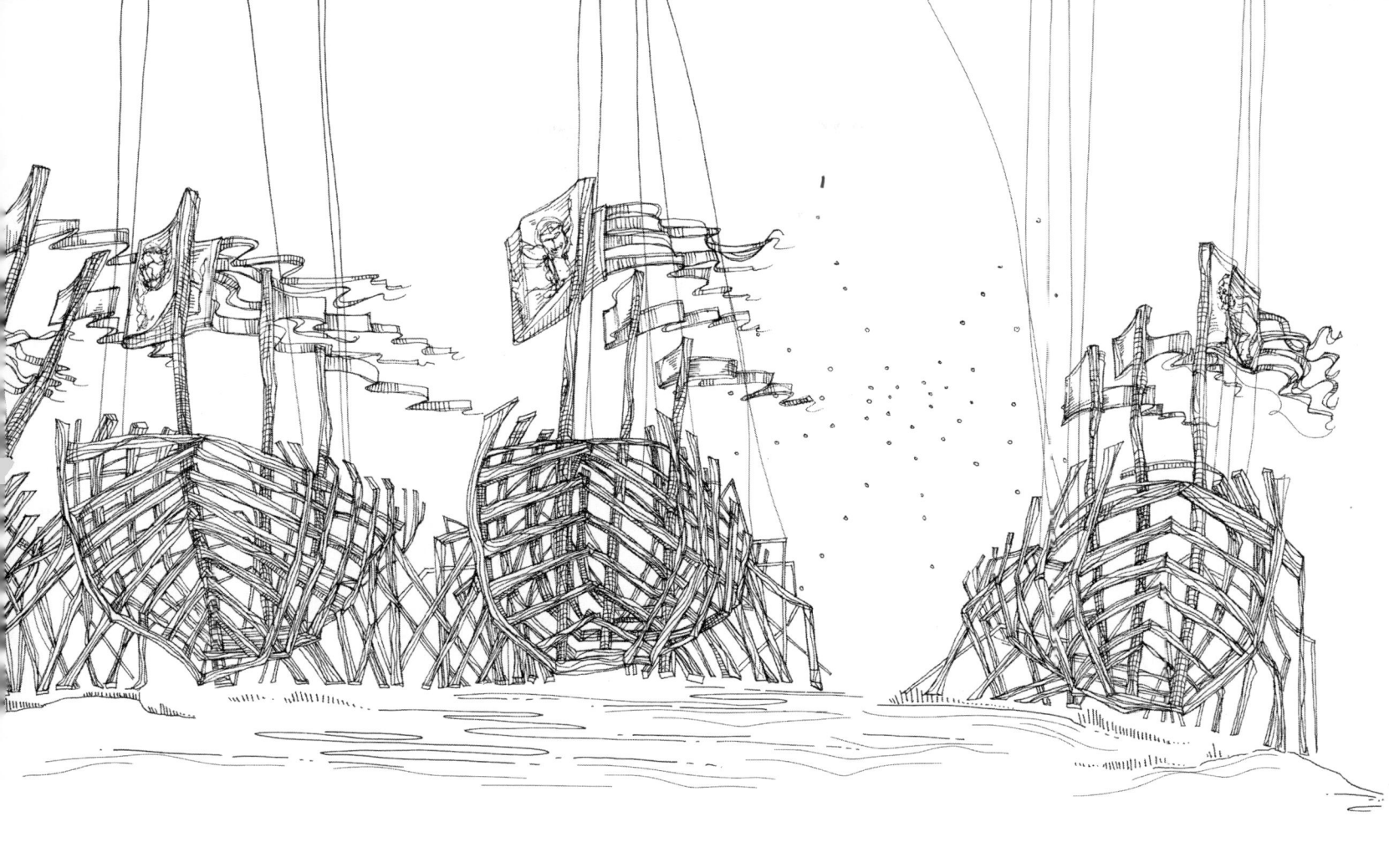

the fourth crusades.

With the advent of the Crusades, Venetian foreign relations continued. By this time, the Seljuk Turks had notably attacked Byzantine territory in the East and the Pope had urged Western Europe to unite and restore Europe's access to Jerusalem. Venice generally preferred to let others sort out their disputes, but she grew deeply torn between her affiliations and to remain an idle spectator.

Although her fleets sailed under the cross, they remained more focused on protecting her trade than engaging her Muslim neighbours in battle. The Venetians fought to prevent their dreaded Italian rivals, like Genoa and Pisa, from gaining any advantages in the East. They also protected the Byzantine Empire and their Syrian and Egyptian markets in order to gain more trade and port privileges. And they shamelessly looted vulnerable ships and cities for a quick profit.

By the time the French princes were preparing for the Fourth Crusade, the *doge* was keen to exploit their excursion. The Crusaders had come to the lagoon and zealously ordered over five hundred vessels from the *Arsenale*, which would give them the grandest fleet created since the Roman Empire. But when less than one-third of the expected Crusaders arrived in Venice, it was more than evident that they would not be able to pay the large sum owing for their ships.

A skilled negotiator, *doge* Enrico Dandolo waived the Crusaders' outstanding debt and even agreed to ferry them to Jerusalem if they helped serve the Venetians along the way. En route, the Crusaders complied; they vanquished pirates, settled down rebel uprisings in foreign ports, and recaptured the city of Zara along the way, almost losing sight of their original intentions.

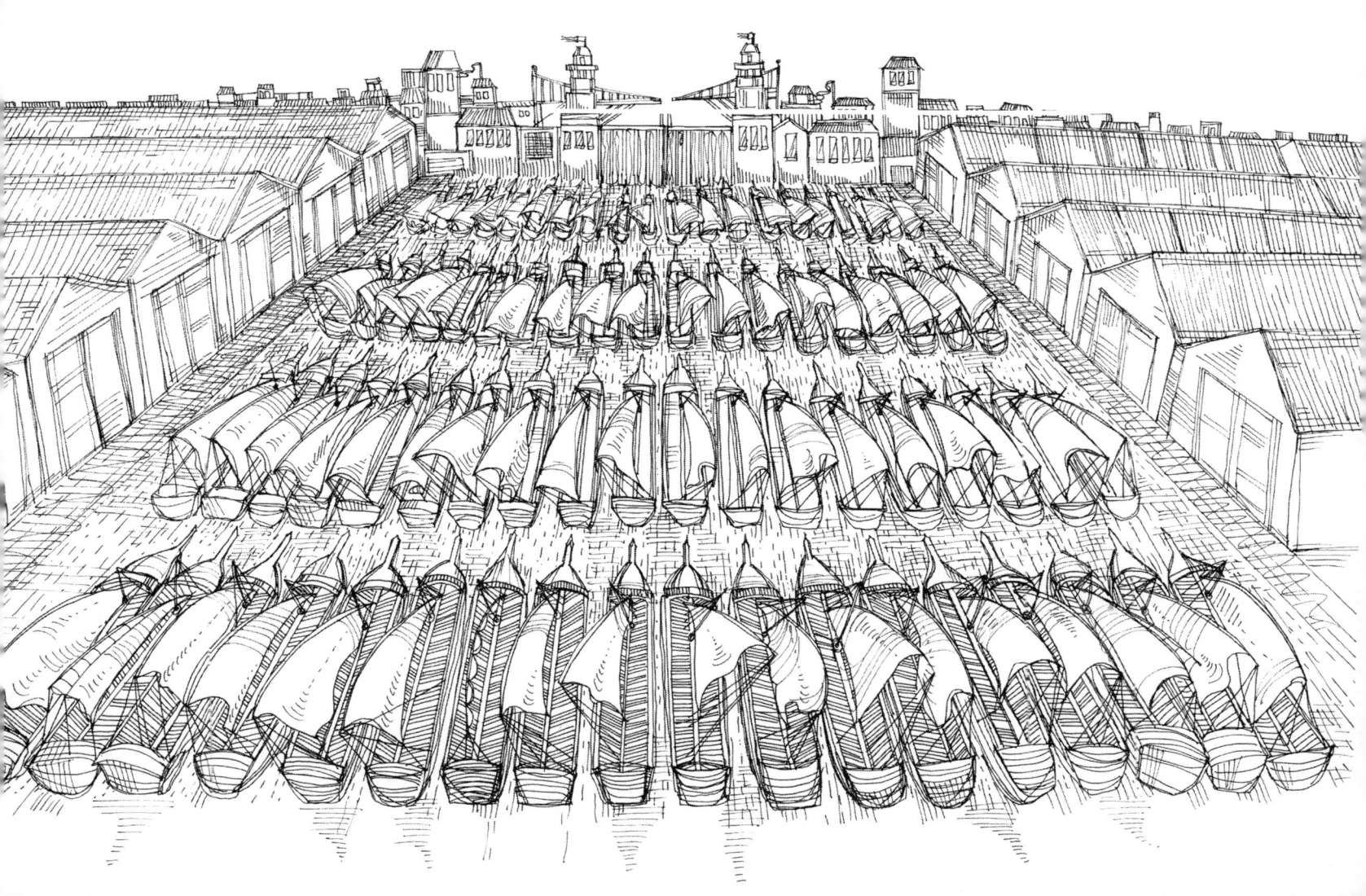

the lion overthrows her master.

Dandolo's final revenge was cast. Using Crusader troops as his pawns, in a move which completely shocked their allies, the contriving *doge,* funneled the European armies into his one, true target - the most Christian of cities, the great Constantinople.

In 1204 C.E., the combined fleets sieged one of the most impressive walled defenses of any city in the world. From below, they knocked out holes and burrowed through. While others attacked the wall from above. They lashed their boats together in pairs, built their masts up high, laid planks across their ramparts and improvise ladders to scale the walls from the sea. Once inside, the soldiers killed thousands in cold blood. Nothing and no one was spared. The city was desecrated and torched, its population shamelessly, ruthlessly massacred.

In just few days, the heart of the Byzantine Empire was smashed for the first time in all of its nine hundred years. The invaders looted all of the city's splendour. Greek marble, Persian onyx and Syrian reliefs were lustfully scoured from her surfaces. Statues were melted down, elaborate artworks were decimated, while gold, silver, and precious stones were plucked from their remains.

Glorious fragments of the world's wealthiest metropolis were shipped to Venice and blatantly affixed to *Basilica di San Marco* to display to the world the new order of things. Its barnacled façade was crowned by four grand, bronze, prancing horses above the main doorway, hailing from Constantinople's Hippodrome. Despite the severe penalty of excommunication by the Pope, this brutal conquest undoubtably marked Venice's callous maritime supremacy and her transformation into a more ruthless empire.

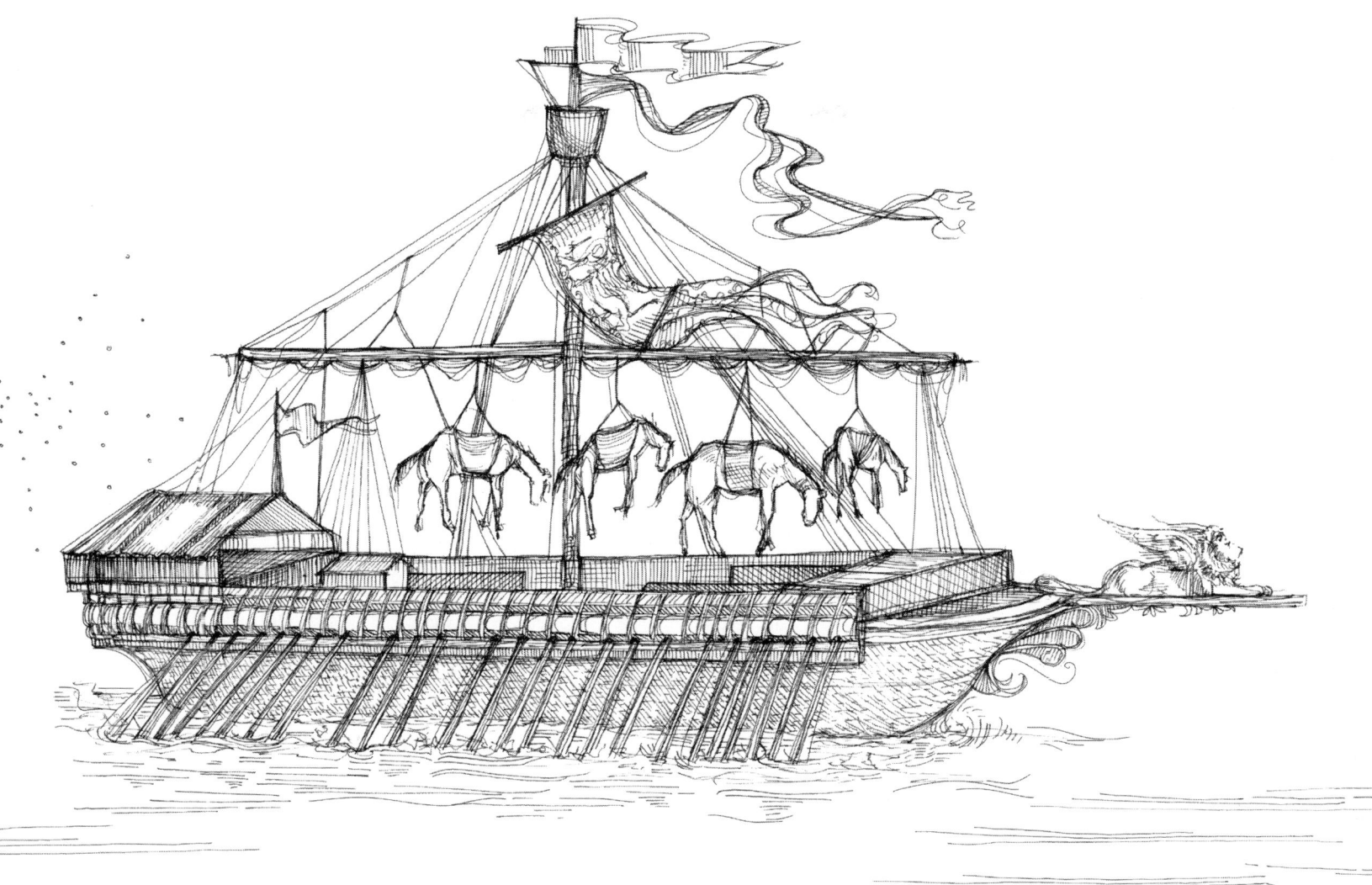

spice monopoly: the lion dominates the sea.

Almost overnight, a population of less than 80,000 had brought their massive colonial empire to its knees. Wanting no part of the Byzantinum inland, the Venetians took half of Constantinople, much of the Aegean coast and some islands in the Ionian Sea, including the key outposts of Corfu, Zante and Cephalonia. They also added the south of the Peloponnese, Crete and Cyprus to their lot, and secured their monopoly on a trade route that stretched to the far reaches of the Black Sea. However, to keep these holdings, Venice would be in constant warfare for the next seventy years.

While her conquests were emblazoned with red and gold lions, Venetians reaped the many resources of her growing dominion. In due season, wine was collected along the Istrian coast. While olive oil from the Ionian islands, like that of Paxos alone, fueled her street lamps, making Venice the first city in Europe to be completely illuminated at night. Yet, the most transformational import in the thirteenth century was certainly the warm and exotic spices brought in from the East; cinnamon from Ceylon, nutmeg from Malacca, ginger from Malabar, black pepper from Hindustan and cloves from Egypt, all sold at insatiably high prices in Europe. This potent and medicinal "black gold" brought in the bulk of her wealth.

As Venice changed her flavour, she remained tactically similar. She created a strict monopoly on her aromatic imports, manipulated the markets, and ruthlessly policed every sale in her ports. She continued to capitalize on her position long before her contemporaries on the *terra firma* had even realized the value of a market economy. More expensive stone slabs, bricks and marble continued to replace her early wooden buildings. Her people were also transformed from their humble beginnings; fishermen became wealthy merchants, who showcased their decadent riches: intricately woven carpets, smooth silks of every colour, and perpetually sparkling gems came to fill their expanding palaces on the Grand Canal.

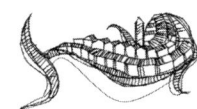

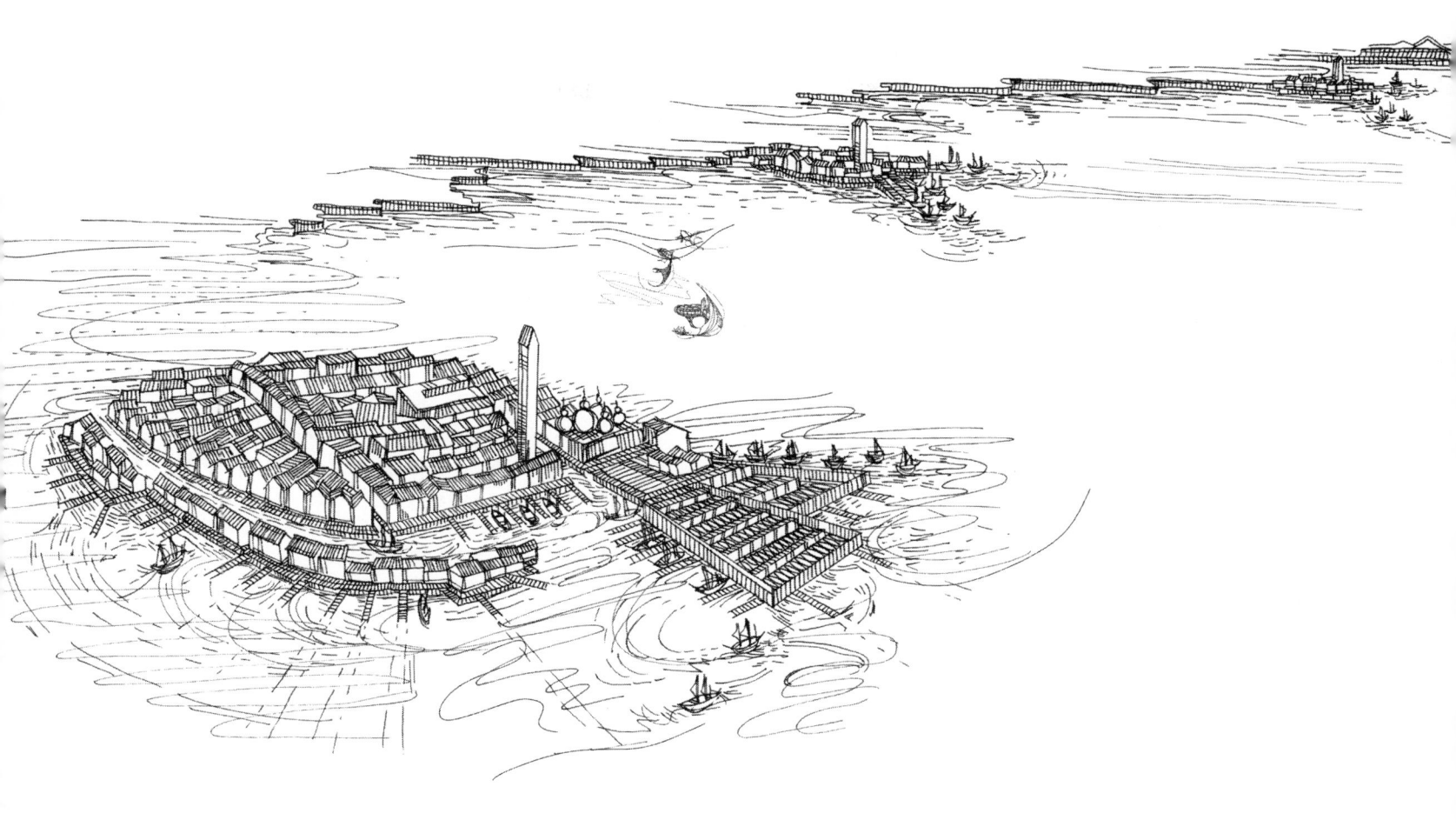

journey to the far east: the travels of marco polo.

Facing outward to the expansive, blue horizon, with all the world passing through her ports, Venice naturally instilled a spirit of travel in her citizens. In 1260 C.E., just as she was losing hold over Constantinople, two Venetian merchant brothers, Nicolò and Matteo Polo, fearlessly pushed past known boundaries to explore the remote reaches of the Far East. Apart from the odd missionary, they became two of the first Europeans to cross the Great Wall of China and enter the elusive court of the powerful Kublai Khan.

Having a father and uncle embark on such an incredible journey, just a few months before he was born, left Marco Polo to dream of an odyssey of his own. And so, in 1271 C.E., when the opportunity arose in his late teenage years, he joined his kin on their return to the Khan's court. Marco immediately charmed the great Mongol Emperor with his elaborate accounts of their journey on the Silk Road and shared tales of his own tiny, yet dominating, in an area of the world which the Mongols had spared.

For the following twenty-four years, the Polos traveled the whole of the Khan's lands as honoured guests. They acted as his emissaries on visits to grand palaces and were free to trade rare silks and gems and spices flowing in and out of the exotic cities. Marco was amazed at everything he saw; he retained remarkable details of the strange and fantastical sights, smells, and customs of their incredible wanderings.

Ironically, after decades of travel and several brushes with death, the Polos faced their most perilous trek on their way back to Venice. They were granted permission to leave the realm of the Great Khan only if they escorted a Mongol Princess on a dangerous sea voyage to Persia. Although they were raided, the Polo family survived the arduous journey and retained a great deal of wealth by strategically sewing precious jewels into the lining of their clothing. Thus bejeweled, they protected their riches, but neared home with priceless stories and new discoveries to share.

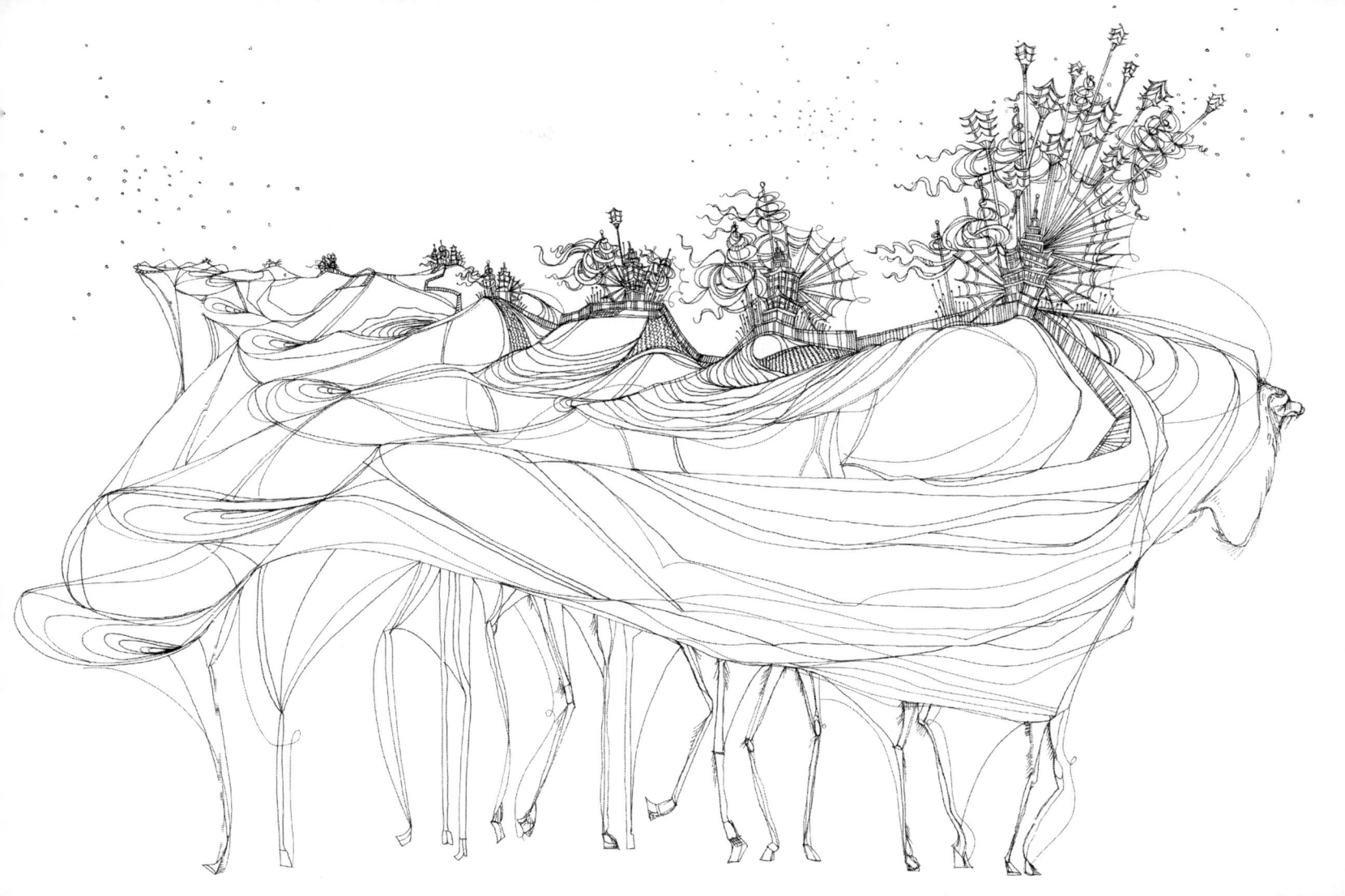

il millone.

When the Polo family returned to Venice in 1295 C.E., the unrecognizably tattered Marco transfixed audiences with a glimpse into the wonders of the Orient.

He offered fantastical descriptions of the unfamiliar. Creatures sounded like absurd impossibilities; elephants reached around with long noses, monkeys scrambled up trees, and horned rhinoceroses charged with intimidating speed. Marco also depicted numerous unheard-of inventions, such as odd paper currency, energy-packed coal, explosive powder, magical printing presses, translucent porcelain, and powerful eyeglasses, which would all change the nature of European life many years later. He also detailed his travels and the enthralling dramas, battles and court intrigues of the Royal Palace at Xanadu. To help subdue any doubts about his unbelievable stoires, Marco simply revealed handfuls of dazzling jewels bursting from his pockets. Luckily, his words still live on; just three years after his return, Marco was captured by the Genose and chance would have it that he was imprisoned with the talented writer Rustichello da Pisa. Although he typically wrote captivating stories of romance and chivalry, Rustichello was compelled to pen his prison mate's captivating accounts in *Il Millone*.

Many to this day still question his elaborate tales, even though he stated "I did not tell half of what I saw" up to his death bed. For the most part, his observations still stand consistent with how we know China to be at his time. Unfortunately, Marco's journey became impossible to replicate; just before the Polos returned to Venice, the Khan died and much of the Mongol empire collapsed. The once prosperous trade routes along the Silk Road were reclaimed by tribal groups, who made it dangerous and largely impassable for Europeans. Regardless, Marco's stories provided important sketches of the unchartered lands in the Middle East, China, Japan and Russia. Future generations were fuelled by his spirit. Even when Columbus hoped to make contact with the Khan's successor, but mistakenly travelled to the New World instead, he kept his well-thumbed copy of Marco's accounts safely tucked at hand.

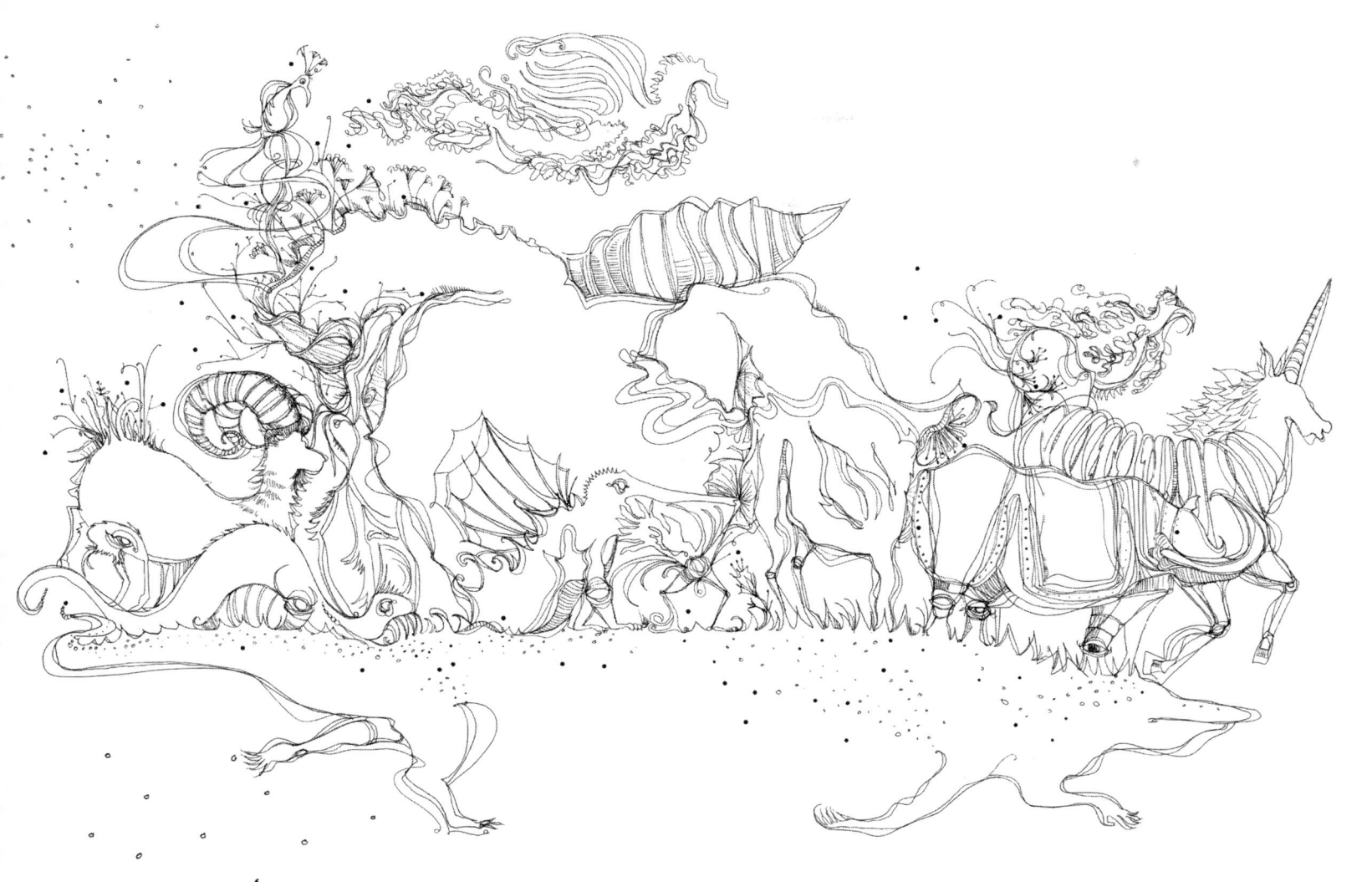

maturation of the state.

In the thirteenth century, while the Republic was expanding to the furthest parts of the world, much of Venetian society was rapidly changing within the lagoon. Many of her governing bodies were diversifying and maturing into their stable forms; new councils, offices, magistratures, and an efficient bureaucracy also emerged.

The advising nobles in the *maggior consiglio* frequently pushed their threshold of 2,000 members and eventually grew too large to be effective. And so, a smaller Senate was elected to counsel the *doge*. In time, select members concentrated into even smaller bodies, such as the Council of Forty, then the more cunning Council of Ten. In times of war, ruling power went to the fierce group of Three Inquisitors. These ruling parties all oversaw the state, ensured that laws were enforced, and quickly extinguished any conspiracies.

Permitted to dress only in black, to signify their submission to the Republic, these powerful nobles used any means necessary to ensure security within the Republic. Like bats, they worked at night and reached into their city's dark corners to listen to concealed whispers and plots. They worked swiftly and their very presence sparked tangible fear amongst foreigners and locals alike.

Although power came to be exercised by a few, intricate systems of checks and harsh punishments ensured that the state was always put at the forefront of any individual power for centuries to follow. For example, in 1355 C.E., just a few, short days after the poorly designed *coup d'etat* by *doge* Marino Faliero was uncovered, the Council of Ten had him arrested, judged, and beheaded; and his ten fellow ringleaders were publicly hung between the columns in *Piazza San Marco*.

A black flag was placed over *Doge* Faliero's portrait in the Ducal Palace, and it still admonishes to all *Hic est locus Marini Faletri decapitati pro criminibus,* meaning "This is the space reserved for Marini Faliero, beheaded for his crimes".

At her core, the majority of Venetian people firmly supported the state and they did not hesitate to post accusations against others. Every anonymous complaint fed into the *bocca della denunce,* or "mouth of denouncement" protruding from the stones of the Ducal Palace was thoroughly investigated. Individual frustrations, desires to have neighbours quietly disposed, or serious plots against the *doge* fell into a tightly controlled bureaucratic response which would have made even Kafka gasp.

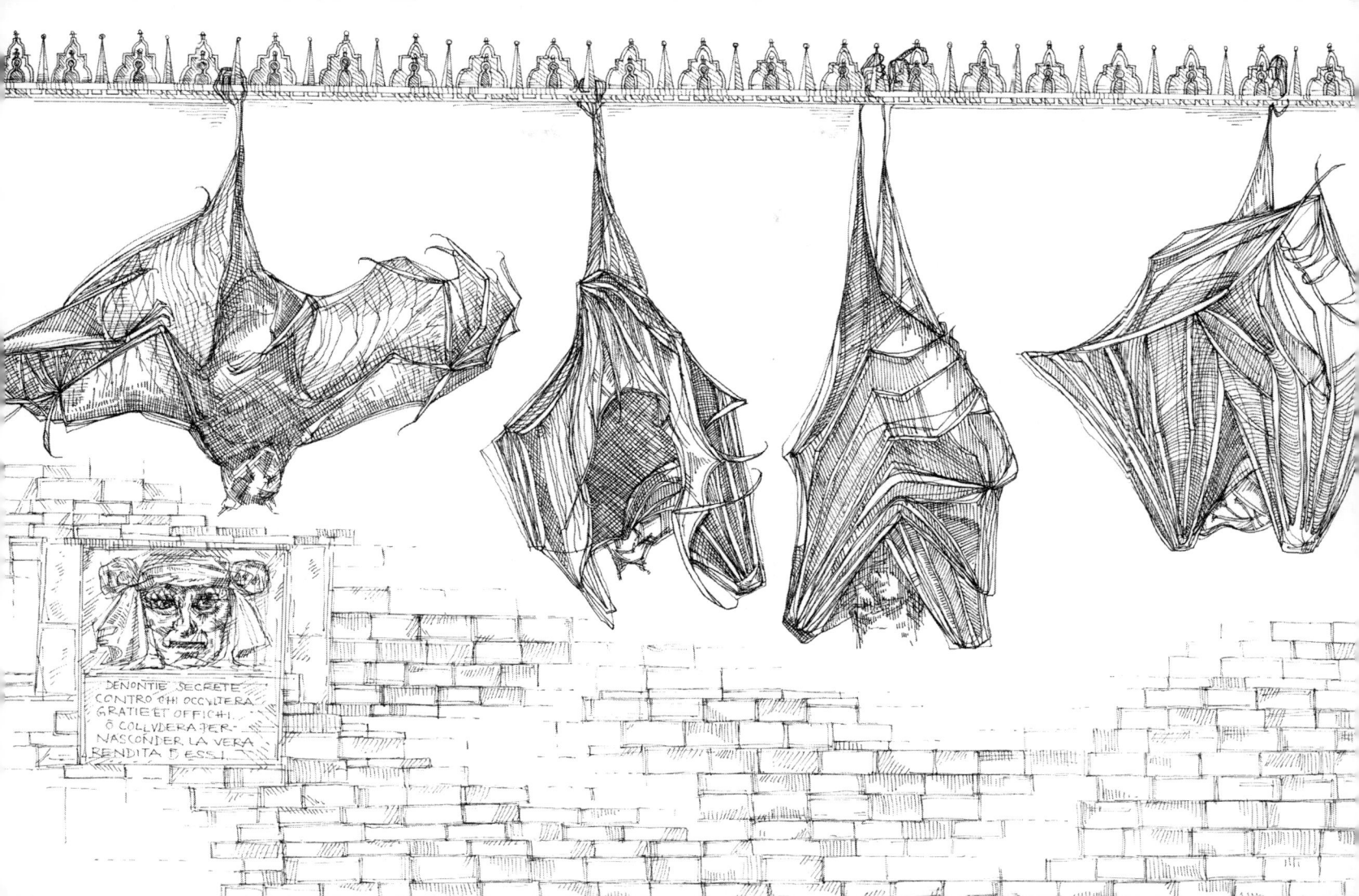

la serrata.

Over time, as the roles of power became more dispersed, convoluted, and intricately woven, the *doge* came to hold very little personal power. Although this life-long position granted much honour, it also involved much self-sacrifice. For example, he could not receive any personal gifts, or meet with a king or powerful ruler in private, or even leave the Ducal Palace without an escort.

In order to prevent the formation of an overpowering dynasty, the ruling class even devised an elaborate ritual and algorithm, unparalleled in complexity, to select each new *doge*: After an election was called, nobles drew lots to choose thirty representatives. From these thirty, a vote was cast and nine were nominated. These nine then named forty, who drew lots to become twelve. These twelve then voted for twenty-five, who were reduced by lot to nine. The nine voted for forty-five, who became eleven, who then voted for forty-one. It was these chosen forty-one who finally nominated a new *doge* for approval and eventual coronation.

Despite these exhausting precautions, in 1297 C.E., the Venetian noble class came to sanction *la serrata*, or closing, of the *Libro d'Oro*. This denied any new and aspiring entrant noble status and political participation. Instead, they greedily passed their exalted privileges down their own familial lines, and locked them within a restricted group. Still, even as her societal roles became more rigid, as a noble, or a citizen, or a *doge*, all Venetians continued to work together under a stable hierarchy; they united against the water, the mud, and any other threats to their hard-won prominence.

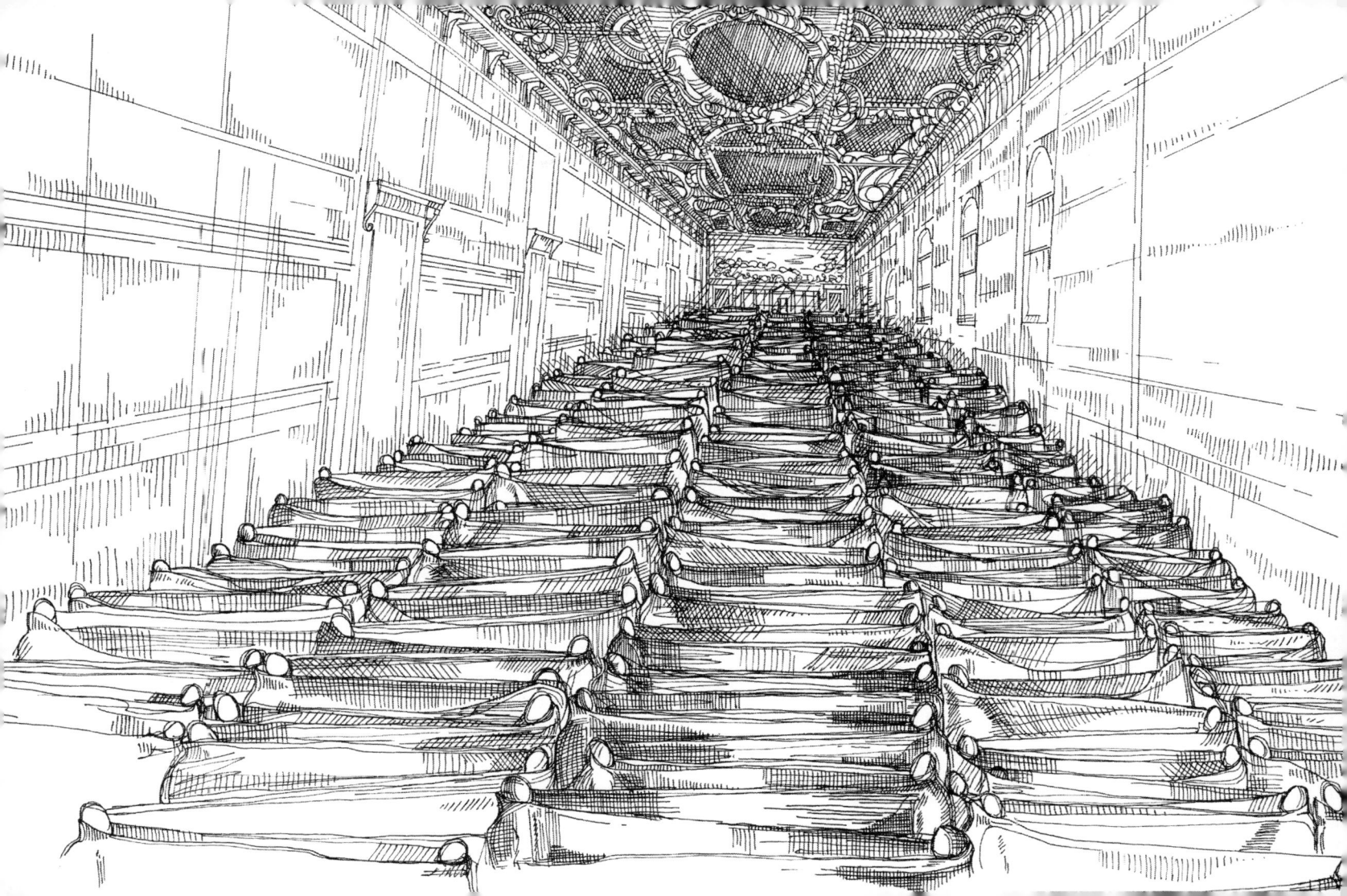

part three: struggles

(14th century - 16th century)

the plague & war with genoa.

Despite precautions, the seemingly unbeatable Republic could not withstand the natural forces of history. During the thirteenth century, the bubonic plague latched onto Venetian imports travelling along the Silk Road. By 1334 C.E. it had already destroyed over two-thirds of China's population, and unsuspecting merchants had shipped the invisible, contagious horror back to their beloved lagoon.

The plague was hidden down deep in the coats of rats, who were carrying lethal fleas, whose stomachs were infected with the undetectable bacillus, *Yersinia pestis*. After contact, the victims developed swollen eyes and painful boils, which burst and formed a thick, black crust over their skin. They suffered from high fevers, severe chills, and insufferable vomiting episodes.

The horrifying plague spread quickly and wreaked havoc upon the lagoon, halving the Venetian population of 150,000 before subsiding. In any given day hundreds were buried in the same open grave. The city's resources were becoming exhausted and drained. The rich plunged to the middle class, while the middle class became poor and the poor found little compassion.

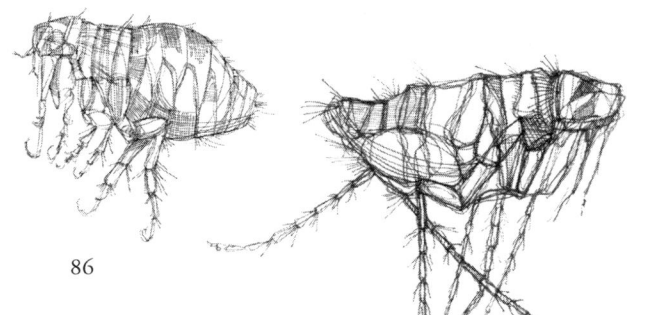

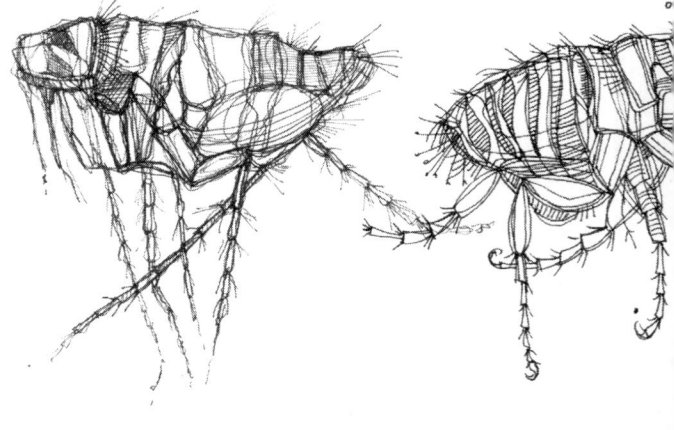

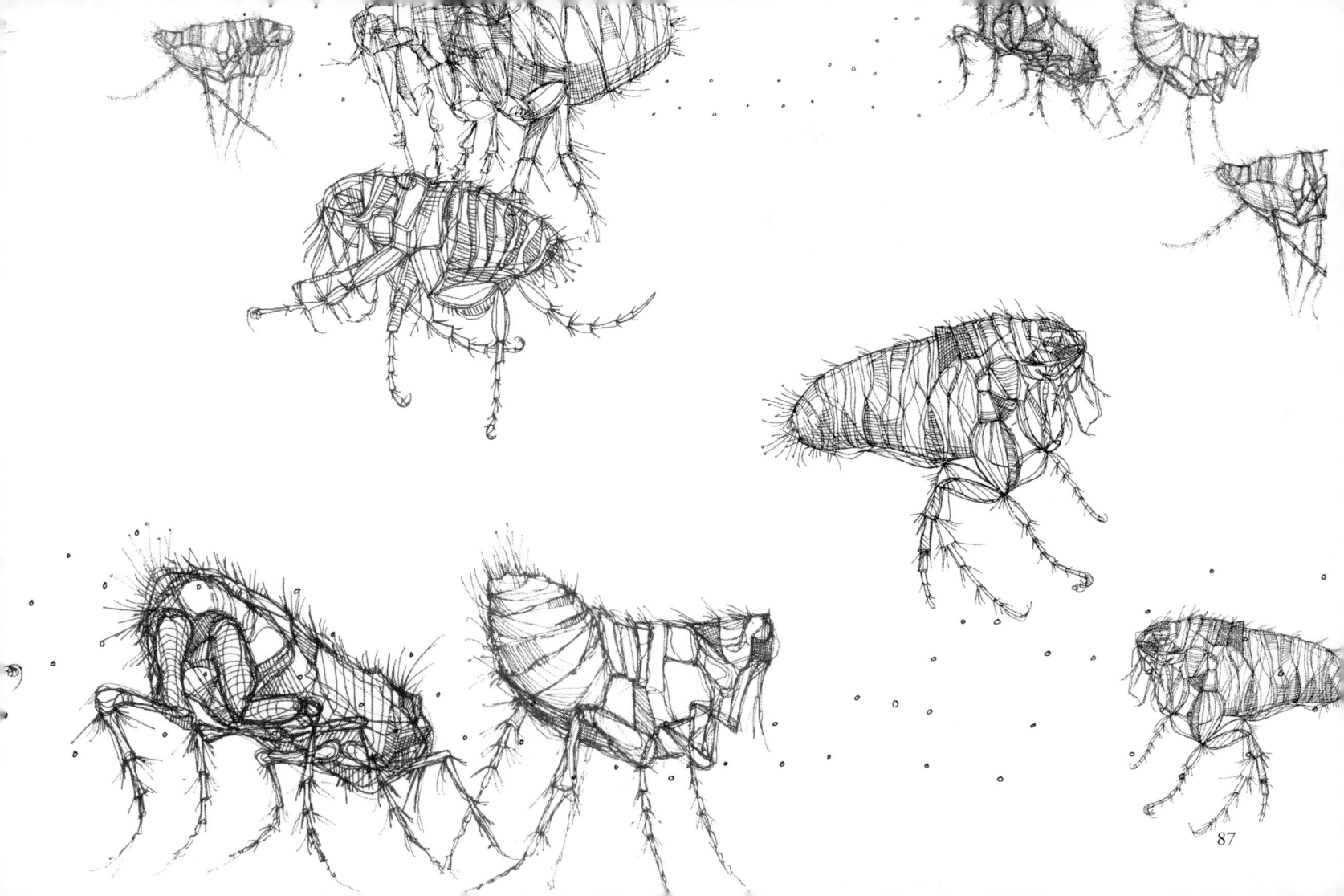

dottore della morte.

To add to her detriment, Venice's long-standing Italian competitors attacked at this vulnerable time, and so began her wars with Genoa and Chiogga (1378-1381 C.E.). Astoundingly, even in their depleted state, the Venetians kept their enemies at bay. Compared to her rivals, the Venetians were better seamen, more accurate navigators, faster and more skilled at shipbuilding, and their opportune location allowed them to reach to the lucrative eastern markets for added financial support during times of desperation.

Motivated by her first deadly encounter with the plague, Venice established a public health system far in advance to that in the rest of Europe. Yet, when the plague returned to the lagoon in 1527 C.E., it still baffled physicians. They carefully patrolled her alleys and canals to identify and isolate the ill. But they treated them with ineffective practices, such as bloodletting, induced vomiting and impotent ointments. Despite their best efforts, the elusive plague continued to decimate the lagoon.

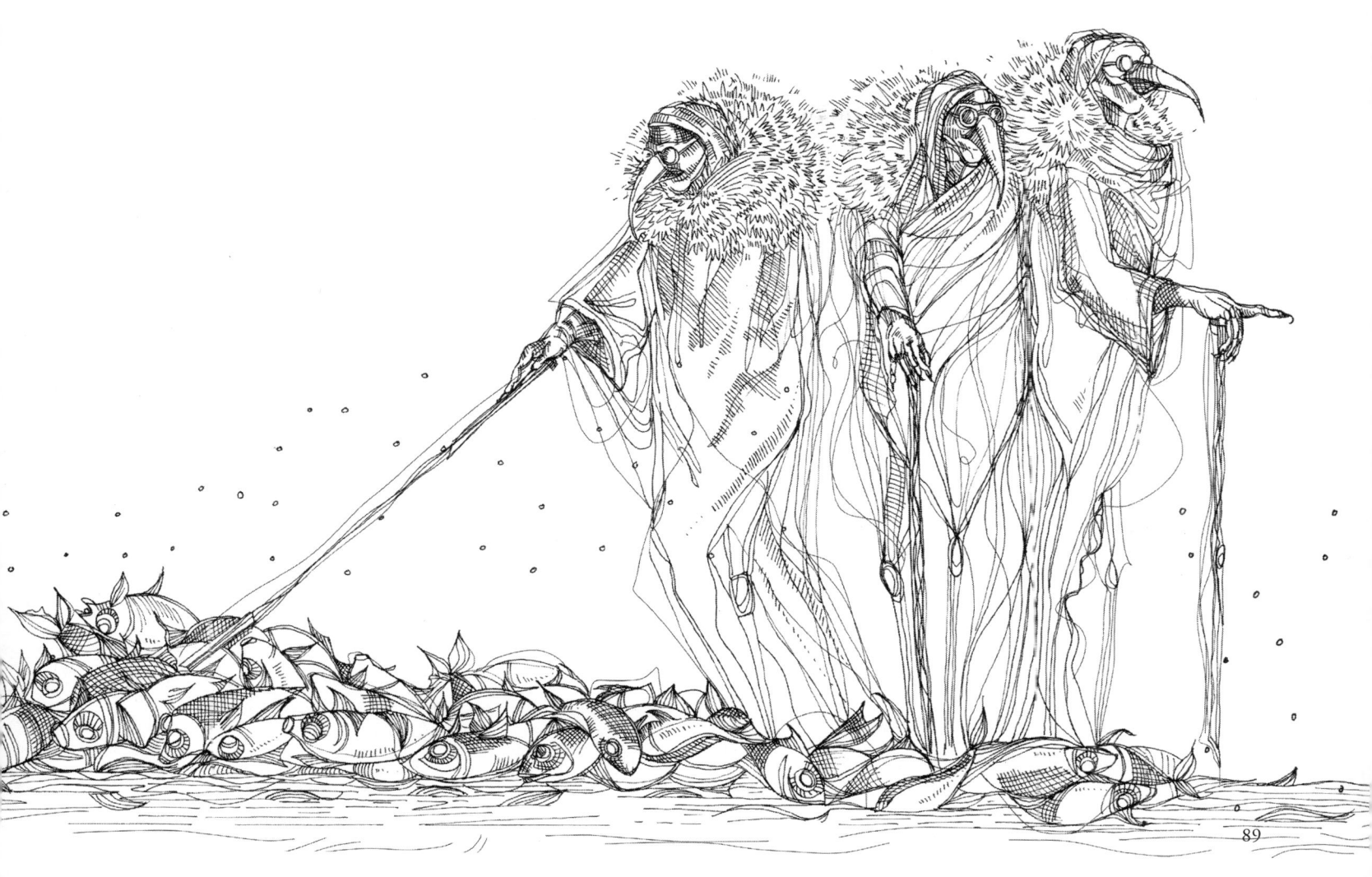

deliverance.

The plague was relentless; it returned again and again. To make matters worse, gravediggers recklessly trafficked infested clothes from the dead, innkeepers disregarded health controls, medical passes were forged, and many of the rich thoughtlessly ignored health inspections, quarantines and trade restrictions. Doctors had little protection. They improvised thick, black overcoats, and coated them in wax as an extra guard. Masks, with long, curved beaks that reached over their noses, were also used; they were packed with pepper and aromatic oils to cover the stench of the dying.

The worst impact of the plague was documented the years 1575-6 C.E., when remaining survivors were confined to their homes. They watched as a dark ash accumulated in sky above, over the island where the infected corpses were burned. Hospitals, overcrowded, held up to four patients to a bed. Many hopeless infected surrendered to the disease and threw themselves into the canals amongst the floating dead.

Nearly every Venetian lost one or more of his or her close relations, and over one-third of those in southern Europe died from the plague. Afterwards, this devastating episode, the city commissioned Palladio built his grand *Chiesa del Redentore*, as symbol of their immense gratitude. After its completion, Venetians formed a somber procession through the city, across a long bridge of boats, to its entrance on Guidecca island. Each step served as a reminder for all that was lost and all that was in front of them. This ritual still continues on each year, in July.

When the plague finally ceased in the winter of 1631 C.E., many survivors fervently embraced religion. Amongst many churches constructed, *Santa Maria della Salute,* was built to honour the Venetian's long awaited release. Their reflective baroque-style spaces were filled with consoling, sacred music, like that of Claudio Monteverdi, born in the Republic's mainland holding, Cremona. While in the synagogues the end of great suffering was lauded with fasting and penitence. The infinitely small virus had brought the zealous Republic to its knees.

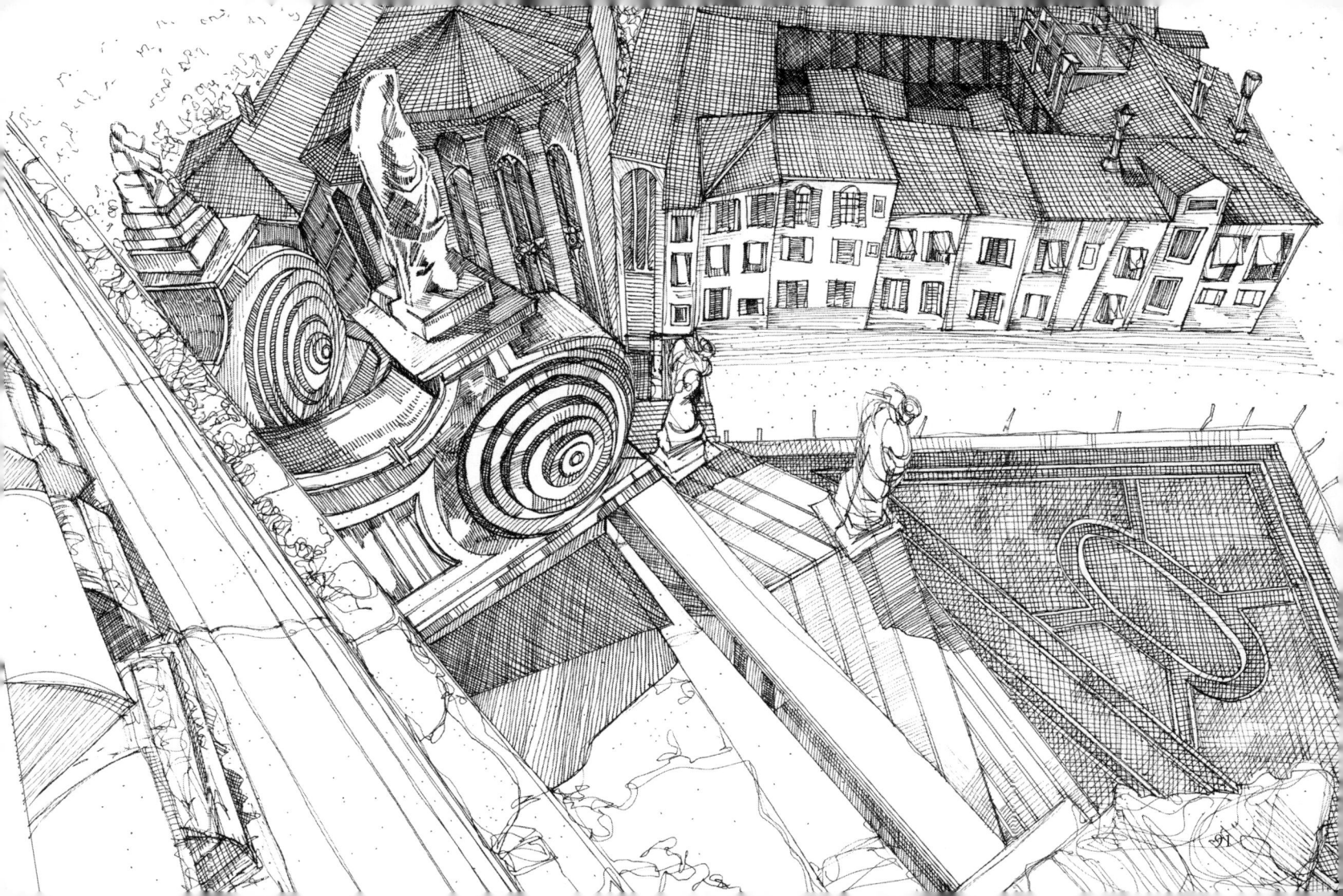

the age of discovery: a race to the new world.

While Venice recovered from the plague, an even more subtle danger was cultivating around her. Seafaring countries were rapidly modernizing their technology. They designed stronger and sturdier vessels, with larger rudders which could better handle the vast, open oceans. More sophisticated navigational tools, like the magnetic compass, also allowed sailors to reach further into the unknown waters. New courses were charted and global maps were quickly being refined.

This rising class of bold mariners were charged with the spirit of discovery. In addition to the tales of Polos, many sailors were inspired by the travel accounts of the equally restless Venetian brothers, Nicolò and Antonio Zen. In the fourteenth century, they explored the outlandishly beautiful coasts along the north Atlantic, up Viking trade routes to Greenland and onward to North America. Luckily, Nicolò's great-great-great-grandson pieced their route and story together from a few surviving letters.

The Zen Brothers' travel narrative fueled a sensation for those hoping to find a northwest passage into the highly desired markets in China. Furthermore, their updated map helped the great German cartographer, Gerard Mercator, to complete his version of the first modern map of the world in 1569 C.E., making such desires more plausible. By the late fifteenth century, global fleets of explorers were on the move.

Driven by their palates for sugar and spice and an equally strong hunger for colonial profits, European monarchs raced to find new courses to the East and new lands to exploit. Ships crept south, along the west coast of Africa, and by 1488 C.E., Bartolomeu Dias reached the Indian Ocean for Portugal. Thirteen years later, Vasco da Gama dared the daunting waters at Africa's southern tip and opened a new, direct sea route to the thriving spice centres of India. During this Age of Discovery, the seas were filled with dreamers encountering the new and unexpected.

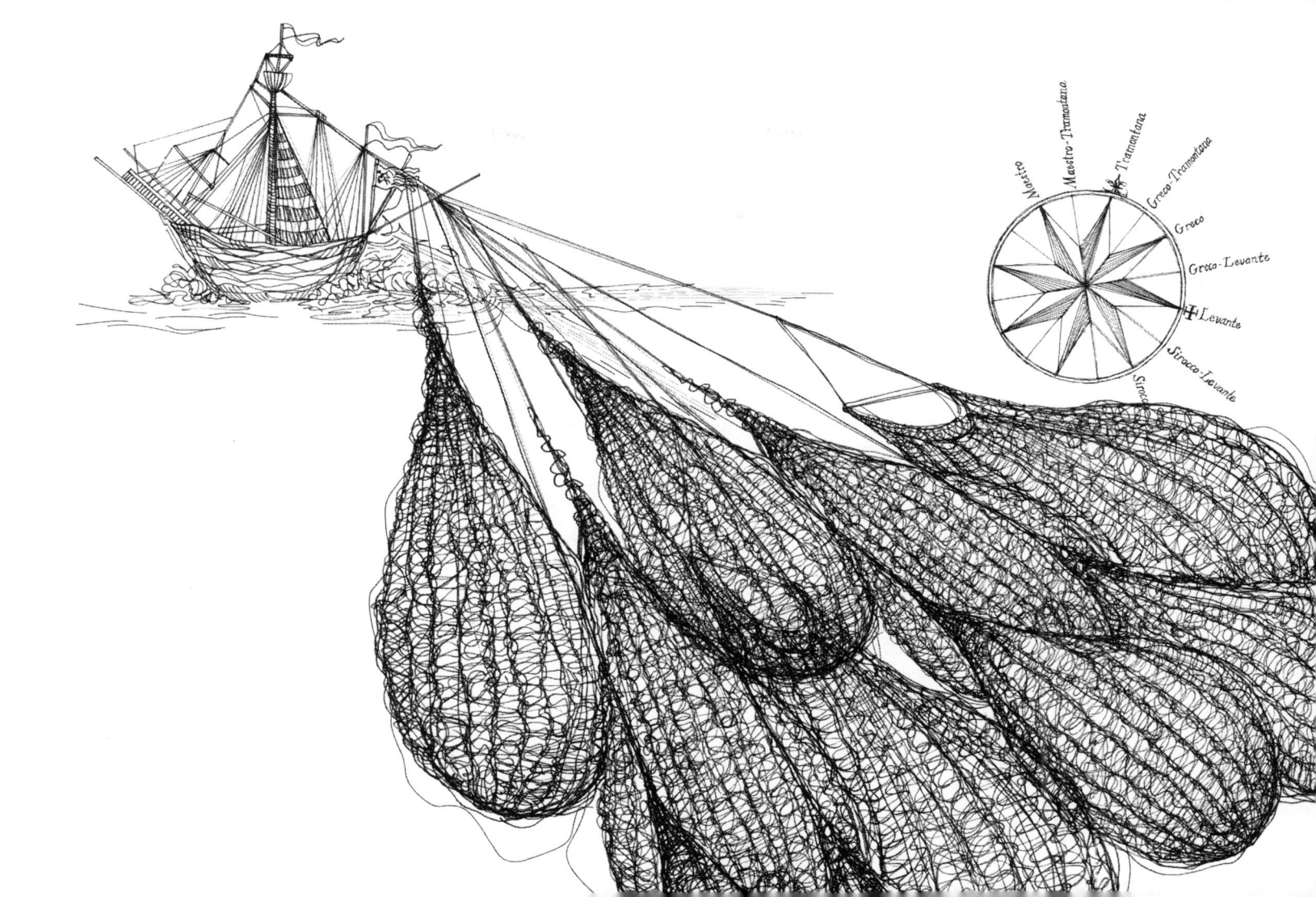

changing worldviews.

After the Portuguese successfully opened a new, direct sea route to Asia, France, England and Holland soon followed suit. They bypassed Venice's trade route monopoly to the East, along with its unreliable camel caravans, threatening pirates, and increasing tariffs.

Perhaps overconfident and not believing that their routes could be made redundant, Venetians kept to their tested systems and design. They even continued to build their traditional oar-powered *galere*, which could not even dare to traverse the great oceans. Regardless, Venetian markets connections were still undeniably strong. For example, when the Portuguese finally arrived in India, they found Venetian *ducati* as the major trade currency. It is difficult to understand whether Venice was left behind or chose to stay behind during these New World developments. Nevertheless, even the most skilled and knowledgeable Italian explorers had to elicit support from elsewhere.

In 1492 C.E., Genoa native, *Cristoforo Colombo* sailed for Spain and five years later, the Venetian-born *Giovanni Caboto* set off for England. While heading west, Columbus landed on uncharted islands in the Caribbean, convinced he had reached China, and Cabot set foot on the shores of North America; both remained unaware of what they had actually encountered.

By the end of the fifteenth century, amongst others racing across the ocean, another Italian, Amerigo Vespucci, reached the coast of South America and returned to Spain certain that it was a new continent. Shortly after, another Florentine, Giovanni da Verrazzano, sailed for the French and mapped the extensive coast stretching from Cabot's Newfoundland down south to the Carolinas, in the United States. Each new voyage revealed endless possibilities, lapping at and eroding the foundations of the reigning, yet abstaining Republic.

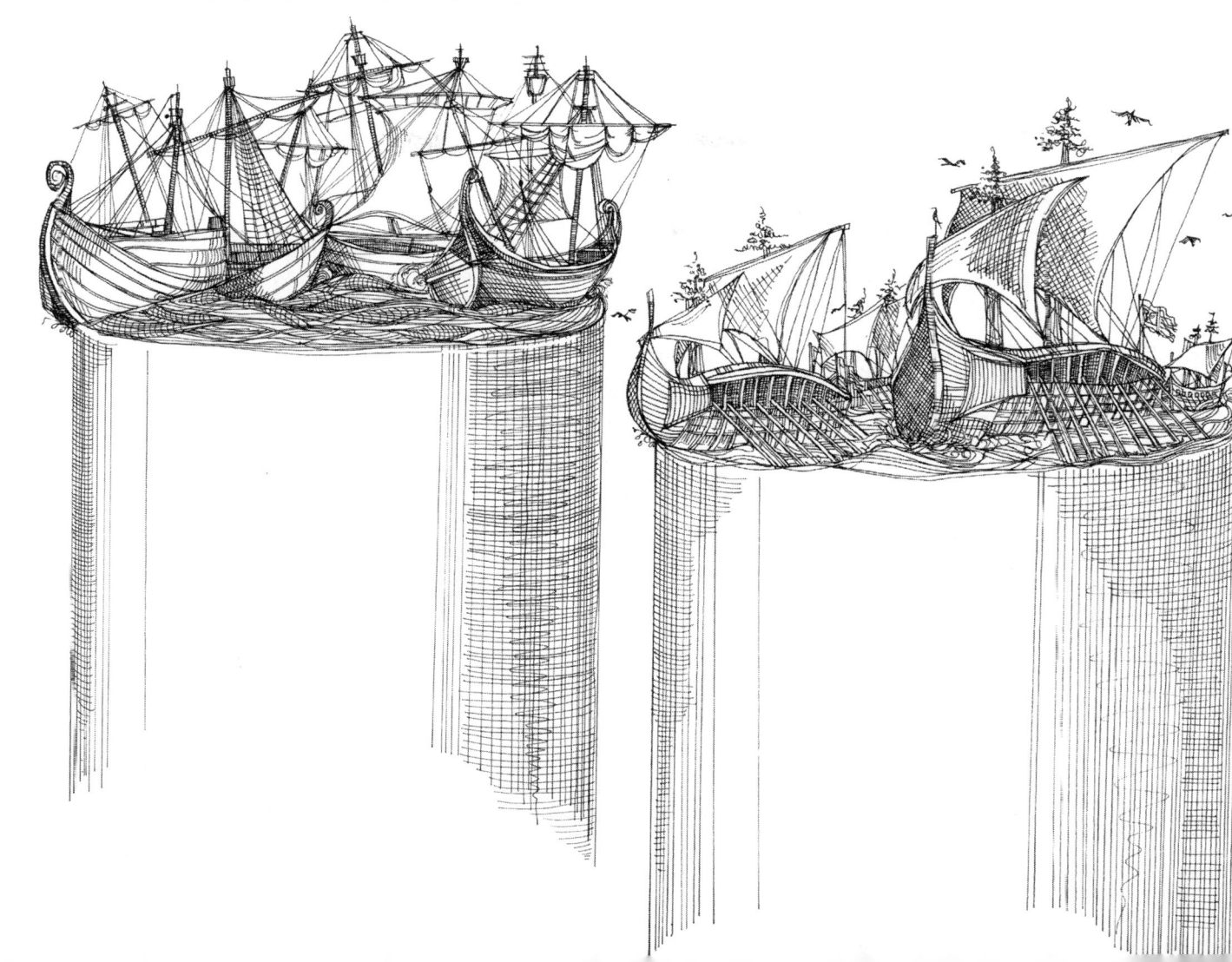

clash of empires.

Not only were her European neighbours exploring nebulous opportunities in the New World, but the Ottoman Turks had gained a great deal of strength. In 1453 C.E., they brutally overwhelmed the still ruined city of Constantinople with massive cannons and the deadly scimitar. The Turks continued to aggressively expand their terrain on the eastern horizon.

In lieu of risking exploring the unknown in the West, Venice remained focused on the crux of her survival; she charmed her prospective enemy. While carpets and textiles were exchanged within the lagoon, Turkish envoys indulged in familiar comforts; they could visit mosques, a pampering *hamam,* and rest in special lodgings in the *Fondaco dei Turchi*, right on the Grand Canal.

With much diplomacy, Venetians continued trading in all major cities of the Ottoman Empire, and her profits ensued. In 1479 C.E., the Republic even sent her most prominent painter to the Sultan's court as a cultural ambassador. Gentile Bellini painted the ambitious Turkish conqueror Mehmed II in a flattering style, wearing a red caftan, trimmed with fur, and an enormous, wrapped turban, to amplify his exceptional power.

Still, this delicate balance was not to hold out indefinitely. After the Turks increased tariffs on Venetians, seized more of her colonies, and entertained merchants from Florence, war was soon declared between these two superpowers. This time however, the resulting stance did not fall into Venetian favour. The surprisingly strong Turkish fleet expelled them from much of the Mediterranean. They took her beloved Cyprus and Crete and reduced her vast eastern dominion down to a few meager fragments. The humbled Venetians retreated and heavily reinforced their final holdings with massive, stone fortresses and weakened navy.

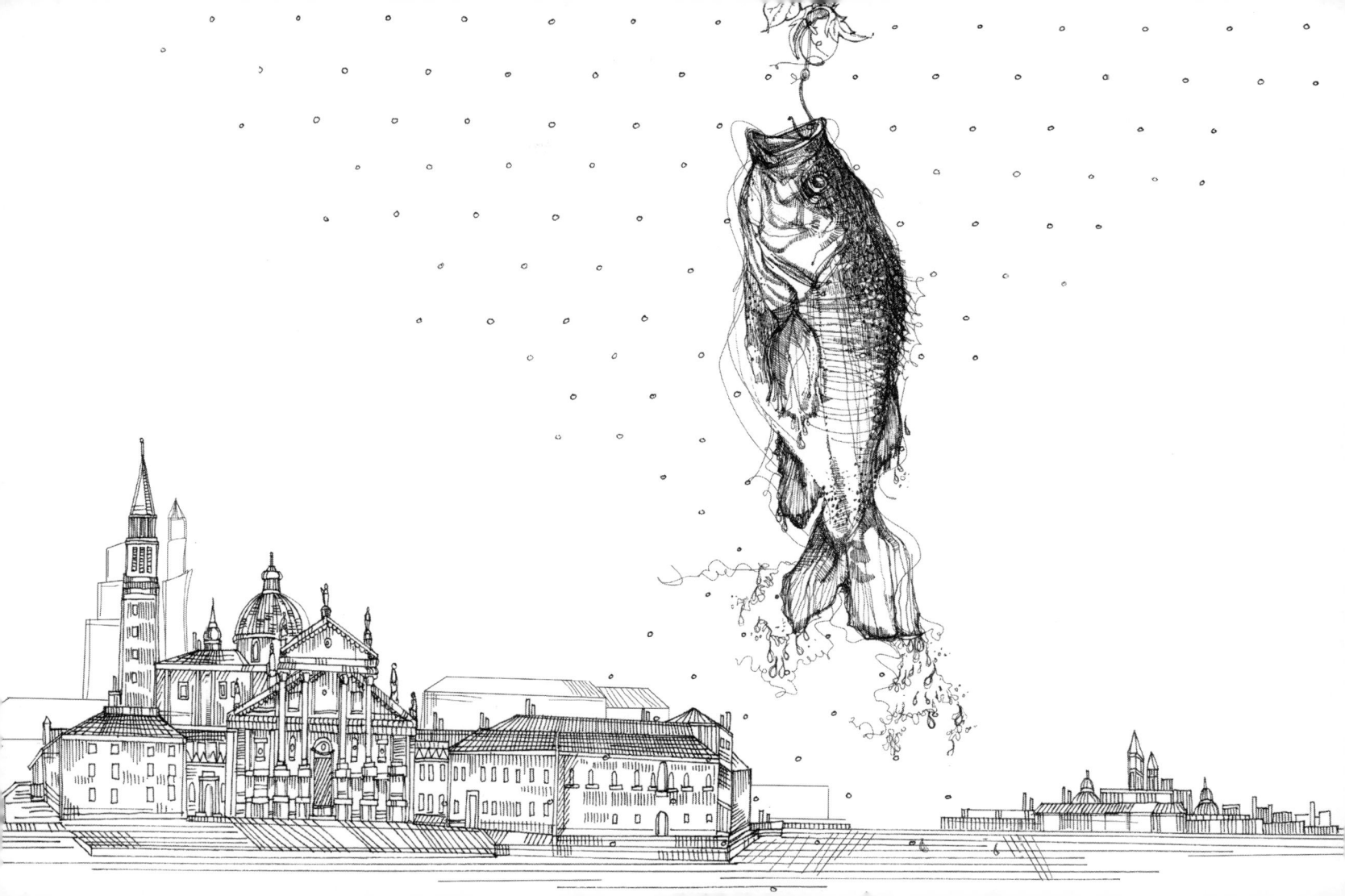

mainland infiltration.

Without the life-support of her navy and merchant ships, Venice was forced to turn to the very land from which she had originally fled. The *terra firma* was too enticing to resist any longer. It promised rich agricultural land in the fertile plains of the Po valley, thriving industries, and extensive road and river connections to more supply routes and merchant cities within Europe. With little alternative, over many generations, Venice engaged in a series of exhausting land battles and set deep roots on the Italian mainland.

However, another power sought to smother any further Venetian encroachment. Pope Julius II saw her expansion as an immediate threat to his bordering papal territories. Towards the end of 1508 C.E., he aligned with France and Spain, who also held ambitions in northern Italy, as The League of Cambrai.

In just fifteen days, this powerful, combined army brutally seized all Venetian territories on the mainland that took them centuries to acquire. This particular humiliation was promptly underlined by the observing Nicolò Machiavell, in his codex entitled *The Prince*, in which he analyzed complex mechanisms of power in politics.

The Venetians had to confront the unthinkable notion that their lagoon sanctuary could one day be invaded. However, this fear never materialized. Over a ten year period, diplomacy rather than force won Venice back her mainland holdings. Even during this courageous revival, she kept outside of most conflicts on the *terra firma* and chose not to aggressively expand. Peace and neutrality became her new mantra. She transformed into *La Serenissima*, or "The Most Serene Republic".

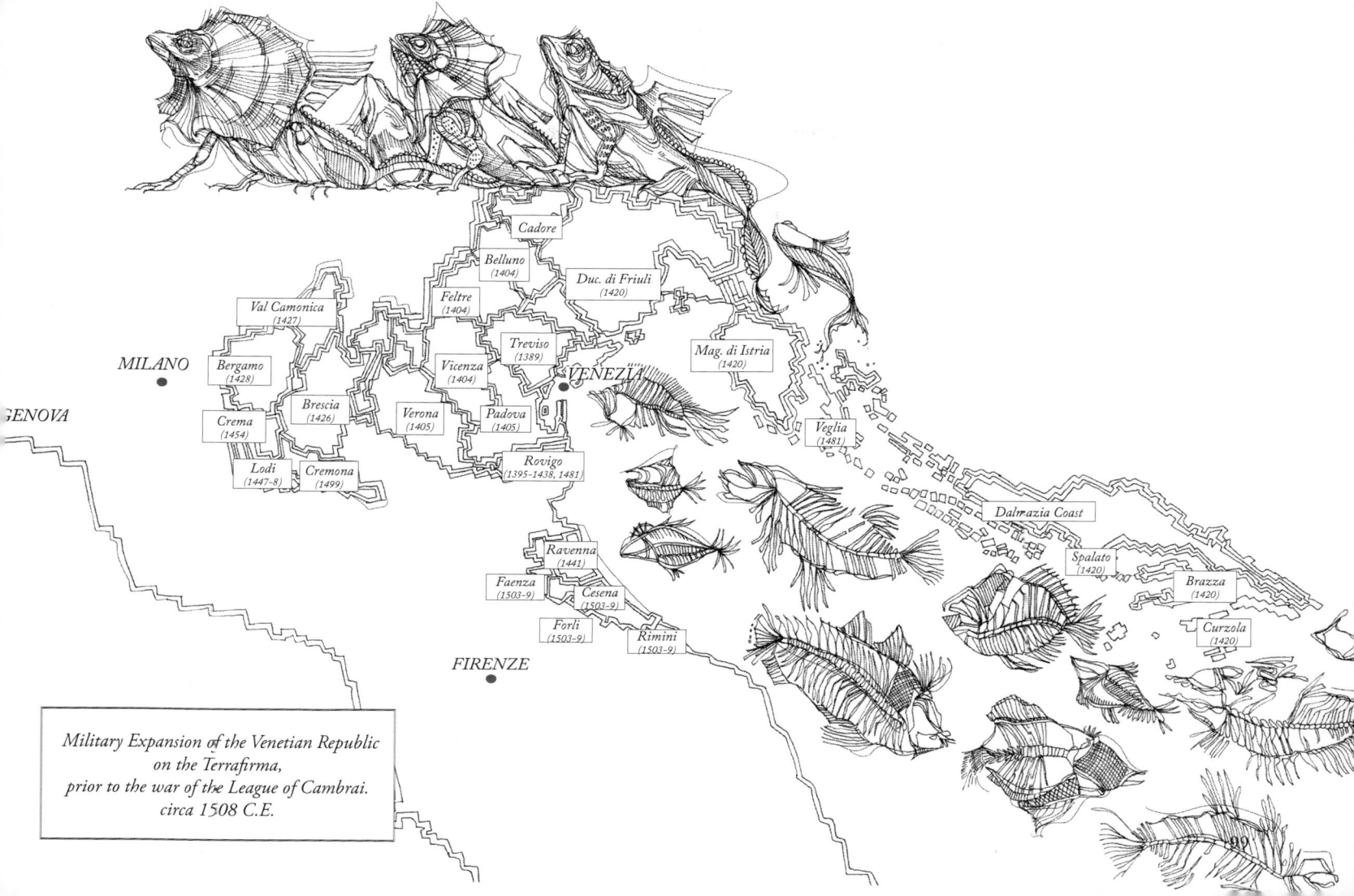

inquisition, reformation & heretics.

During the fifteenth century, powers on the mainland continued to clash and drastically shift. For example, in Spain, King Ferdinand II and Queen Isabella, the same royalty who granted Columbus his ships, expelled Muslims from the Spanish peninsula, and together with the Catholic Church, used a ruthless Inquisition to exile any remaining heretics from their lands.

La Serenissima largely remained neutral and, being a natural hub for trade, was more open than other European countries to foreign cultures. She offered a home to many displaced persons regardless of their religion or orgin. However, backlash was brewing on the mainland.

In the small German town of Wittenberg, which was the furthest university north of Rome and its politics in Europe, a fevered monk, Martin Luther, started to freely question the Catholic Church. He criticized prevailing papacy behaviours as nepotism, usury, and selling indulgences to the poor to raise money to rebuild St. Peter's Basilica in Rome.

Eventually, in 1517 C.E. Luther's *Ninety-Five Theses* was famously posted to a weathered church door. Normally, his readership would have been limited to the Wittenberg faithful. But, because of the newly invented printing press, his ideas, along with vernacular translations of the Bible, were copied and widely distributed throughout Northern Europe. Within a few short months the Protestant Reformation was set into motion. It invited theological debate, catalyzed the formation of various sects, and began to shape new ideals of freedom on the mainland.

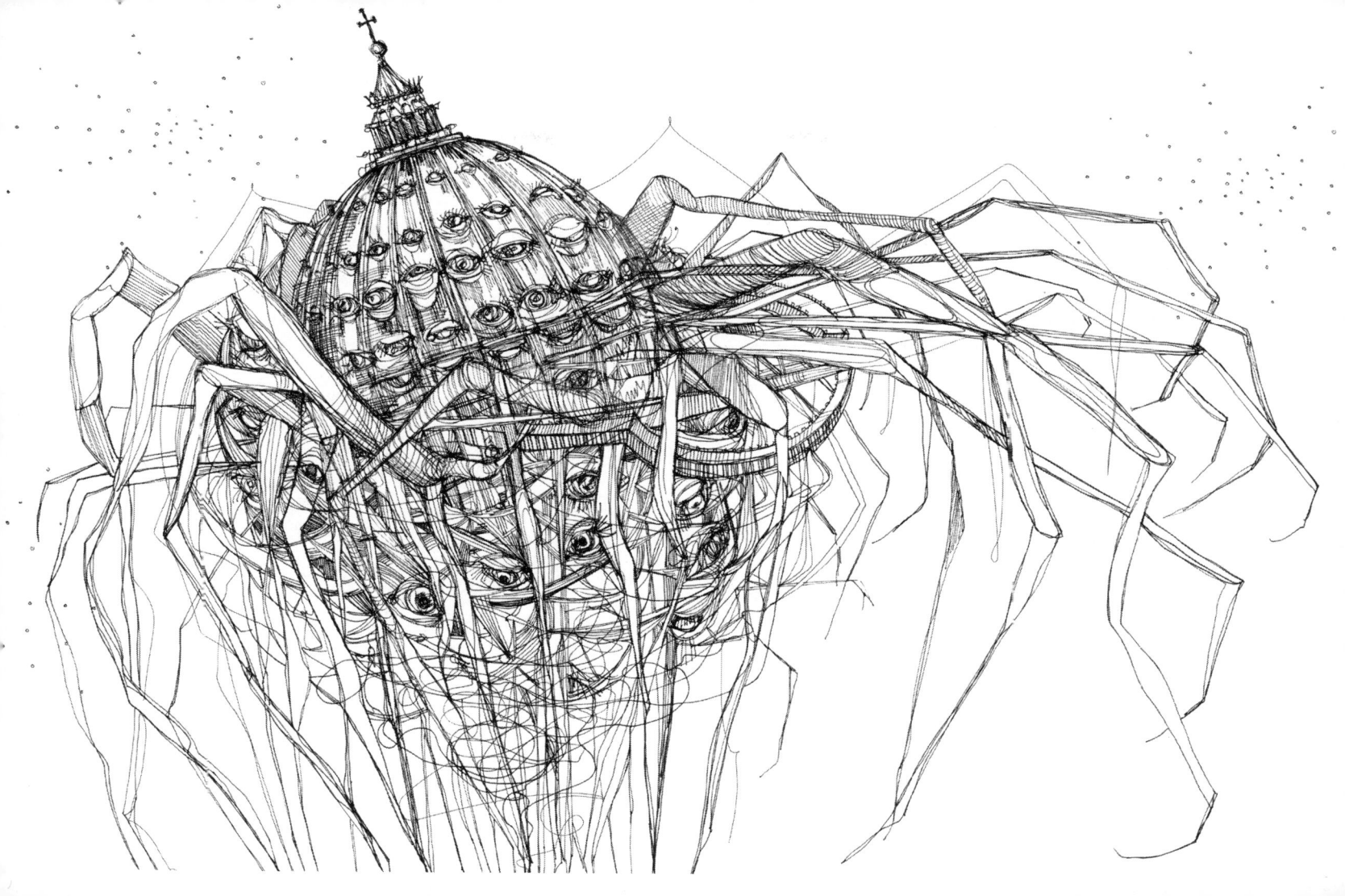

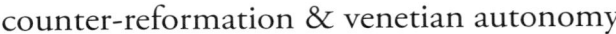

counter-reformation & venetian autonomy.

The main currents of Lutherism and Calvinism, along with many other rapids and ripples of the Protestant Reformation, began a fight inside the Catholic Church. In an attempt to avoid being lacerated into pieces, it formed the *Concilio di Trento* in 1545 C.E., for European bishops to discuss their next steps. While *La Serenissima* remained outside of mainland politics, her chief theologian, Paolo Sarpi, meticulously documented the events of the *Concilio di Trento* throughout its ten years. He encouraged the Church compromise with the reforming forces and open itself to more contemporary ideas, but the conservative approach prevailed.

The Princes of the Germanic North, along with Luther, broke away from their religious ties and joined with similar-minded individuals to escape its power and control. The Church went back into its fortress of doctrine, protected by walls of firm canon, and set in motion the Counter-Reformation with its new Inquisition. While it tightly gripped hold of Italy, the Church fought well into the seventeenth century to win back northern Europe and its smaller states undergoing the Counter-Reformation.

Although Venice initially agreed with the orders of the *Concilio di Trento*, she was quick to resist their practical application if it interfered with her own sense of progress. She remained true to her maxim: *"Venetians first, Christians second"*, and used her stronghold of Saint Mark to keep from being saddled with Rome's dictates. When the Inquisition arrived at Venetian shores, it criticized many of her broad-minded practices and divergent politics. Venetians were denounced for publishing prohibited books, for offering work to Jewish inhabitants, and for providing asylum for typically mistrusted *marrani*. Accordingly, the Counter-Reformation did not take hold as strongly in Venice as in other parts of Europe.

Even when *La Serenissima* was threatened with excommunication again, she did not relent. From her earliest days, Venice sought to exercise her autonomy in all respects, and understood that her survival was only possible through assimilation and adaptation. She had to stay open to the world around her; if she was too rigid, or too hard, she would simply sink.

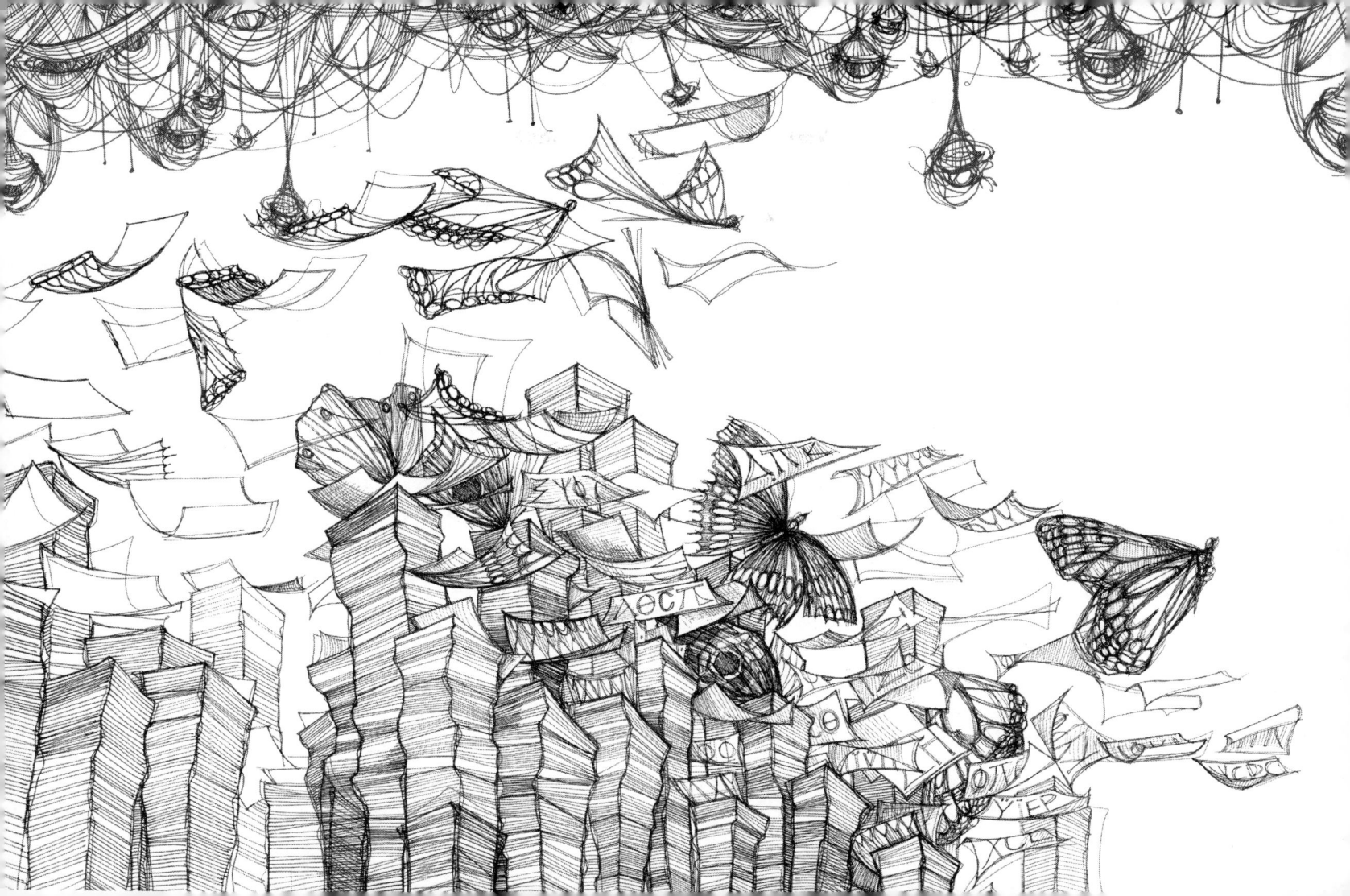

money lenders, a new economy, & the ghetto.

While rebounding from years of malaise and grueling wars, *La Serenissima* held a diminished work force, who faced the unpleasant realities of poverty. Consequently, in as early as the thirteenth century, they opened their markets to Jewish workers to stimulate their ailing economy. Venetians desired their fresh capital and thriving trade network along the Mediterranean. They also hoped Jewish moneylenders would offer small loans to help to lift the Venetian poor out of debt, which was a practice strictly forbidden to Christians.

Unlike anywhere else in Europe at this time, Venice provided charters for Jews to reside and carry out business in the lagoon. However, clear lines were drawn to keep the Jewish and Christian populations distinct. Within Venice, Jewish residents could not go to school or educate Christians; they could not have relations with Christians, or work in any sector which would compete with their Christian contemporaries.

As in the rest of Europe, Jews could not own land or property and were kept as a mobile population. They could be banned from the city easily, but in time, this served more of a hallow negotiating tactic. Even so, in time, the Venetian Jews came to be commonly slandered for their practices in a business which they were encouraged to take up. Despite this backlash, along with heavy taxes and tightly imposed restrictions, the freedoms in *La Serenissima* were still more abundant compared to those in rest of Europe.

Still, with added pressure from the Church and its Inquisitions, reins eventually became tighter; in 1516 C.E. the city's Jewish communities were moved to her more isolated *Ghetto Nuovo* area. The *ghetto,* a term which originated in Venice, was enclosed by a wall and separated from the city except for one drawbridge. Space was tight and controls were put into place to closely regulate their behaviours and activity.

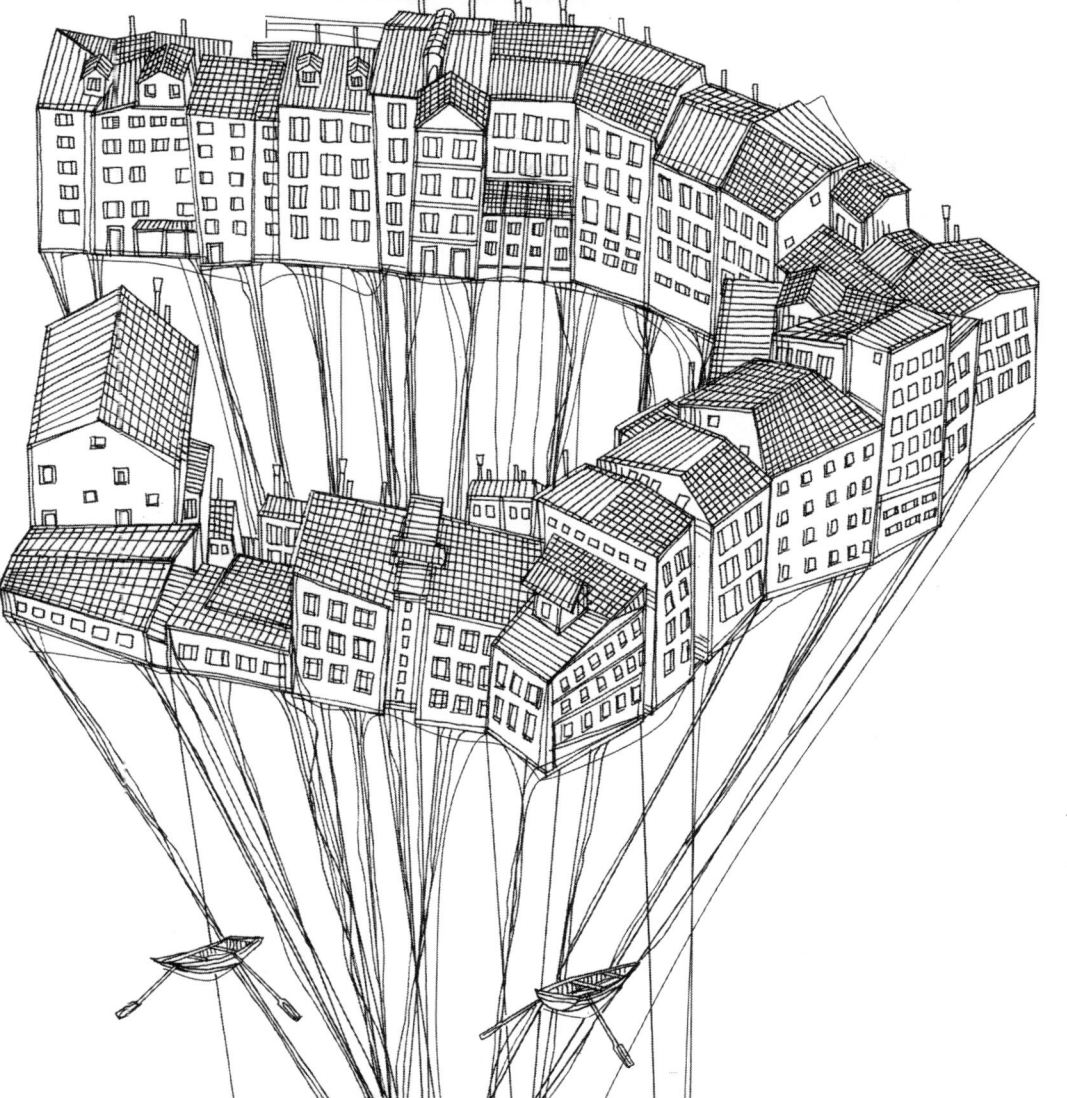

In the confines of the *ghetto*, Venetian Jews were forced to pay Christian guards surveilling their surrounding canals, who were placed to protect them from any conflicts arising outside their walls. They also had set curfews and identifying dress codes mandated.

In time, the *ghetto* became overcrowded. With limited space, it was forced to grow upward; some of its buildings reached seven stories high. Still, space was lacking, and many took shifts sleeping on the floor. The *Ghetto Vecchio* area was soon constructed. This larger space became a vibrant and diverse community of Levantine, German and Italian Jews, who travelled a difficult path together, and found a small haven in the lagoon.

marrani & the revenge of joseph nasi.

Many foreigners found a sense of safety within the lagoon. Many *marrani* who were persecuted in Europe for converting from Judaism to Christianity during the Inquisition found more tolerance in the Republic. But, if one had elusive community ties, or retreated to the *ghetto* to celebrate Jewish customs only to attend Church the next day, or ate both kosher and non-kosher diets, or was accused of having multiple baptisms for money, he or she was promptly investigated. Those who challenged her intricately woven social organization, especially during the Inquisition, were commonly banished to monasteries, colonies and hospitals. While the most unfortunate were killed and hung throughout the city. *La Serenissima* had little tolerance for any dishonest, threatening, subversive, or overly predatory behaviours.

One exceptional case the noteworthy *marrano* named Joao Micas, alias Giovanni Miches, alias Juan Migues, alias Joseph Nasi. This man of many names was part of the extremely wealthy Mendes family, which caused *La Serenissima* an unimaginable set of problems alone. After marrying his wealthy cousin, who was herself banished from the Republic, Joseph Nasi was exiled and condemned to death between the two columns of *Piazza San Marco*. He quickly fled to Constantinople with his wife, and compelled five hundred other *marrani* in Venice to join them.

Using his vast trading ties and financial influence, Nasi tenaciously built up his political career. By 1561 C.E., he had already gained the favour of the Sultan and tried to create his own Jewish settlement in Tiberias. However, after disappointing results, Nasi came to focus all his efforts on revenge. He plotted with the Turks to take the beloved island of Cyprus away. In 1570 C.E., when the Turks attacked and claimed it for their own, Nasi became a feared legend in the Republic.

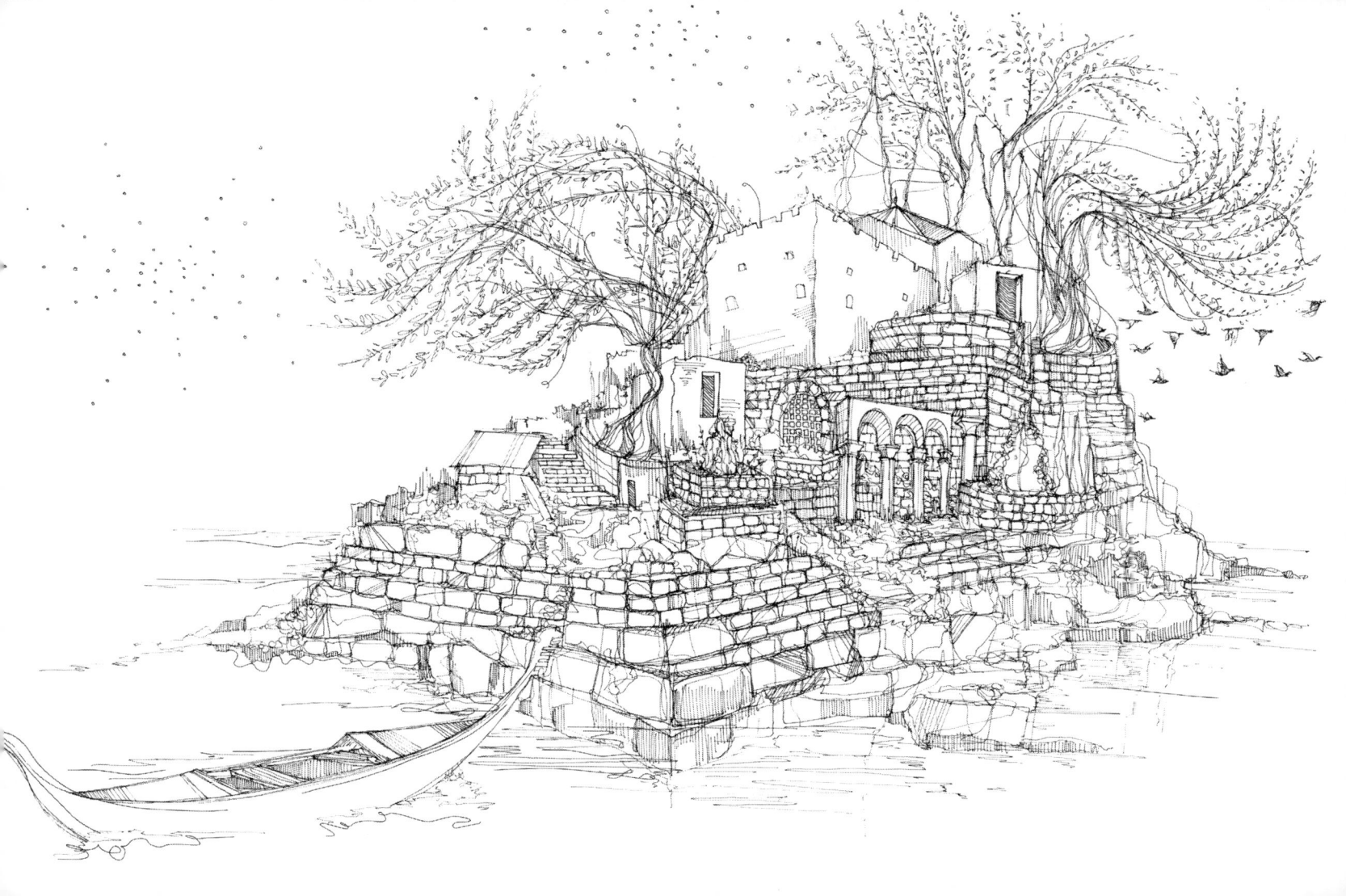

turkish contenders & the battle of lepanto.

The Ottoman Turks continued to aggressively expand. After taking Syria, Egypt, Rhodes and Algeria, they seemed unstoppable, and ready to advance into Europe. Faced with this pivotal threat, the Serene Republic stepped out from her veil of repose and aligned with the Holy League and Spain. Together they challenged the Sublime Porte in one of the largest naval conflicts of the sixteenth century, the *Battle of Lepanto*.

Off the western coast of Greece, hidden deep inside the Ionian sea, over two hundred oar-powered *galere* engaged in brutal, hand-to-hand combat on trembling waters. Ships bearing crescent moons and crosses smashed each other, burned, and grounded themselves ashore; the blood pouring from maimed and fallen bodies was enough to turn the water red. However, the European fleet had a significant edge; they introduced larger, more formidable *galezze* into the battle. Their ships were specially designed by Venetians and fitted with an unsurpassable amount of guns, canons and ammunition by European metalworkers. These enormous, wooden sea monsters advanced quickly and burst into battle. With projectile iron spheres and pellets, they tore apart the Ottoman fleet, draped in green, silk banners. After its flagship was defeated, the remaining Turkish fleet retreated in shock and grieved its first loss in over a century. The Ottoman expansion was deflated and this decisive defeat ultimately denied the Turks access to the Atlantic and Americas.

However, just two years after such a monumental battle, the Venetians signed a treaty with the Ottomans, separate from their Christian allies, which formalized their loss of Cyprus, but maintained their friendly trade relations with the Levant. Always focused on self-preservation, *La Serenissima* continued to pursue diplomacy and peace from its guarded, gilded barge, safely perched above the sparkling Adriatic Sea.

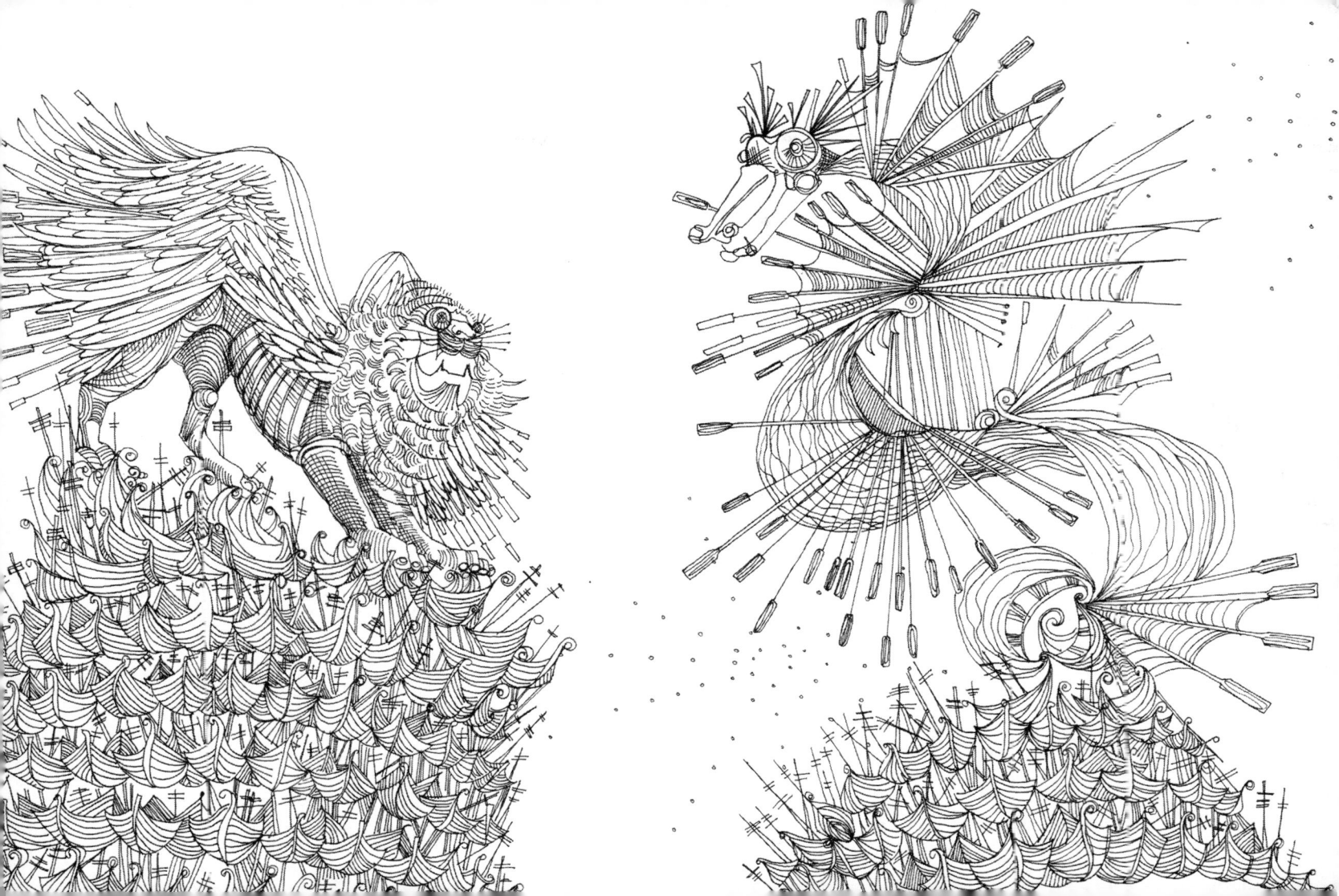

part four: exchanges

(15th century - 16th century)

venetian renaissance & the printing press.

Throughout her development, the Serene Republic trod both eastern and western Roman Empires. But during the fifteenth century she associated more with her Florentine and Roman neighbours who were embracing the Renaissance and its revival of ancient Greek and Roman ideals.

Meanwhile, her entrepreneurs quickly capitalized on Gutenberg's novel moveable-type printing presses to rediscover the classics. In just thirty years, Venice became the printing capital of the world. Her leading printer, *Aldus Manutius*, published over 130 titles, with the help of many Greek scholars fleeing from ruined Byzantinum. Together they translated nearly all known works of the Greek era. Their first editions of Aristotle, Homer, Thucydides sold in unprecedented quantities.

As Humanism exploded in the lagoon Venetian architects endeavored to externally express its ideology. However, many designers struggled to replicate ancient proportions. Coincidentally, in 1527 C.E., the Holy Roman Empire challenged the Catholic Church and rampaged through much of Rome, diverting many classically trained artists into Venice. They brought with them the missing expertise to initiate a High Renaissance.

Amongst these incoming talents, Jacopo Sansovino was assigned to give the *Piazza San Marco* a face lift. Once full of convoluted, medieval stalls, Sansovino transformed the *Piazza* into a refined entrance, which immediately asserted power. Of his many creations, his library, with rows of ionic columns stationed above a doric arcade, was revered as one of the most richly ornate Renaissance structures built since ancient times.

However, the challenge to make its support completely out of bricks, and thus fireproof, proved insurmountable. Its base buckled and collapsed. Even a *maestro* like Sansovino paid for his error dearly; he was imprisoned until his building was fully restored.

A humble stone mason from an impoverished background, Andrea Palladio, emerged from Sansovino's shadow to direct future architectural developments. Compared to Sansovino, he applied a more radical vision of classicism by using an exceptionally astounding scale. His most renowned design, a gleaming white, massive, marble church, with gigantic columns and dome, still dominates the small island of *San Giorgio Maggiore* from across the *Piazza*'s shore. With works like this, the stage was set for other architects to recast the Venetian form beyond any ancient aesthetics, and evolve an irreplaceable façade for Venice, one unlike any other.

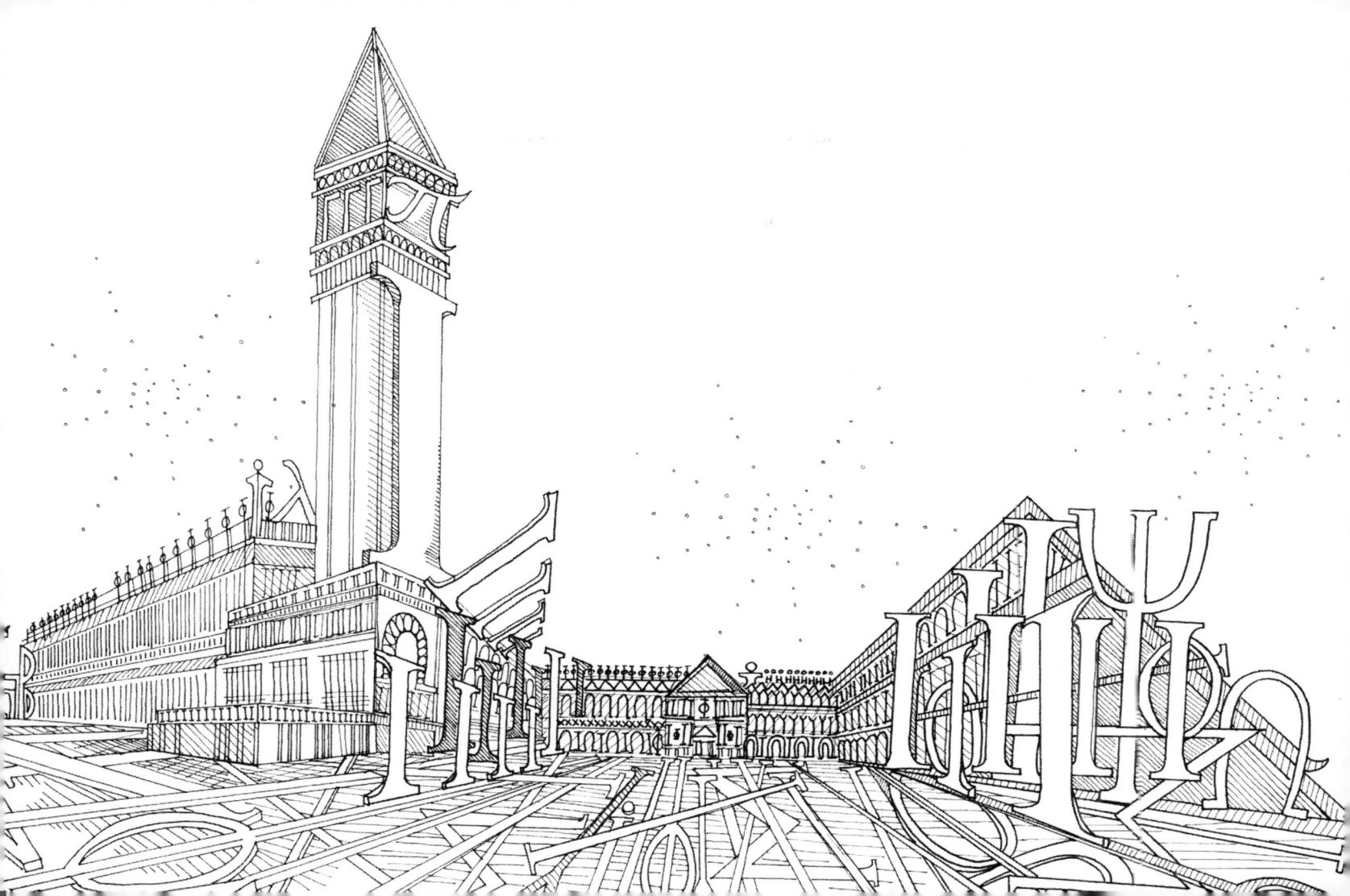

observation and liberal learning.

Despite a public focus on classicism, many Venetians did not avidly study ancient literature. Instead, nobles tended to study such topics as: mathematics, geography, astronomy, trigonometry, physics, sailing and horticulture, in order to advance the Republic's development in trade, economics and food security. A young noble only studied the classics so that he might serve as an ambassador to a Venetian colony in Greece. In actuality, many classic texts were neglected in the lagoon. Even when Petrarch, who was considered to be the father of humanism, bequeathed his impressive library to the Republic in 1374 C.E., it sat unused in damp room in the *Basilica di San Marco* for over two hundred and fifty years, where it severely decayed.

Enquiring Venetian minds studied in the many schools and academies within the lagoon. They had access to public lectures, private tutors, as well to the progressive University of Padua, which is amongst the oldest universities in the world. It was founded in 1222 C.E. by students and professors who sought more academic liberty, who dared to break away from assumed, medieval practices and favoured direct, hands-on observation as their only reliable source of knowledge. While founding the basis for much of modern science, medicine and law, many discoveries made in the Venetian Republic that conflicted with popular religious theories took longer to diffuse into public acceptance. For example, although human dissections were banned by the Church, University of Padua became renowned for its anatomical theatre, which attracted many scientists and artists to clearly observe investigations from above.

As chair of Surgery and Anatomy, Andreas Vesalius frequented the space and published his ground-breaking anatomical discoveries about the intricate vascular and circulatory systems, in *The Fabrication of the Human Body* in 1543 C.E.. Vesalius' work was deemed heretical during the Inquisition for disproving not just Galen but also Aristotle, and his discoveries were quickly burned on the mainland. In spite of this, many Venetian presses reproduced Vesalius' detailed anatomical drawings and notes. Other banned material, as well were made available to those who dared to be more open to new ideas and methods of investigation.

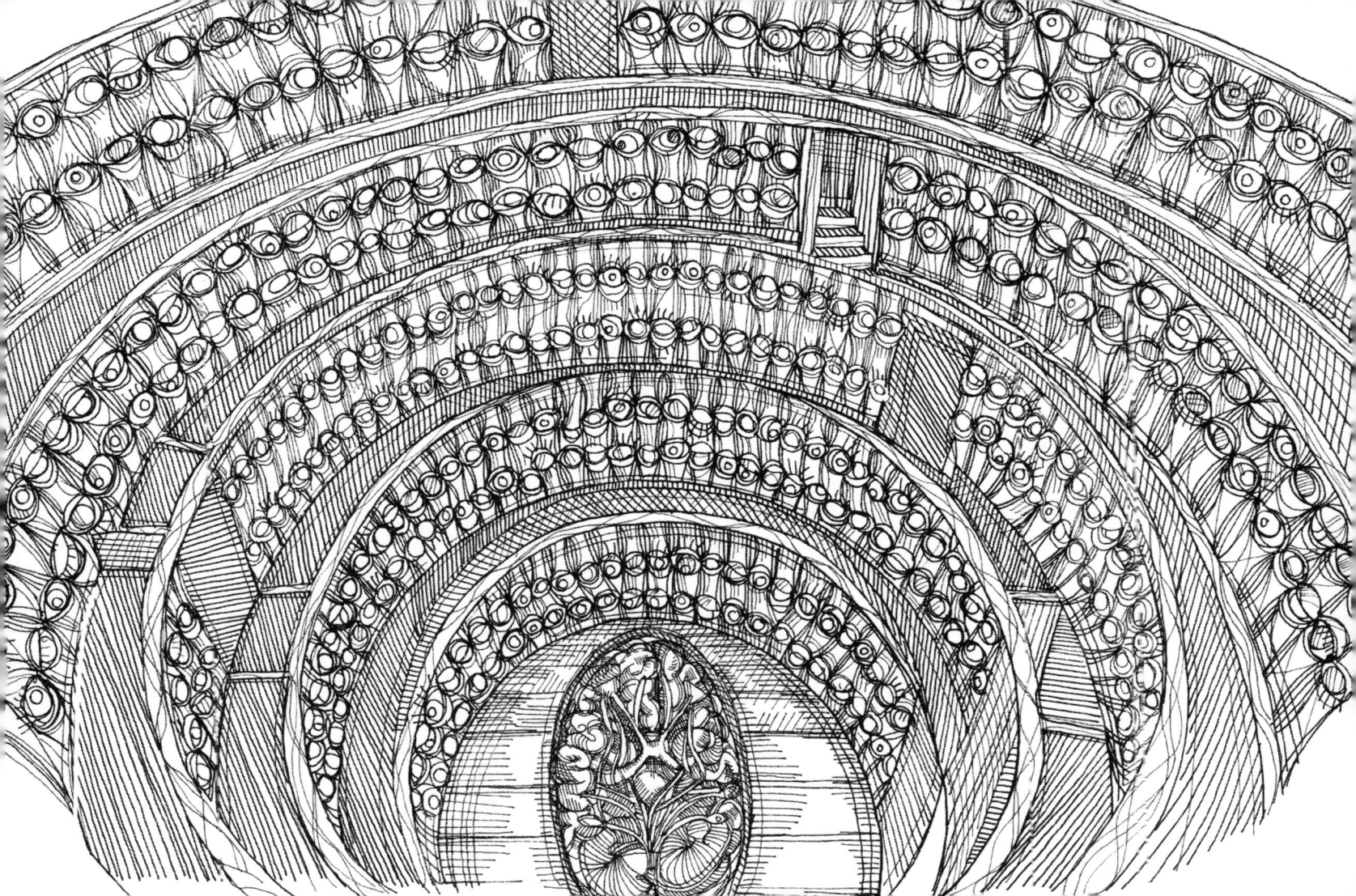

the great cosmopolitan.

The Venetian Republic evolved from a wild, island refuge, which survived from interacting with vastly diverse communities in far reaching ports. By the sixteenth century, Venice had become a great and fascinating metropolis. Her astonishing layout was captured by maestro printmaker, Jacopo de' Barberi, who studied and sketched the city from its many *campanili*. His meticulous and painfully detailed, massive print of the surging city in 1500 C.E depicted an original, bird's eye view of the city. Impressively, his plates are still comparable to modern aerial photographs and satellite imagery of Venice to this day.

Like her very substance, Venetian inhabitants came from all over the world. Communities of Armenians, Turks, Albanians, Greeks, Jews and Germans were neighbours along the Grand Canal. There was certainly friction between these groups, it wasn't as severe as in the rest of the world. Even in the beginning of the sixteenth century, when many of her minority communities faced tighter regulations and were confined to certain districts in order to be monitored and taxed more easily, *La Serenissima* upheld her reputation for being extremely well-governed and controlled. Individual workers found much support in the lagoon by joining specialized trade guilds. Each small sub-community of silk weavers, mask-maskers, leather workers and embroiderers, to name a few, helped to care for their own elderly, widows, orphans, and others in need of compassion. In addition to *campi*, guilds further strengthened the threads of Venice's ever-expanding, tightly woven social fabric.

Countless merchants, pilgrims, refugees and visitors came to fill the *Piazza* with an enduring orchestra of languages and a tonality of accents. Here, unlike in other port cities, foreigners were intentionally been protected; they could easily find accommodation, interpretation and reasonable prices for their needs. From her earliest moments, tourism has been integral to the Venetian economy; one of her proverbs reminds us, *"He who loves foreigners loves the world"*.

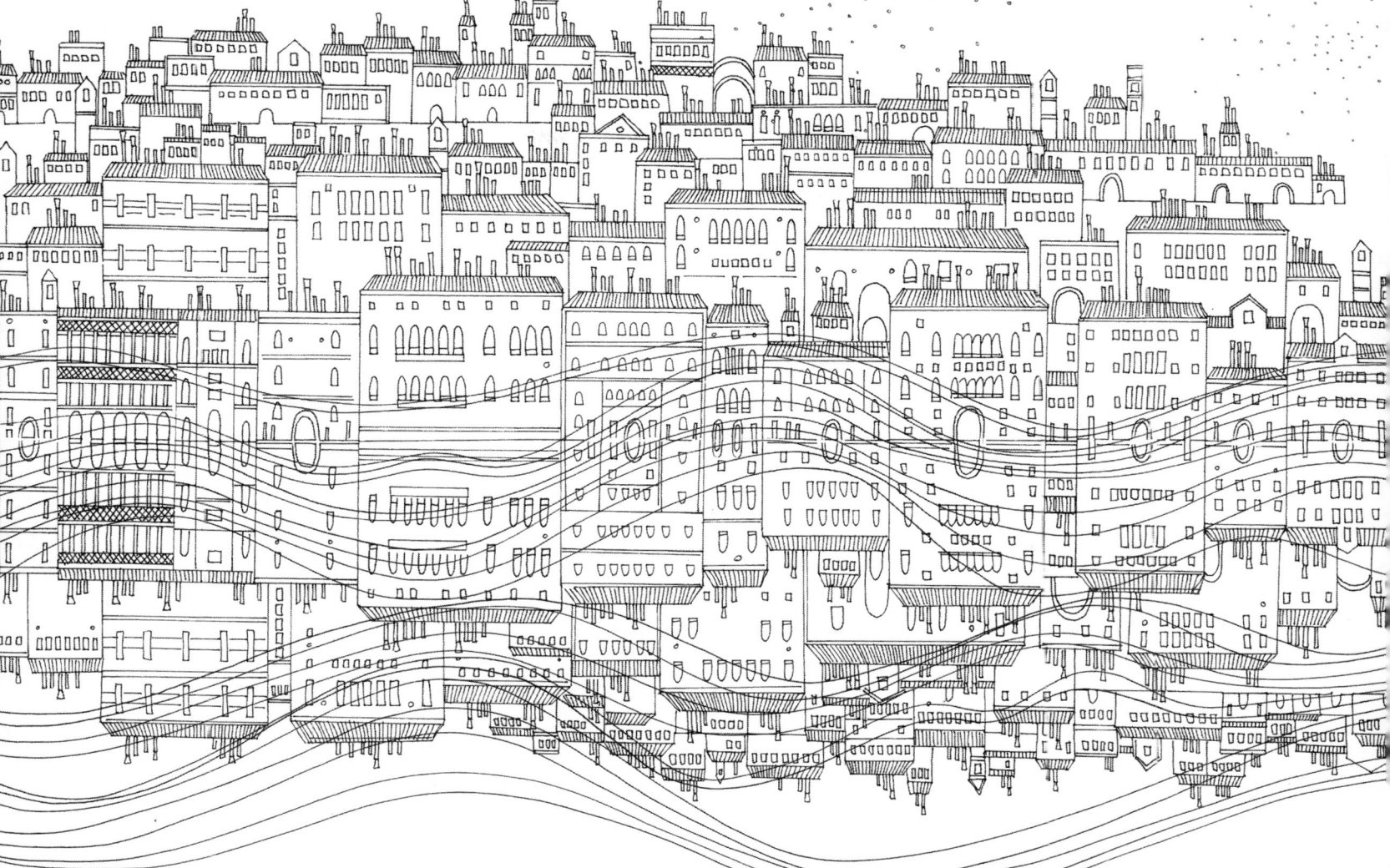

murano, burano: artistic refuge & artisan conclaves.

Although Venice seemed to welcome everyone into her domain, she was also in some ways a very closed society, which held on tightly to its secrets. For example, foreign craftsmen were encouraged to settle in Venice, but they could just as easily become imprisoned by their remarkable talents.

In the earliest days of the Venetian Republic, glass-makers inherited their ancient skills from Byzantine and Islamic artisans. They learned how to masterfully heat clumps of sand into hot, molten paste, which they carefully twisted around a long, iron rod. Then, using only their breath, they transformed this pliable, translucent medium to take on any imaginable form or colour, and brilliantly capture light. Without this manipulation, rudimentary glass could only be found if one were to sieve through endless dunes for extremely fine, snakelike ribbons of silica, which had been fused together by spontaneous bursts of lighting, or dare to confront bubbling, molten lava to search for pieces of hard, glossy, black, obsidian stone.

Endowed with such rare abilities, Venice was extremely protective of her venerated artisans; they were forbidden from moving and anyone caught escaping or revealing trade secrets was put to death. By the thirteenth century, all Venetian glassblowers were tucked away from prying eyes to Murano island. In this creative incubator. They created some of the most impressive chandeliers, goblets, beads, mirrors and works of grandeur, in all of the world.

Venetian glass makers developed unique recipes to mimic other materials. Each formula was transcribed into secret books, which only passed from a glass-making father to his son, who would inevitably inherit his exalted skills. For example, *lattimi,* or milk glass, became an elegant substitute for porcelain imported from China, whereas *ghiaccio* was made to look like ice, and *calcedonio* could delightfully replicate marble and stone. They also formed the brightest, most purest, transparent glass called *cristallo*. It was molded into elaborate ornaments, like small animals and balancing dancers, made solely to amuse the eye. Venetian glass-makers could recreate any object existing outside of the lagoon's shores, if not in function, then at least in form.

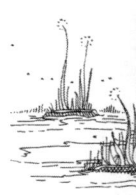

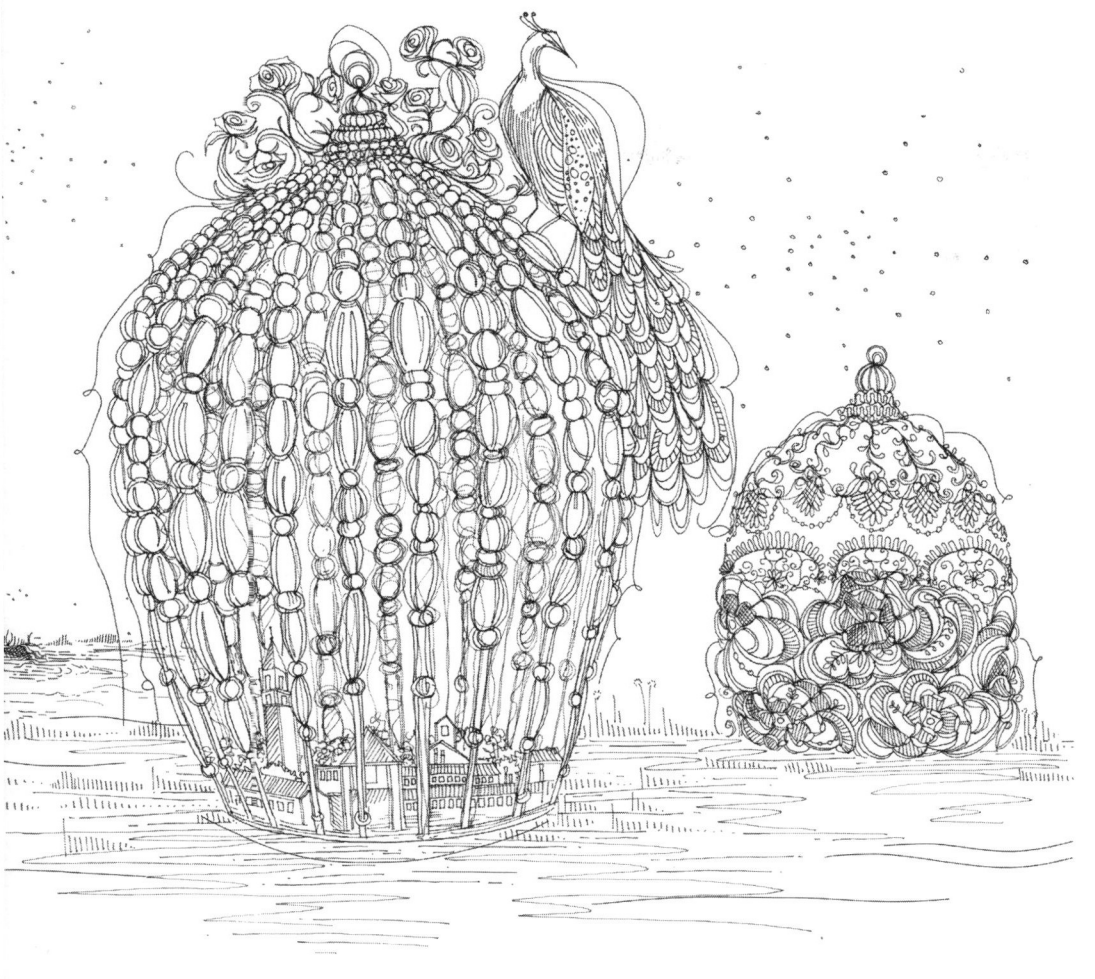

Her artisan sector greatly benefitted from her power and strong trade. Venetians manufactured wool, wax, marzipan, and lace, a cornucopia of transplanted products; the area of *Dorsoduro* was used by her renowned silk-workers, while sailors and shipbuilders inhabited the *Castello* region, cloth stretchers occupied the west, and tin makers plied their trade along her north-east flank.

The city held many trade fairs to celebrate its commerce and craftsmanship, which possessed a spirit similar to vibrant religious celebrations. Guilds held parades and processions in the streets, with elaborate ceremonies and fantastical displays, like musicians masterfully playing long, glass trumpets. Only the newest exotic and luxury goods arrived at her ports; whether fine wine from Crete, caviar from Caffa, sugar from Cyprus or dates from Palestine; ivory from Tanzania was displayed alongside scarves from Kashmir and musk from Tibet. *La Serenissima* became a market of the world; everything imaginable was for sale in her shops, stalls and under her awnings, for all to taste, touch and discover.

the golden age: painting & palladio palaces.

Amongst her exotic imports, rare pigments also traveled to Venetian ports; saffron yellows were harvested from the pollen of handpicked flowers in India, and *ultramarine*, or "over the sea", blue was ground from *lapis lazuli*, a semi-precious stone from an obscure mountain valley in Afghanistan. Only the most successful artists with extremely wealthy patrons could afford such prized materials. Because of the lagoon's harsh and salty air, Venetian artists innovated special measures to protect their precious colours from evaporating. They suspended pigments in a clear, slow-drying oil, and gave their works an added layer of sensual richness.

By the fifteenth century, the *Venetian School* for painters was a thriving centre for art. It rivaled talent in both Florence and Rome. The lagoon showcased the meticulously detailed cityscapes of Carpaccio and Bellini, the Renaissance colourist portraits and landscapes of Titian, Giorgione, and Guardi, and the dramatic Mannerist canvases of Veronese and Tintoretto. Venetian artists celebrated secular life and dared to be delineated. Titian painted seductive nudes and Veronese stirred tradition by depicting religious stories in modern settings; his *Last Supper* was deemed blasphemous for placing drunkards and dwarves in the company of Jesus.

Venetian painters flaunted Venice's many festivities and enchanting atmosphere, all crowned by her extraordinary architecture; they avoided confining lines and restricted forms, and painted with a sense of fluidity. Like the waves around them, they moved colour across their canvas with rhythmic harmonies and an eager, lapping tempo, and attempted to capture the essence of the Venetian experience within their frames. While the city was being rendered, her own architecture continued to blend Gothic, Byzantine, and Ottoman influences from around the world. Moreover, Venetian aesthetic diffused out of the lagoon thanks to the likes of Palladio, who designed many grand estates on the *terra firma*. In the sixteenth century, during the first days of summer, affluent nobles packed their belongings onto large barges. They floated their furniture, paintings, and servants down the Grand Canal, through an extensive series of rivers, to their country estates, in order to escape the unbearable summer heat. In their peaceful and expansive mainland properties, the affluent Venetians grew crops and vines and reconnected with the natural cycles of organic life. When the cooler autumn months arrived they drifted back to the city, in time for the reopening of the Great Council and *Carnevale* celebrations. Life at this time was beyond prosperous and full of possibility for the swelling ranks of Venetian aristocrats.

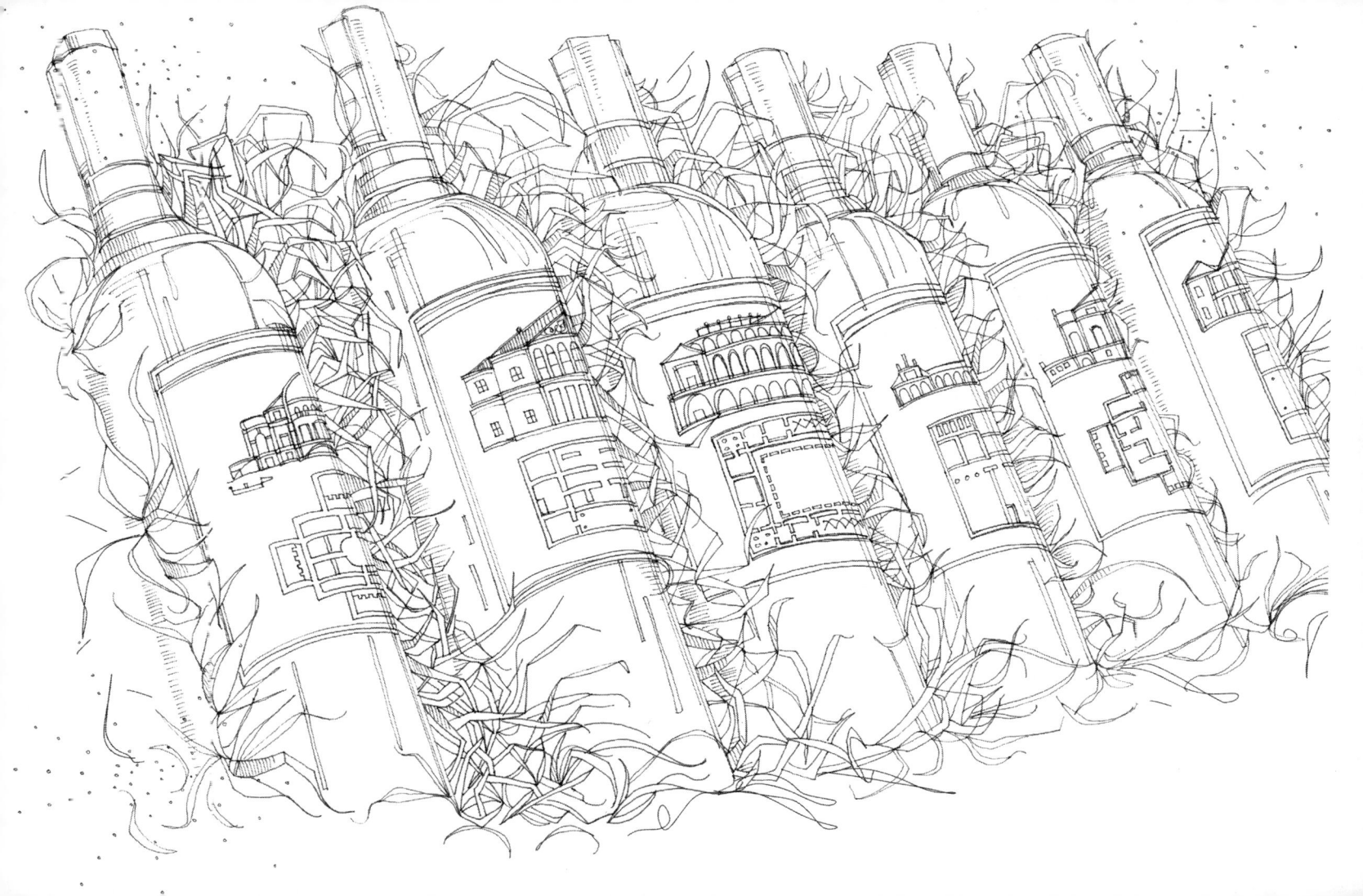

the spyglass and new heights.

During the seventeenth century, while Venice expanded and spilled style onto the mainland, a principal mathematics professor at the University of Padua, set his focus on something even further in the distance. Galileo Galilei spent each day and night considering gravity, the universe and distant stars, and pushed past Venice's highest imaginable boundary. At this time, the Ptolemaic concept of universe prevailed. The earth was placed at the centre of creation, and everything else moved around it, in perfectly round orbits.

Being surrounded by notions of predictability, Venetians were known to be quite superstitious and avoid ominous situations. To keep any evil at bay, they would paint large eyes on the fronts of their ships, sailors reflexively saluted statues of the Virgin Mary for protection, and when storms approached, they took out a knife and defiantly cut into the approaching, dark sky.

Horoscope readers were often called upon to read out a client's future from their highly organized star charts. They happily continued on to scrutinize the symmetry of one's face and disclose the secrets in the fine lines etched on one's palm. However, this seemingly foreseeable notion of the universe soon came to a halt after a simple, Dutch spyglass reached Venetian ports. This new device inspired Galileo to combine his expertise in optics with the clearest of hand-blown glass from Murano. After carefully grinding and curving lenses over a cannonball, he fabricated a version of the spyglass twenty times more powerful than any other.

In 1609 C.E., from the top of the tallest *campanile* in the lagoon, he demonstrated its power to the Venetian senate. They scoured the horizon, and spotted ships approaching two hours earlier than with the unassisted eye. For its obvious military advantage alone, the *doge* awarded Galileo copious funds to pursue his studies.

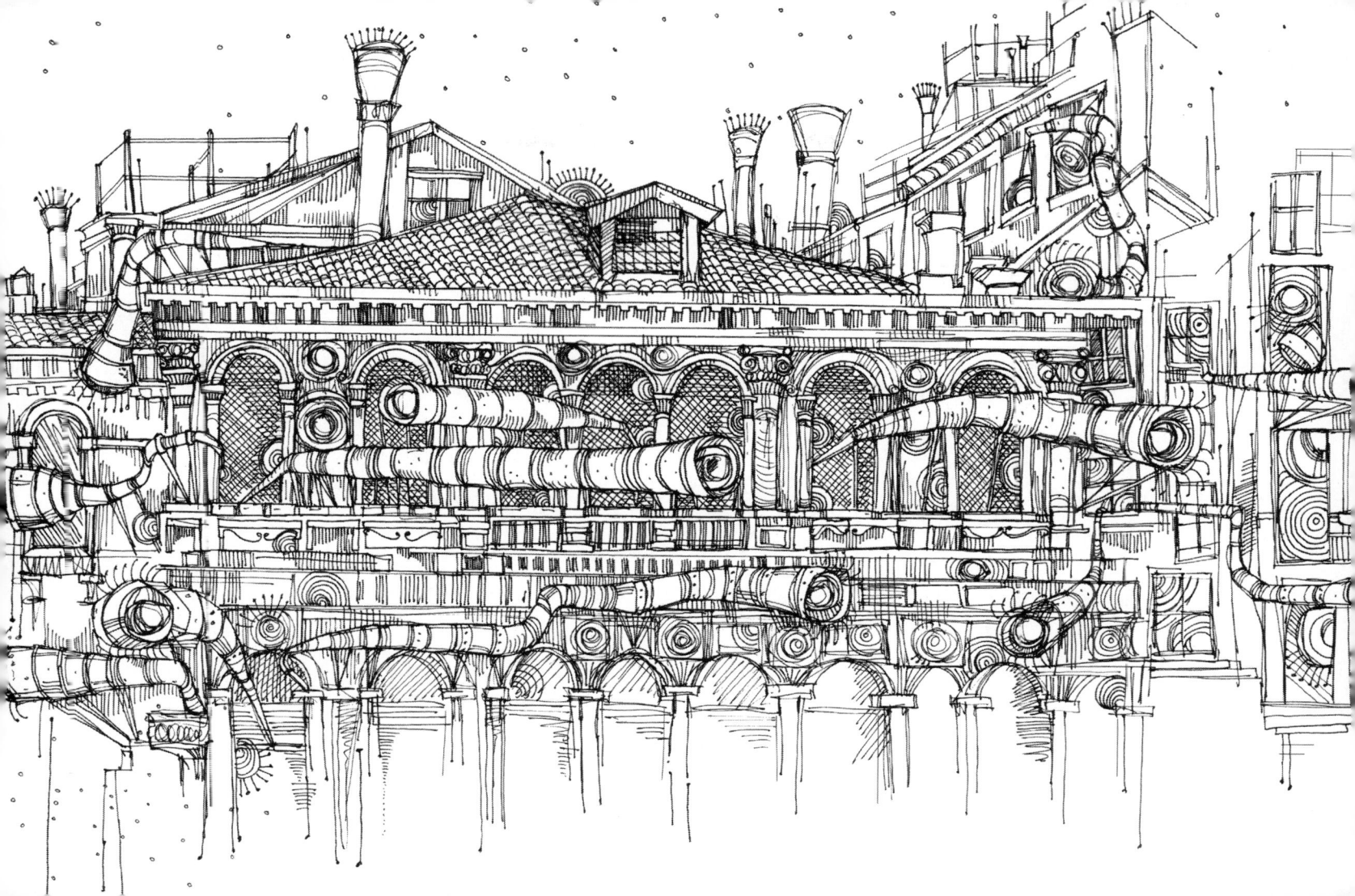

the man who opened the skies.

Soon, everyone in Venice was seeking new vantage points with their own spyglass. Salt-makers focused on distant pools to see if high tides threatened their precious assets; merchants pointed theirs to determine the true nature of approaching cargo and crew; and the less ambitious simply enjoyed the thrill of peering into the private, mundane lives of their neighbours.

Galileo, however, kept his spyglass aimed at his main intrigue, the night sky. He observed and carefully plotted a startling number of celestial discoveries for a single lifetime. He was the first to see that the moon had mountains and deep valleys, and that it was not a perfectly smooth sphere. He also observed unexpected spots on the sun, rings enwrapping Saturn, and four moons dancing around Jupiter. As Galileo meticulously analyzed these sights, the universe opened before him.

He observed that the earlier, heretical, heliocentric concept of the universe proposed by Copernicus was in fact accurate. Galileo also courageously affirmed that the sun, and not the Earth, was at the centre of the universe.

Using the many available presses, he took the papal bull by the horns and published his revolutionary notes in *Sidereus Nuncius*. Although his findings caused an overnight sensation, many did not trust his new instrument and were not ready to turn their understanding of the universe inside out. The Church, still in its fight against the Reformation, used the Inquisition to censor Galileo's writings. They silenced his teachings, placed him under house arrest, and forced him to recant. However, Galileo's ideas did not vanish. Many of his writings were smuggled out of his house unknowingly, but not shamefully, in his visitors' breeches. His writings were welcomed in northern Europe, which was busily laying the foundation for the modern scientific method.

In time, as others also came to carefully observe the world around them rather than rely on the ancient authorities, Galileo's truth was brought to light with more diligent research in physics and astronomy. With this revelation, the vast cosmic ocean holding our tiny, fragile world came to be something for every age to investigate and marvel at with its own refined instruments and extended eyes.

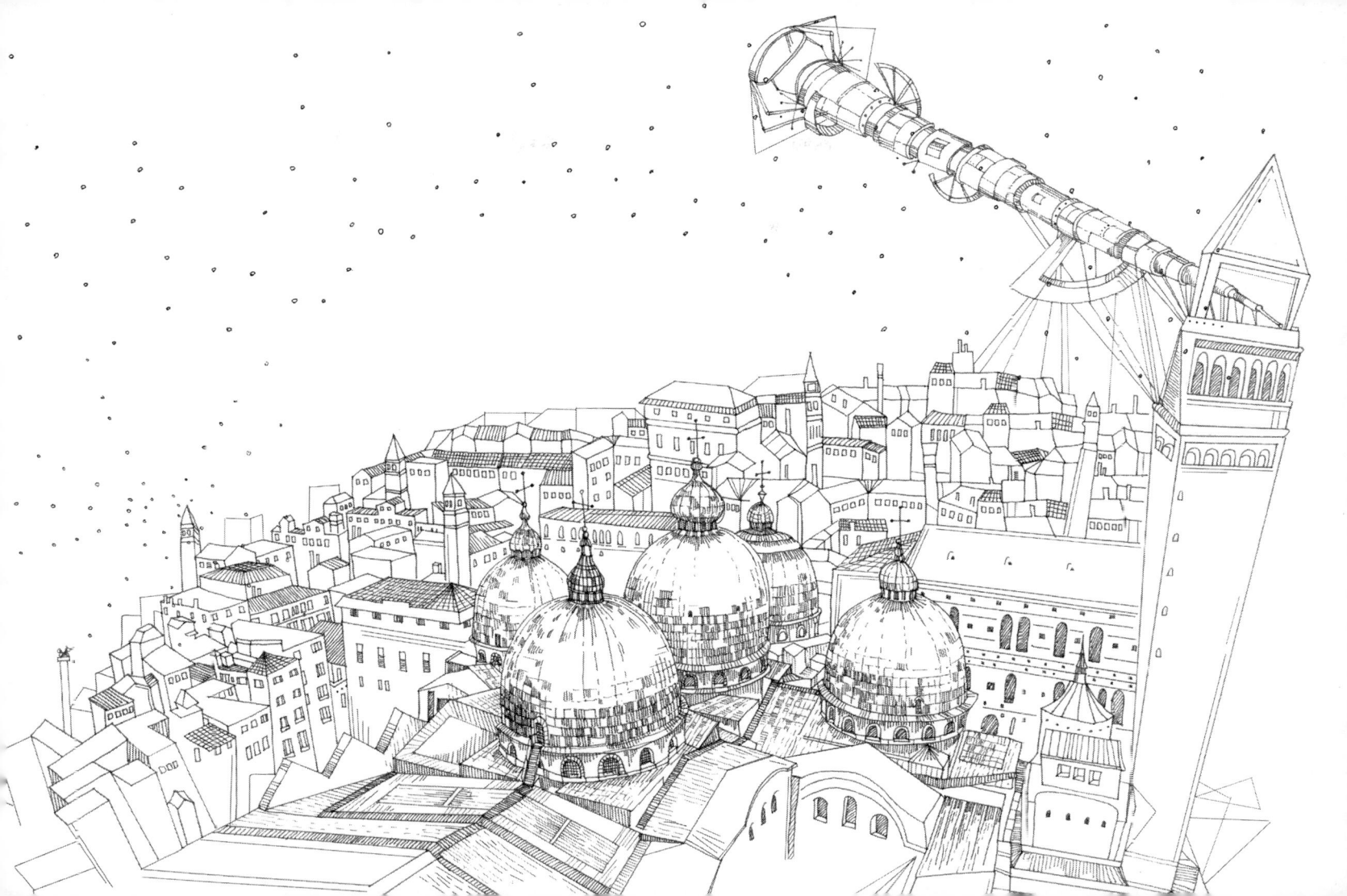

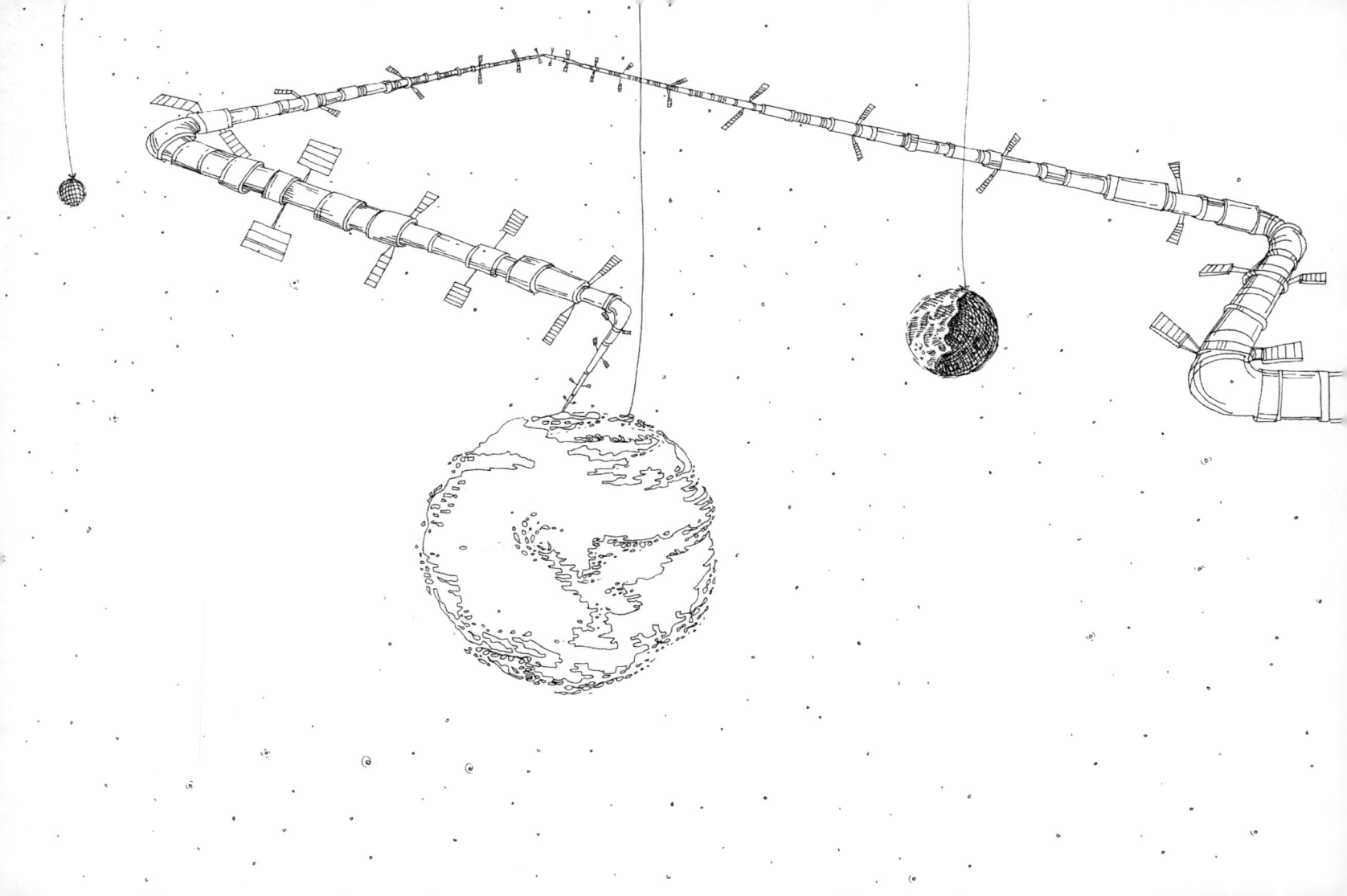

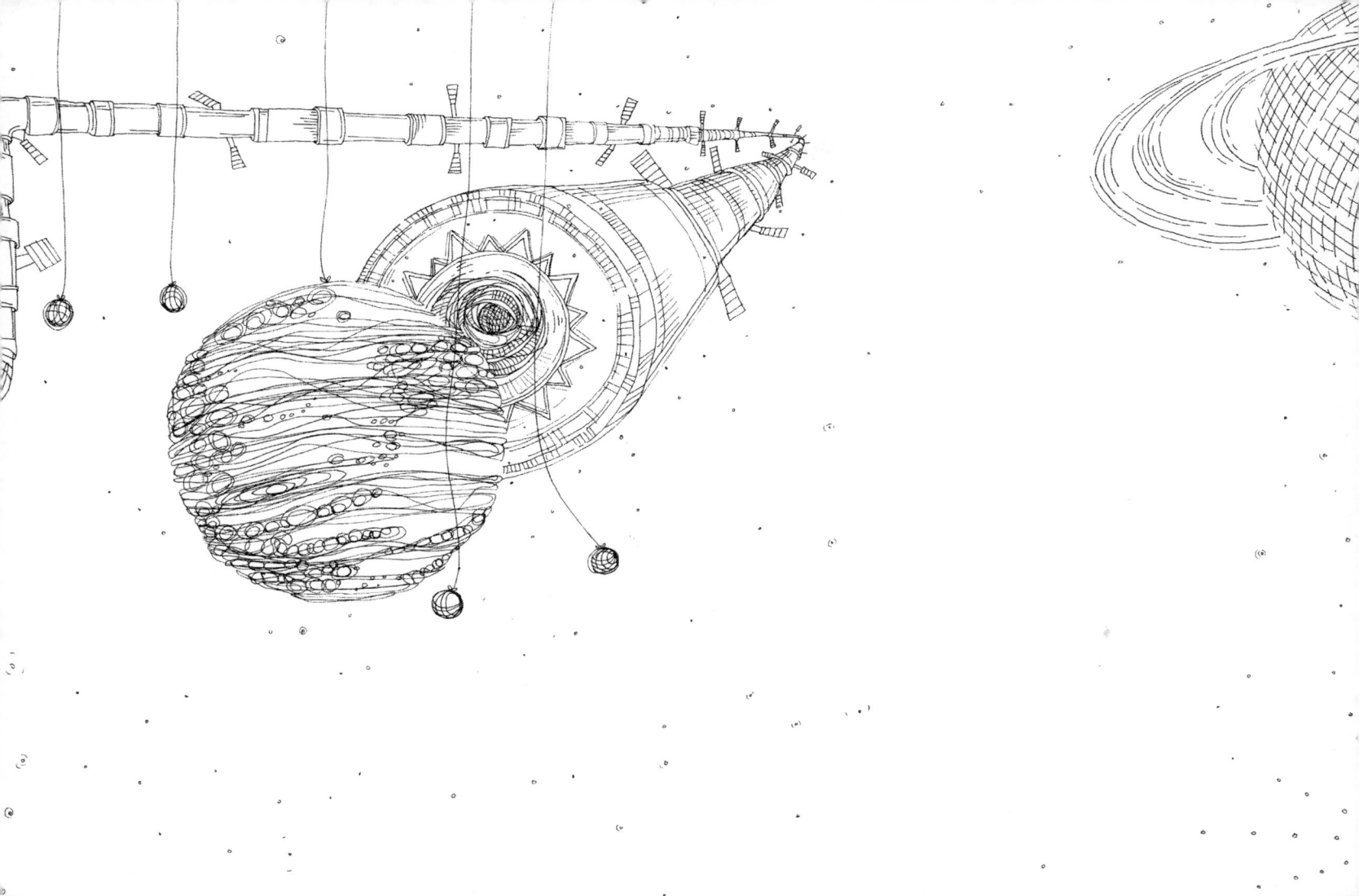

part five: implosion

(16th century - 18th century)

decadence & unrestrained indulgence.

While the earth shifted its position in the universe, so too, inevitably, did the Venetian Republic. By the end of the seventeenth century *La Serenissima* had faded into a shadow of her former power and entered a period of slow, economic decline. Yet, Venetians chose to celebrate their remaining days in their brazenly beautiful lagoon, and end with a bang!

Once again, *La Serenissima* transformed, this time into a powerful manifestation of decadence. Resilient as ever, the Venetians certainly manipulated the many pleasure-seeking travelers who arrived at their extraordinary setting to splurge on an endless stream of luxury. Gambling alone drew in thousands; many travelers came to play cards in her small, private *casinos*. Enticing chance became so popular that by 1638 C.E., the Republic opened the first public gaming house in all of Europe. However, the notorious *Ridotto* was closed a century later, after too many nobles gambled away generations of hardwon inheritance. When this thrill ceased to satisfy, Venice boasted a lively red-light district to offer condolences. Over 12,000 prostitutes were registered in the city during the sixteenth century alone, while alluring courtesans, trained solely in the art of seduction, attracted more expensive tastes. Those seeking catharsis were also known to bypass her *casinos* and brothels completely and head to the city's nunneries, where many young women, whose families were could not offer dowries, held the liveliest, most unrestrained soirées of all.

As pleasure became the ultimate goal of life, the art of love poured throughout the lagoon. A famous epitome of intrigue and seduction, Giacomo Casanova, penned intimate details about this era of Venetian madness. In his memoirs, *The Story of My Life,* he disclosed first-hand encounters with royalty and luminaries, such as Voltaire, Goethe, and Mozart, along with drama incurred in *casinos* and ballrooms, scandalous affairs, and his subsequent arrest, daring jail break, and life on the run in Bohemia.

Those who came to the lagoon to study language, culture, art, and architecture were easily distracted by charming beauties cruising the canals, or courtesans hiding behind angled fans, reciting erotic poetry in the popular *Caffè Florian*. The more studious did manage to return home with refined Italian, and could even commission souvenir paintings of the city by the likes of Canaletto. His vibrant, realistic scenes made Venice into a highly coveted beauty in her own light.

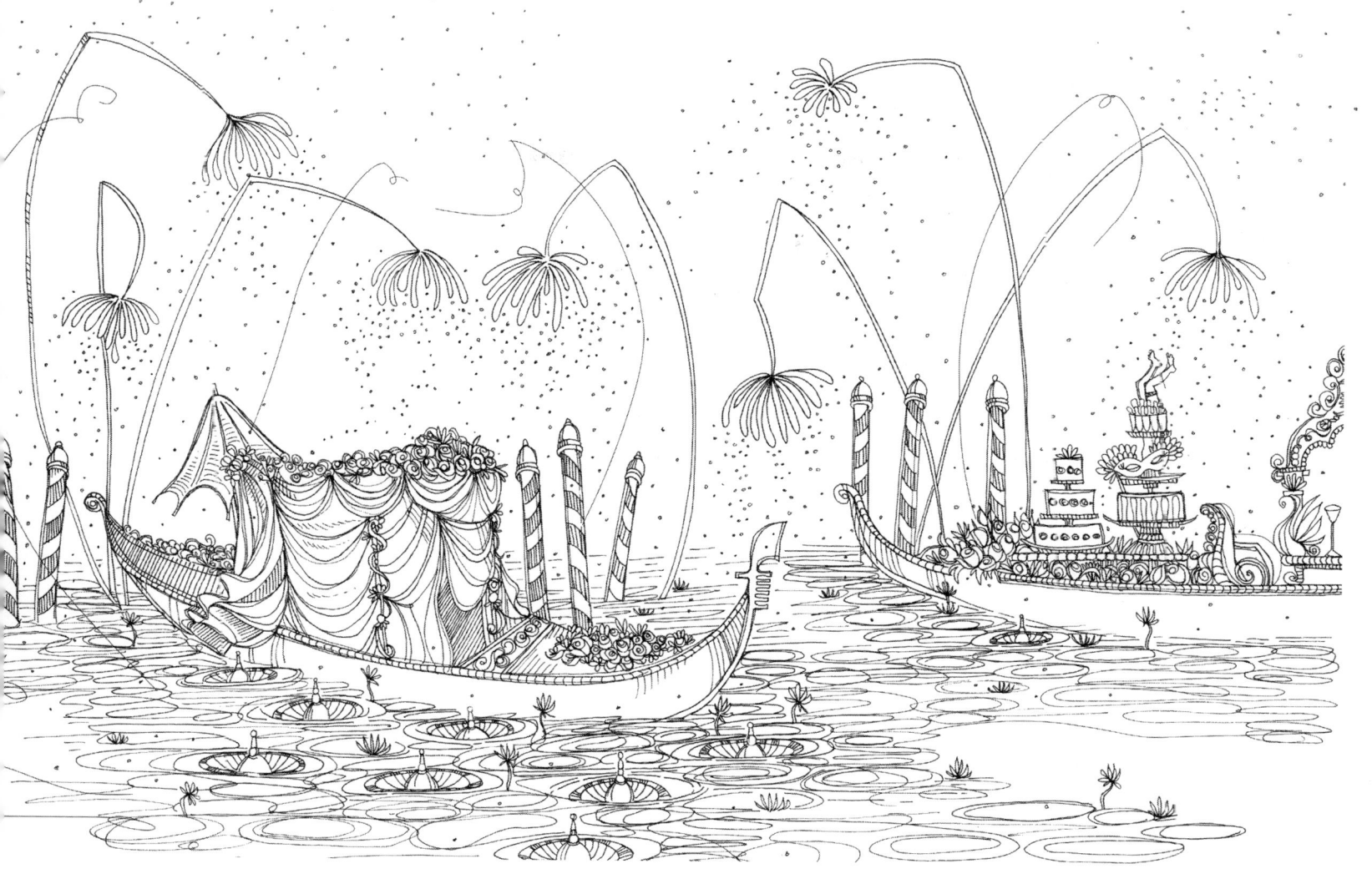

the stage & commedia dell'arte.

Bragging both the first commercial theatre and the first public opera house in Europe in the sixteenth and seventeenth centuries, high-brow audiences flocked to Venice to experience her latest artistic performances. From tiers of identical boxes, lined with red velvet upholstery, and surrounded by elaborate, marble figures, golden balconies and carved pillars, visitors witnessed the works of some of the greatest composers and playwrights from around the world, including the local talents of Carlo Goldoni and Carlo Gozzi.

Curious onlookers also gathered in her outdoor squares and gardens to watch the ubiquitous street theatre. Teams of travelling players regularly staged popular *Commedia dell'Arte*. They improvised overtly stereotypical characters with exaggerated gestures, distinctive masks and costumes.

To name a few, there was *Pantalone*, the miserable, old Venetian merchant, always dressed in a red waistcoat and black cloak, who became the ironic victim of every imaginable trick. While, the colourful trickster *Arlecchino*, performed energetic back flips and was conversely cheered on when he outwitted his master. A multitude of characters explored themes around jealousy, old age and age-old love.

Although the actors used the same framework for every show, they artfully tailored their liberal scripts to satirize local scandals and include regional tastes. Their overall gaiety and spontaneity came to be favoured by Venetian audiences. With creativity surging through her streets, the line between players and audience became difficult to distinguish; Venetians truly lived all aspects of the arts.

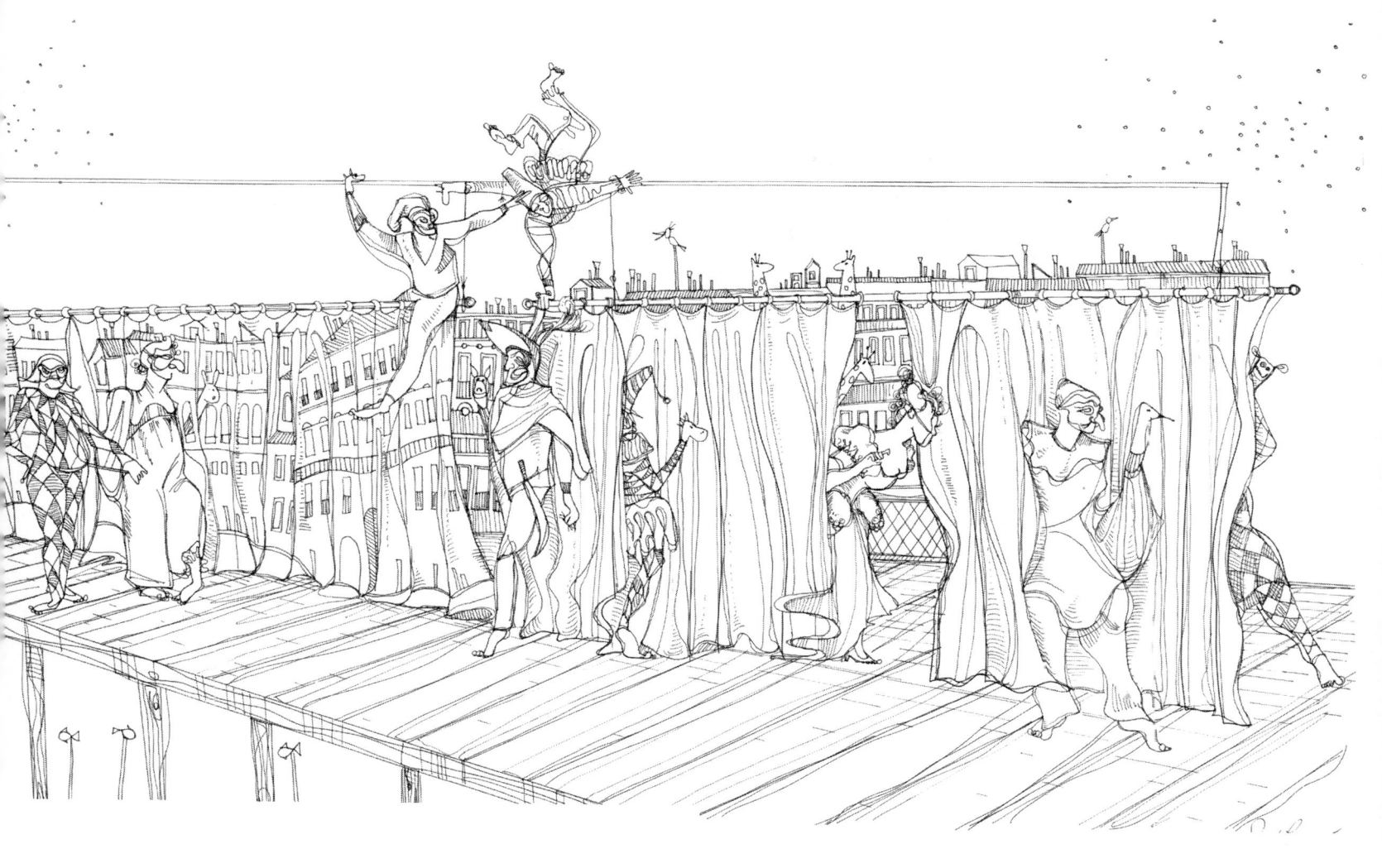

extravagant baroque: opera & music.

During this era of playful indulgence, Venice was the seat of music in Europe. Every corner of the city was filled with melody; the ducal orchestra played in *Piazza San Marco* every day, gondoliers continuously carried song down the canals, while spontaneous serenades and performing gypsies filled her alleys. And no other city could compete with Venice's colossal orchestras. These multiple choruses and instrumental groups, expressed perfect harmonies and order throughout her churches, opera houses, concert halls and in the open air.

Maestros played baroque on specialized instruments in the lagoon, like the fine-tuned *pianoforte,* hailing from Florence, and violins perfected by the Stradivari family in the Republic's mainland city of Cremona. Composers from all over made their way to *La Serenissima* - Scarlatti, Mozart, Wagner, Handel, Medelssohn, and Stravinsky, to name a few. Additionally, since Ottaviano Petrucci made sheet music into a saleable commodity, listeners could also take home their favourite scores. The most fashionable audiences flocked to witness the latest creations of her famous flaming, red-haired priest, Antonio Vivaldi.

Despite being chronically ill and house-bound, he fervently composed over five hundred concertos and forty-four operas. By surrendering to his explosive, impulsive genius, Vivaldi could craft an entire symphony in a single day. For over forty years, he conducted many abandoned, illegitimate daughters of nobles and courtesans, raised in the *Ospedale dell Pietà.*

From an extremely young age, these women were trained solely to excel music; they became married to Vivaldi's orchestra, and in a sense, nuns of his art. Sublime performances, which included Vivaldi's most famous work, *The Four Seasons,* featured an orchestra of up to forty of these beautiful girls wearing pristine, white robes, hidden in galleries above the congregation. From behind wrought-iron grills, the girls played and sang Vivaldi's wildly mischievous music. Each piercing *staccato* perfectly expressed the vivacity of Venice running through their own fragile veins. Instead of applauding, audiences would uncontrollably weep at the divine sounds, astonished by the expressions of glorious beauty presented to their senses.

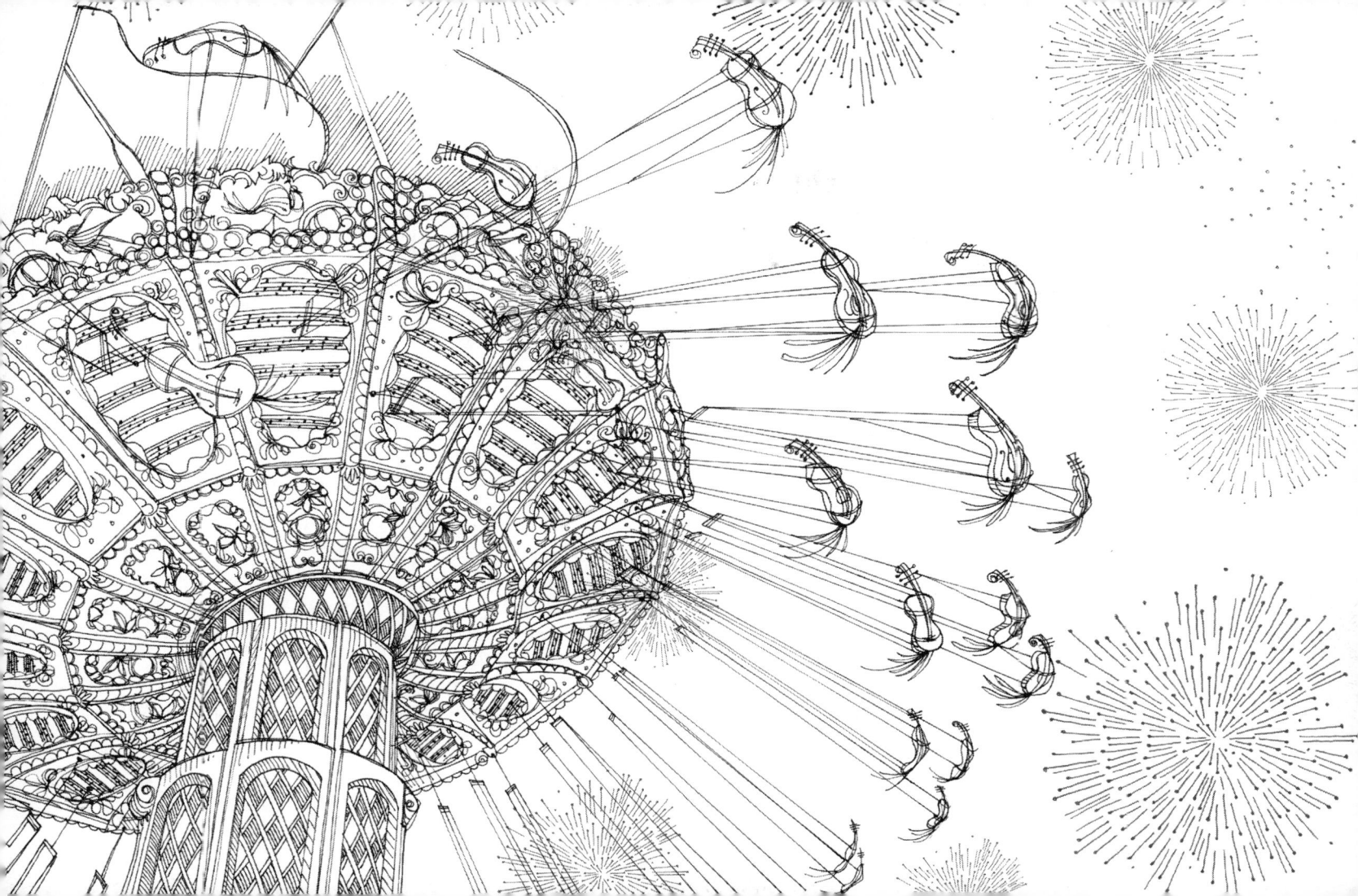

carnevale: festivities & celebrations.

Of all performances in the lagoon, the oldest celebration, *Carnevale,* became the most elaborate. This "farewell to flesh" stemmed from small parties, where families drank and gorged on reserves of meat, butter and sugar before the forty-day fasting period of Lent. As *Carnevale* grew increasingly social, its original connotations were quickly forgotten. In as early as the tenth century, tens of thousands of visitors flooded to Venice for its rousing boat races, masked balls, and florid parties.

By the eighteenth century Venetians had even extended the *Carnevale* season to run for six whole months of the year. During its peak, a steady stream of decorated gondolas emptied boatload after boatload of excursionists at *Piazza San Marco,* to experience the city's arising delights. Here, audiences threw flowers and confetti for thousands of jugglers, acrobats, dancing animals, and magicians; they gasped in terror while rope-walkers slid across a fine wire between the *Campanile* and the Ducal Palace; they jumped for safety as bulls were released and madly chased throughout the city. When exhausted, sightseers lounged in gondolas heaping with gold and crimson fabrics, or indulged in wines, sculpted marzipan sweets, pinnacles of meringues, and excessively delicious, deep-fried and sugared pastries, like *frittelle* and *crostoli.*

Later in the night, for those still able to stand straight, countless masquerades, concerts, productions, *casinos* and brothels beckoned, while mesmerizing firework displays lasted well into the morning. At its height, *Carnevale* was a time to cast away one's winter cloak, don a fantastical disguise, and fully embrace one's vices. Ordinary life, in any moment, truly became extraordinary.

Drama and theatrics were no longer limited to the stage, and at times it was difficult to decipher who was the true cast. Audience members wore masks and costumes, mirrored familiar character gestures, and boastfully cheered, whistled, fought, and caressed in their theatre boxes throughout performances. Meanwhile, outside the theatre, dazzling costume parades and street performers twisted throughout Venice's alleys. All carousing participants came to laugh and act wild together. But by the time the spring heat had set in, life in Venice returned to its highly regimented, ordered structure. Treachery and subversion were once again cruelly punished, until the next round of *Carnevale,* when everything in the lagoon opened again to another set of extravagant possibilities, and reality was once again defied.

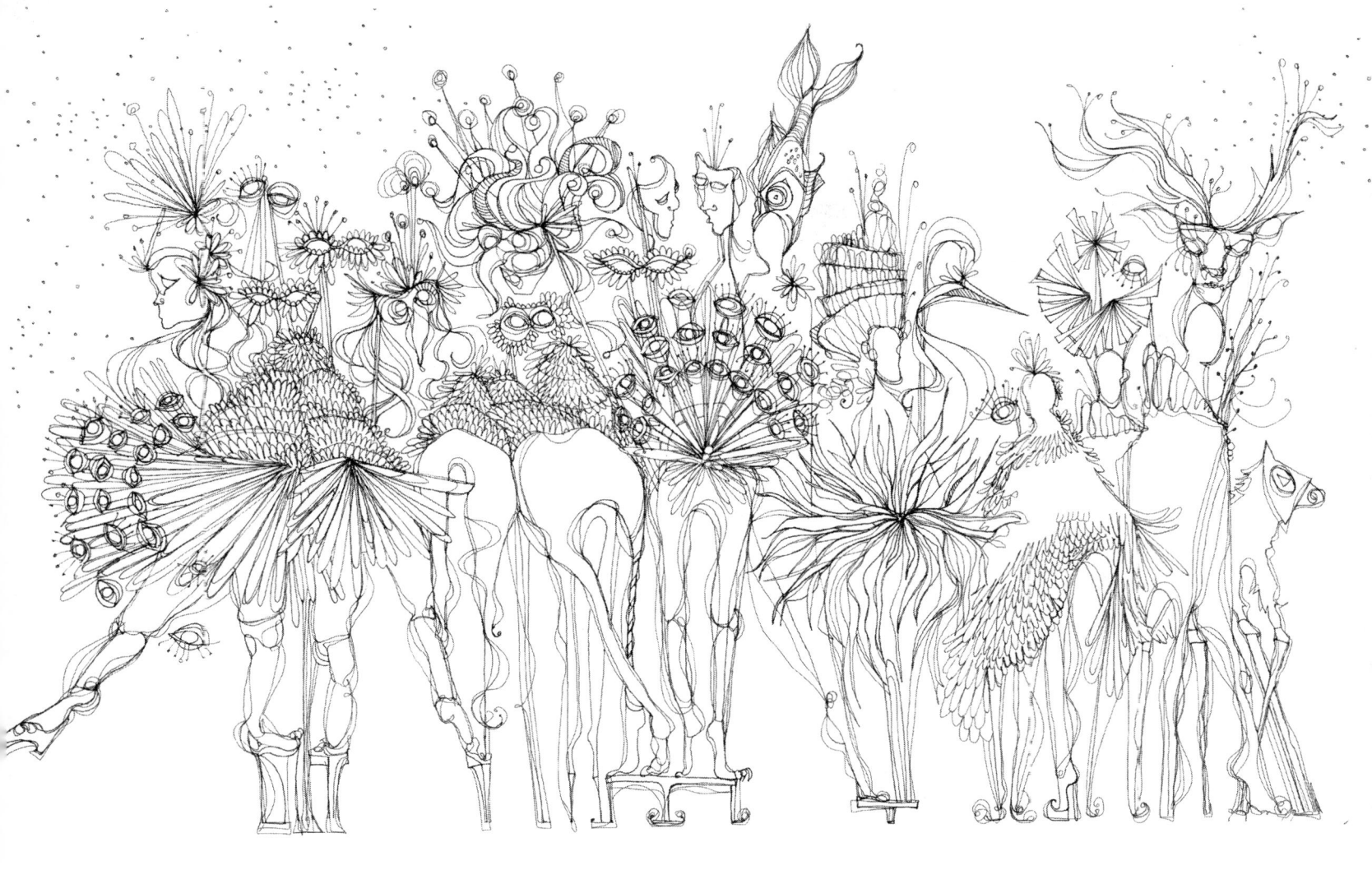

social order, privacy and masks.

Carnevale turned regular life upside-down. Everyone wore masks, both day and night, and anyone without disguise in public was immediately denounced. Barriers of wealth and gender were dissolved; there was little distinction between shopkeepers and beggars, nuns and inquisitors, nobles and prostitutes, and lovers and sworn enemies. Masked vendors outfitted new faces for all.

People dressed as anything imaginable; they imitated beggars, tooth-pullers, nuns, and mythical creatures, and even the bird-like mask of the plague doctor once again returned to the lagoon. Of all options, the most popular costume came to be the more practical white *bauta* mask, with its strong chin line and exposed mouth, topped with a black, tricorn hat and silk cape. This style completely covered any defining characteristics, but still allowed one to drink, eat, play and be merry. Very little was forbidden during *Carnevale*, and everyone found their place in this grand catharsis. Men dressed as women, servants dined with the elite, politicians parodied their rivals, and priests freely entered brothels, all without prudent eyebrows being raised.

In this enclosed community, gossip ran rampant, so costumes gave Venetians a sesnse of privacy. With the aid of masks, state inquisitors could freely question citizens for their investigations, bankrupt nobles had the chance to forget their poverty and find new business opportunities in order to rebuild their lavish lifestyles, and Venetian citizens could express their thoughts without embarrassment and resolve any seething personal conflicts. For at least half of the year, Venetians would live amongst each other as strangers, and experience their own exciting city as foreigners.

However, with such unadulterated freedom, sordid risks, like syphilis, crept in to lie underneath the many layers of capes, taffeta, puffed sleeves, colourful stockings and shimmering, brocade bodices in the lagoon. Rather than suffer this unexpected result of pleasure, many Venetians escaped to the navy. They chose to die in battle than face any boils and ulcers, which ate away at the heart, lungs, and brain, and turned people mad before dying. Still, despite its darker side, *Carnevale* celebrations united Venetians in their passion for life; even while masked, they continued to express their pure love for all that Venice city had to offer.

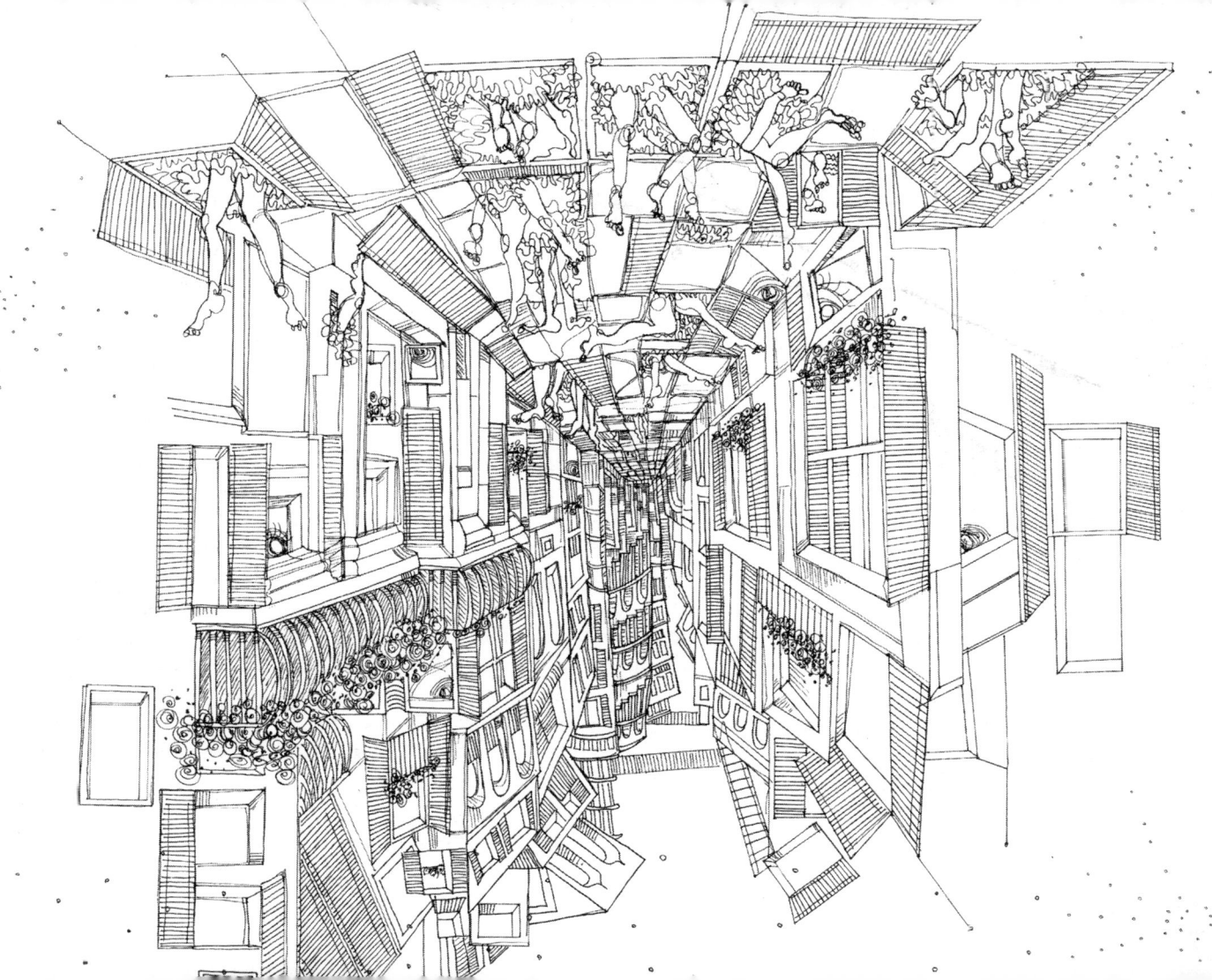

the age of reason: fashion, revolution and coffee.

By the eighteenth century, Venice was clearly no longer a leading power or economy. Yet, when the *Carnevale* season ended each year, Venetians continued to indulge in pomp and frivolousness. They traded fantastical costumes for the most coveted fashions hailing from Paris, and transformed themselves into elaborate works of art. They sought to watch and be watched.

Ladies wrapped themselves in endless metres of expensive, silks, with tight bodices which strategically displayed *décolleté*. They wore tall, sculpted wigs and elaborately twisted and curled their hair, which they even streaked with urine for added shine. By fluttering finely woven lace fans, women directed attention to their perfectly placed beauty spot to signal their passionate nature. To complete their elaborate ensembles, Venetian women slipped on one of the first pairs of high heels, which made walking completely impossible, and gondolas all the more necessary. Noble men, on the other hand, wore modest, black cloaks to outwardly signify their submission to the Republic. Yet, they too could not resist wearing the latest French styles. Beneath, they sported colourful coats with stylish tails, tunics with long, lace wrists, shoes with metallic buckles, and knee breeches attached to the finest of silk stockings. And on top they wore black felt, tricorn hats over white wigs, carefully curled to perfection.

Venetians closely followed French style, but they did not embrace its *avant garde* ideals spreading throughout northern Europe. During the Age of Reason, nobles dismissed Rousseau and Voltaire, while servants smoothed their fussy, lace and silk froufrou. They changed their surface, but not the depths of their essence; During this time, the Venetian Republic was an extremely well functioning governing system. It had already prevailed for over a thousand years without any instance of civil war. The Republic had even come to model a microcosm of well-balanced power to other politicians. For instance, when the American Republic was just emerging, Benjamin Franklin, along with the creators of the American constitution, looked to Venice for inspiration for the New World.

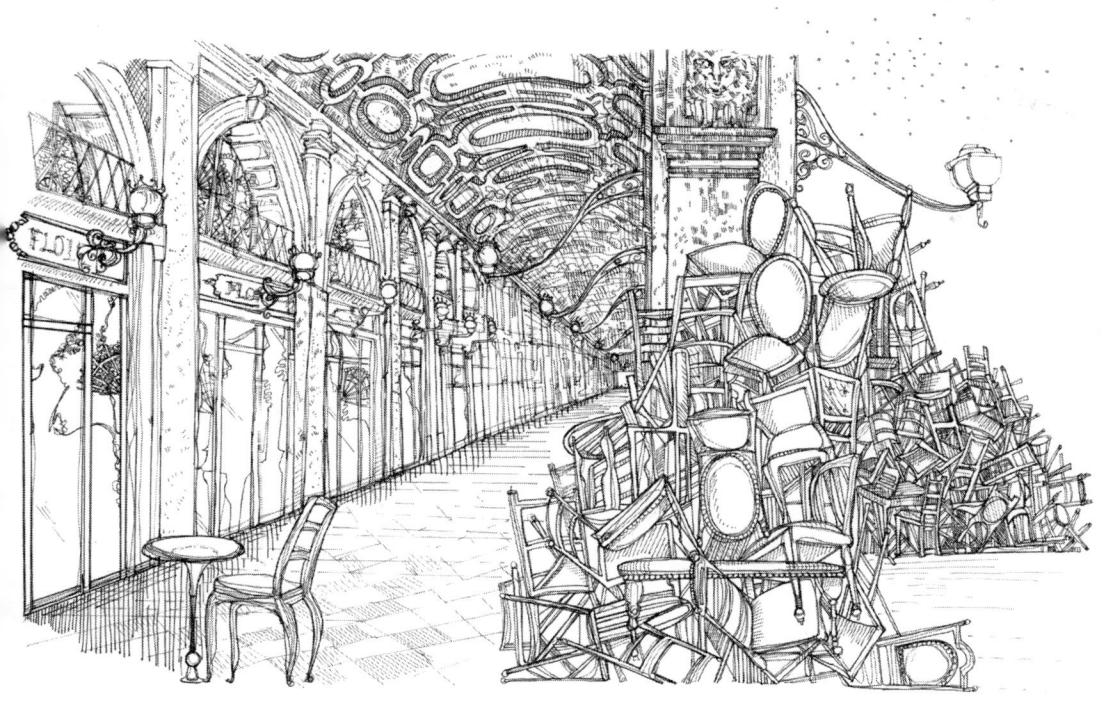

In the eighteenth century, political discourse became concentrated in Venice's many boisterous cafes, which brewed the novel, stimulating Ethiopian beans arriving at her ports. *Caffè Florian*, the city's oldest coffee house, was favoured by many literary intellectuals, such as Goethe, Proust and Dickens. However, their discussions tended to result in creative outcomes instead of political change.

Over centuries, an array of visionaries, inspired travellers, nationalist revolutionaries, and Austrian resistors enjoyed hot, black coffee, chocolate, and spirits, within *Caffè Florian*. They gossiped and debated ideas circulating around the globe. While discussions around coffee resulted in much of the Illumination in the rest of Europe, they were mostly diluted to *chiaccere*, or "chit chat", rather than revolution, within the lagoon's waters. Venetians were open to ideas from afar, but ultimately sought to continue living in their own elaborate societal structure which had granted them peace for many generations.

napoleon and political overturn.

Near the end of the eighteenth century, destitute populations in France shook the bourgeoisie to end their *Ancien Régime;* they expelled expressions of privilege, and promptly beheaded King Louis XVI. Yet, the Veneitan Republic remained withdrawn from revolutions and confined to her vanities. In fact, earlier in the century, Venetians had actually increased their diminishing aristocracy and reopened the *Libro d'Oro*. Noble titles were sold for hefty sums to compensate for languishing commerce, to settle bankruptcies, and to help secure her holdings. *La Serenissima* continued to present herself as the place to enjoy the many pleasures of life.

Meanwhile, the conqueror Napoleon Bonaparte had expanded his cause outside of France, and engaged in wars with every major European power on the mainland. Using espionage, deception, and by moving his troops with unexpected velocity, Napoleon caught his enemies by surprise, and swiftly secured a dominant position. Italy was the first foreign country to fall to his notorious campaign. As the French stepped into the Republic's mainland territory, Venetians concealed any fear and complacently declared themselves neutral. With reduced troops and only scraps of a naval fleet, Venice was defenseless. By 1797 C.E., the twenty-six year old Napoleon was irritated and berated their neutrality as duplicity. Upon command, his 40,000 expeditious soldiers flooded Venice and demanded the abdication of its *doge* and elitist regime.

Fully aware of their end, the remaining Senate members and Lodovico Manin, the last *doge* in a continuous line since 697 C.E., cast their final votes for Bonaparte's desired democracy. To an almost empty chamber, the 120th *doge* calmly deposed his ducal *corno* and submitted to Napoleon. Until that point the Venetian Republic had remained independent longer than any other population in the world.

The Republic was no more. The winged lion was knocked down from its column, the *Libro d'Oro* was thrown into a large bonfire; while many of her palaces were flattened to their foundations. All her gold was melted down, and sent to France. Even her four bronze horses were dismantled and shipped away. Just as Venice had looted Constantinople, she was now recklessly plundered. *La Serenissima* made peace at a hefty price. Yet, her surrender in some ways helped to preserve the city; her enemies never opened fire with their devastating, modern guns and canons, Venice's fragile architecture and vulnerable population were saved from destruction.

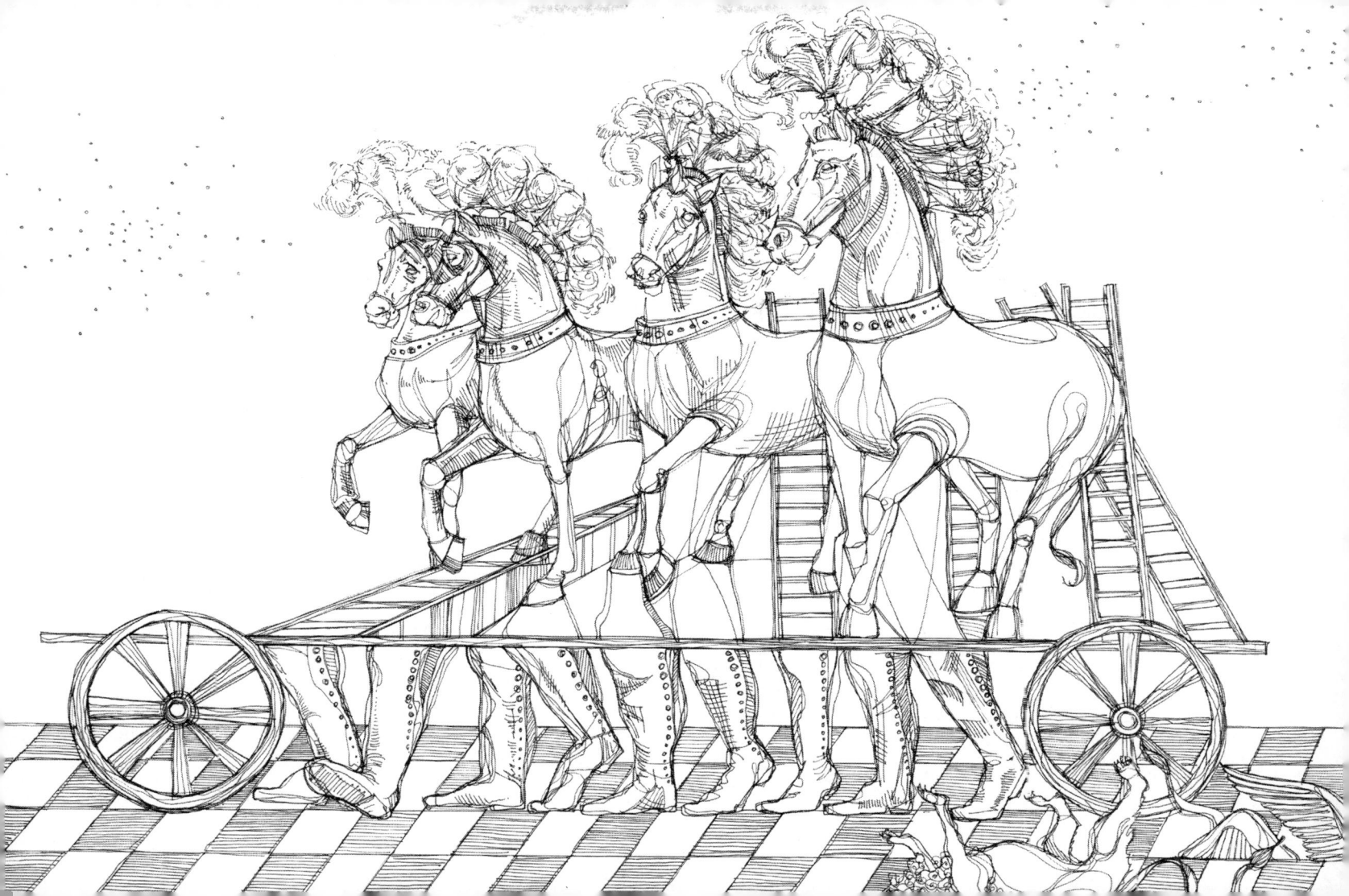

austrian rule and shifting occupation.

After falling at the mercy of one man, Venice was pulled into the torrential and turbid politics storming on the mainland. Just five months after the French invasion, Napoleon forced Hapsburg's Austria into peace and exchanged Venice for other lands. After eight short years, he returned in fury and reclaimed the lagoon. Though he had the intention of making a united kingdom in the north of Italy, nine years later, after a crushing defeat, Venice was nevertheless tossed back to Austria.

As power ebbed and flowed above her, each changing hand pulled the chains more taut. Venetians could do little more then act as spectators to their own fate, while trying not to drown. The French thoughtlessly filled in her canals, looted her reserves, and demolished revered structures. They built frivolous architecture, like a ballroom, for the growing demands of the French emperor. By the time the Hapsburg reign returned to the lagoon, Venetian buildings lay in ruins and much of her economy had seized. Her population was diminished to rags, and over one-quarter took to begging. Some residents barely survived bitterly cold winters and on occasion froze to death in her alleyways.

The Hapsburg's tried to revive Venice's deteriorated condition. They filled her ailing *Arsenale* with their own navy and made her ports tax-free. They illuminated her *Piazza*, reset the winged lion on top of its original column, and returned the four horses to the *Basilica di San Marco*. The Austrians shunted the city to take in more life from elsewhere. They built an extensive railway bridge across the whole lagoon, which allowed trains to bring in cargo and travellers into Venice in just minutes. The Austrians hooked Venice like a fish and permanently fastened her to the mainland.

Under foreign occupation, Venetians lost their voice. Surviving Venetians were even forced to fight under conscription for the sprawling Hapsburg Empire, in brutal battles. Their presses were censored and foreign print was forbidden, education was dictated and travel was carefully policed. All orders came directly from Vienna and were indiscriminately implemented by their authorities in the lagoon. Venice was no longer a remote island refuge, but a distant, subservient domain. She had lost autonomy. Foreign rule had made her almost unrecognizable.

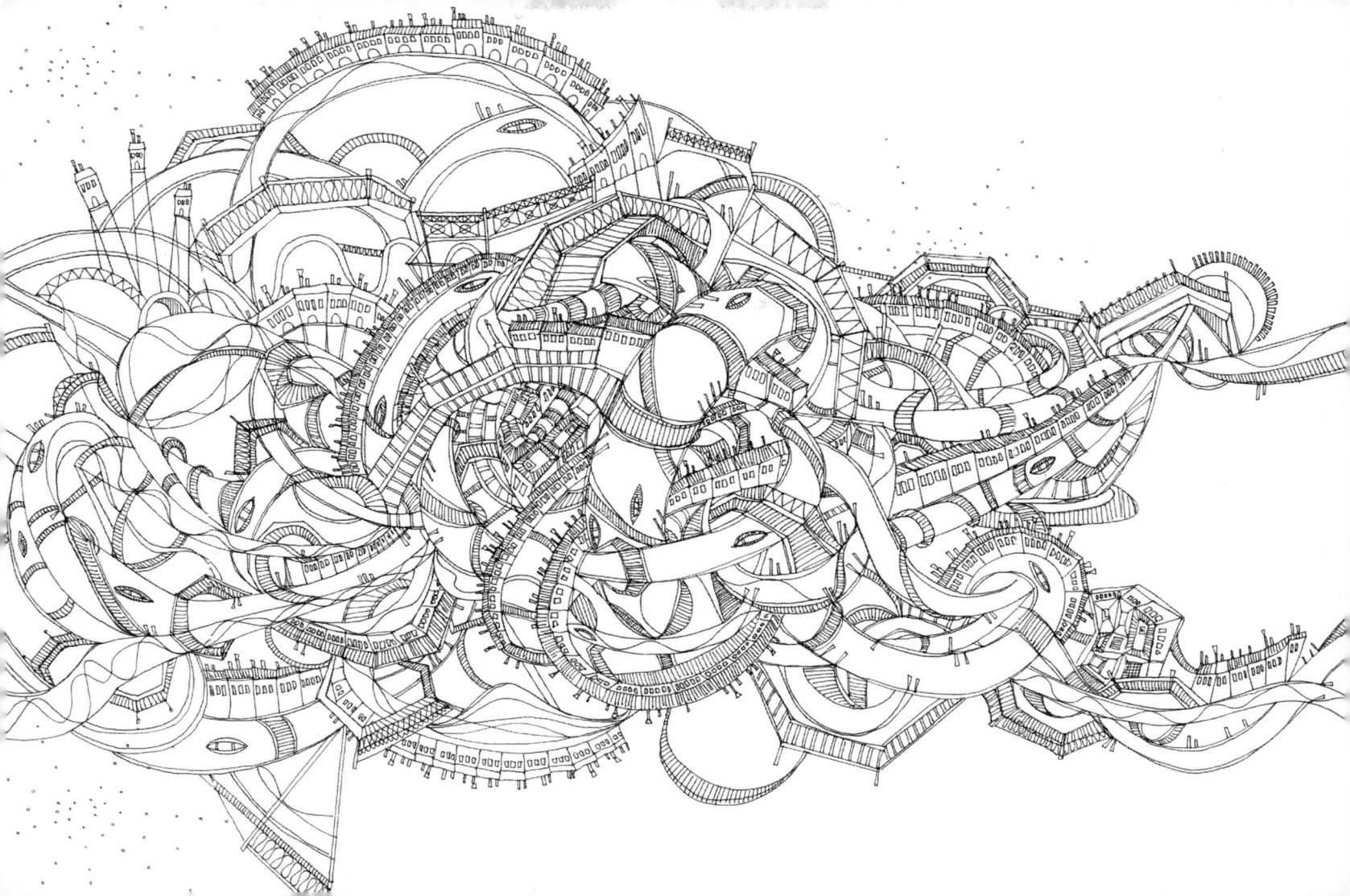

part six: perseverance

(19th century-present day)

foreign reign: suppression & liberties.

While Venice was lashed to the Hapsburg Empire, the European mainland was quaking from heavy protests against various powerful monarchies and its large regions began to fragment into smaller countries. In the late 1840s C.E. a call for independence echoed in the lagoon. A Jewish lawyer and activist, Daniele Manin, joined forces with the renowned patriot Nicolò Tommaseo to protest Austrian reign. They rallied significant support and held, mostly inconsequential, demonstrations outside of the *Caffè Florian*, while Austrian supporters sipped effervescent, orange *spritz* on the opposite side of the *Piazza*. Yet, after these two agitators were imprisoned in 1848 C.E., fiery Venetians protested for their release, reclaimed the *Arsenale*, raised the flag of the *Repubblica di San Marco*, and called for Manin to stand as their president.

The Hapsburg army was quick to extinguish these uprisings. They blockaded the city and relentlessly bombarded the lagoon with canons strategically placed along the railway bridge. For over seventeen months, the Venetians were imprisoned within the very waters that had once protected them. They desperately tried to scrape together a formidable resistance but were overwhelmed by famine and cholera.

For the third time in their history the Venetians fell under suppressive Austrian rule. After this surge, the Austrians increased their military presence and kept the Venetians in a state of cowardice and poverty. They diverted all business into their nearby port in Trieste; they gutted Venice's convoluted interior and constructed cast iron bridges so that they could easily charge through by foot; and in 1854 C.E., they constructed a rigid, steel pedestrian bridge, the first *Ponte dell'Accademia*, to cross over the Grand Canal, to keep the nautical Venetians under tighter control.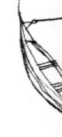

The Austrians dominated the Venetians until 1866 C.E., when they were forced out of their outpost by the Prussians, who had defeated the Austrian Imperial army on the mainland. Italian troops soon alleviated the Venetians, who then joined Cavour's independent Kingdom of Italy. This time around, while uniting in spirit with those on the mainland, a sense of liberty was reinstated within the lagoon. The passionate courage of Manin was honoured; the Venetians placed his tomb in *Basilica di San Marco*, and surrounded it with many fierce, stone lions. Slowly, they set to reconstruct their existence and dream future possibilities with their new hand of opportunities.

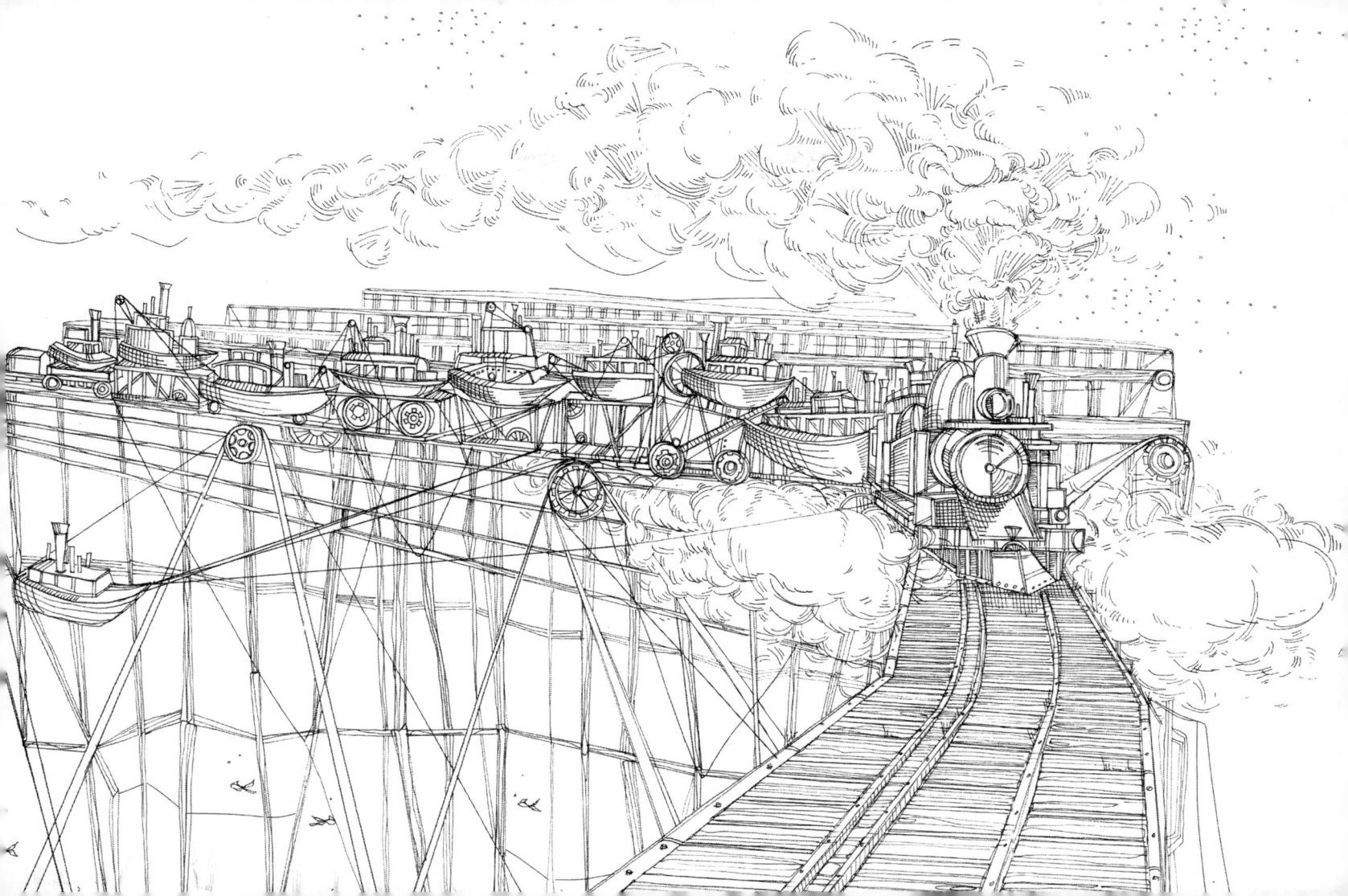

the romantics and beautiful decay.

The Austrians may have smothered Venetian autonomy, but her unique structure kept her immune from the many drastic changes of the Industrial Revolution. Her remote location, and tight, winding canals prevented many pulsing factories and coal-burning machines from dominating her core.

In the nineteenth century, the world around Venice quickly became mechanized: glass was molded in assembly lines instead of by skilled artisans; lace could be fabricated with machines instead of the delicate hands of ladies in Burano; ships moved using steam instead of wind and brawn; printed word flew off modern presses; and weaponry was mass-produced in previously unimaginable quantities. There came to be imitations of the *Arsenale* to produce every major commodity on the European mainland. Meanwhile, Venice had become so neglected that her buildings could have easily crumbled back into the lagoon. Tufts of weeds cracked through her stone. Saltwater fractured rows of bricks underneath layers of degrading plaster. Her petrified base served more as rickety crutches, barely supporting the buildings leaning and cowering above them. Yet, it was Venice's battered grandeur that captivated the English Romantics. They indulged in her remains while they explored their own melancholic emotions and ideas of perseverance.

The poet Lord Byron was one of the first outsiders to visit Venice after the Napoleonic wars. He immersed in her surviving spirit. He brashly swam her canals and raced hesitant Venetians down their own Grand Canal. Like Casanova, Byron fulfilled multiple, controversial love affairs. He expressed her essence in his popular ode to Venice, entitled *Childe Harold's Pilgrimage,* which contributed to her survival. After the Venetian rail linked to Milan in 1856 C.E., many poets and artists travelled to her shores. Foreigners brought back life to the still crippled city. They drafted fantastical impressions from their raw emotional experiences. Like the Romantics, they forever immortalized Venice on paper.

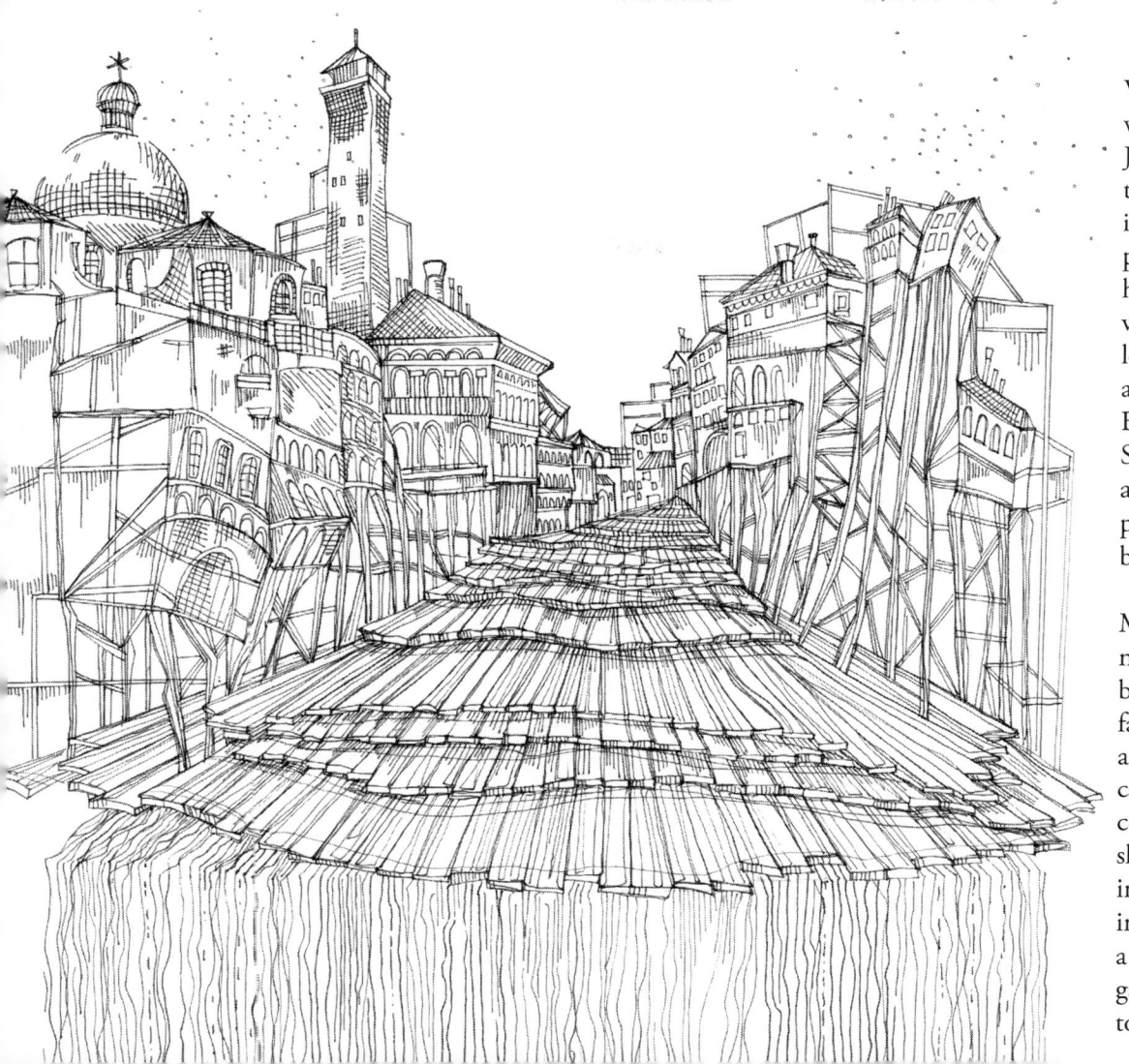

Venice was copiously studied, painted and written about through a variety of lenses. J. M. W. Turner stretched his imagination to paint hundreds of unparalleled, blurred images of the city, which were far from the precise detail of Canaletto. He focused on her dramatic lighting and shifting skies, which commonly devoured the city, leaving haunting, impressions. Venice also attracted the likes of Corot, Liszt, Shelley, Browning, Dickens, Manet, Whistler, Sargent, Nietzche, and Renoir, to name a few. Venice began to assume a new persona, which was mostly constructed by outsiders.

Meanwhile, her own needs remained neglected. For instance, Venice's *Lido* beach resorts began to pamper the more famous who were exploring her developing art scene and emerging *Biennale*, which came to showcase the best in international, contemporary art. Her visitor's notes and sketches glossed over her pressing peril and increasing destitution. Venice was made into a sort of fantasy. She had become a muse at the mercy of her visitors who gawked at her suffering and did little else to help revive her past glory.

preservation, modernism & restoration.

While Napoleon had many of Venice's dilapidated and *passé* buildings torn down, by the nineteenth century Venice was shinning as historic jewel in the rough. Many architects tried to address her crumbling state. They scrapped clean her facades and used modern materials to repair her structures. Her buildings were cast in a pristine and streamlined appearance, which no longer fit within the city's architectural succession. They were out of place. Clumsy.

John Ruskin, a leading art critic of the Victorian era, raged against the city's decay. He supported preservation and berated the destruction of any historical buildings, such as Palladio's church, *Santa Lucia*, when it was torn down to construct its namesake train station. Ruskin obsessively illustrated Venice's historical strata. He tenaciously recorded her details and measurements, and sketched her neglected structures, like the once lavish *Ca' d'Oro*, or "House of Gold". He found the poetry of her decay. He encouraged others to consider the stories beneath her scars.

Ruskin penned *The Stones of Venice,* which catalogued the city's history through her architecture. It fuelled the ongoing debate between the conservation and modernization, which had seemed to hit a standstill. For example, when the incongruous, Austrian-made, *Ponte dell'Accademia* was disassembled, any new designs to replace it were repeatedly rejected. By the beginning of the twentieth century, the prevailing mentality was *com'era, dov'era,* or "as it was, where it was".

This motto is more than exemplified in the recent restoration of the *Gallerie dell'Accademia.* Dating back to 1343 C.E., the building first acted as a *Scuola*, which was a charitable and religious organization within the Venetian community. It was transformed into a place of study by Napoleon, who encouraged its studio painters to access its museum archives. Restoring the *Accademia* raised enormous challenges: where to get funding, how to keep the space financially sustainable after its renovation, how to refurbish found materials in a way which does not destroy them, honouring both its memory and function.

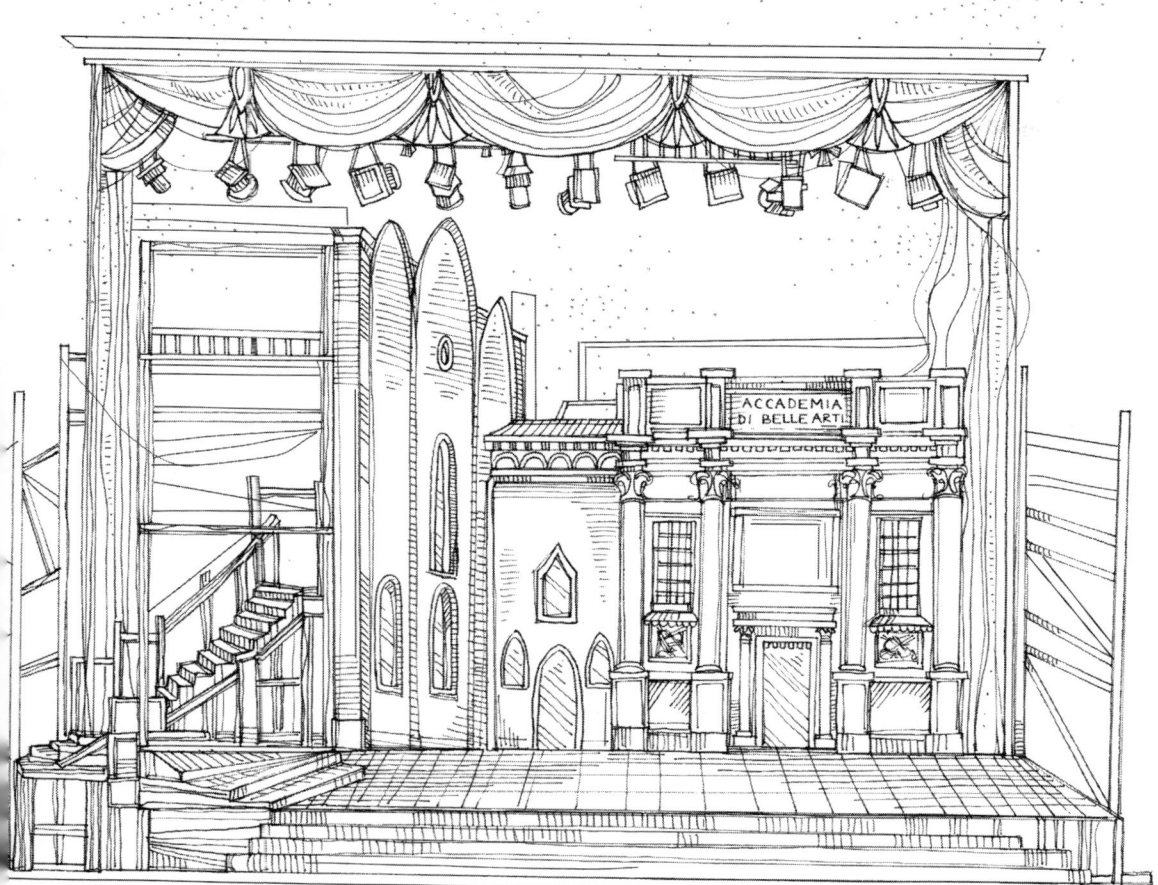

The *Accademia*'s courtyard was dug out, forming the only underground chamber in the lagoon. It was filled with machinery to regulate pumps and control temperatures. Additionally, a specialized mixture of pulverized Istrian stone and *latte di calcio* was painted over its century-old bricks to protect them from the lagoon's abrasive salt and bouts of humidity. While metal plates were placed over other areas of its walls, in order to protect and preserve its historical surfaces underneath. It was quite the effort to integrate new technology while maintaining the integrity of the building.

Similarly, in 1902 C.E., when the landmark, sixteenth-century *Campanile* dramatically crumbled to pieces in *Piazza*, any new building designs were cast aside. With new engineering supports within, and an added elevator, the *Campanile* was promptly reinstated to its previous outward form. With this predominant mindset, *com'era, dov'era*, the city became trapped in a specific space-time.

war, survival, and futurism.

During the First World War, with the Italian front close to the lagoon, Venetians heavily protected their city with scaffolding and sandbags. They swathed her statues in seaweed, and hid away their prized horses and valuables on the *terra firma*. But their efforts proved misdirected. When the Austro-Hungarians retreated it became apparent that Venice primarily suffered from decreased tourism and a stalled economy.

After the war, as Venice gained economic momentum, the Futurism movement exploded on her scene as a radical revolt against the past. Filippo Marinetti led other artists, such as Boccioni, Russolo, and Severini, to worship the machine, motors, velocity, revolving artillery, and everything that the Romantics would have rejected. In 1910 C.E., in opposition to the *Biennale*, from the top of the *Campanile* in *Piazza San Marco*, they released hundreds of thousands of provocative manifestos. Futurists implored the Venetians to make way for more industrial factories, to burn their gondolas, fill in their canals, eradicate their monarchy, and expel the Pope from their realm. They wanted release from their traditional identity and cultural stagnation.

As the Futurists sought a societal transformation, they also became intimately involved with Fascism in the 1920's and 1930's, and tied to Mussolini and Hitler, who led Venice into another world war. Even though many Italian partisans rallied support from Venetians while standing on the table tops in the *Caffè Florian*, they could not stop the Germans from invading the city in the summer of 1943 C.E. or from deporting large segments of her Jewish population shortly thereafter. The mainland was soon heavily bombed and, as they had in the earliest days of their civilization, many mainlanders fled into the lagoon, until they were liberated in 1945 C.E.

As the twentieth century whirred on, more factories and large smokestacks crowded the mainland's coastline. Cars roared alongside her railway line, while motorized boats, buses, and fire brigades, fueled by the fossilized remains of sea creatures, burned through her waters. Still, her canals were never filled in. Venice remained largely unhampered by the ubiquitous sounds of industrialization, and at any point within her city, one can still hear her surrounding waves kicking against her seawalls.

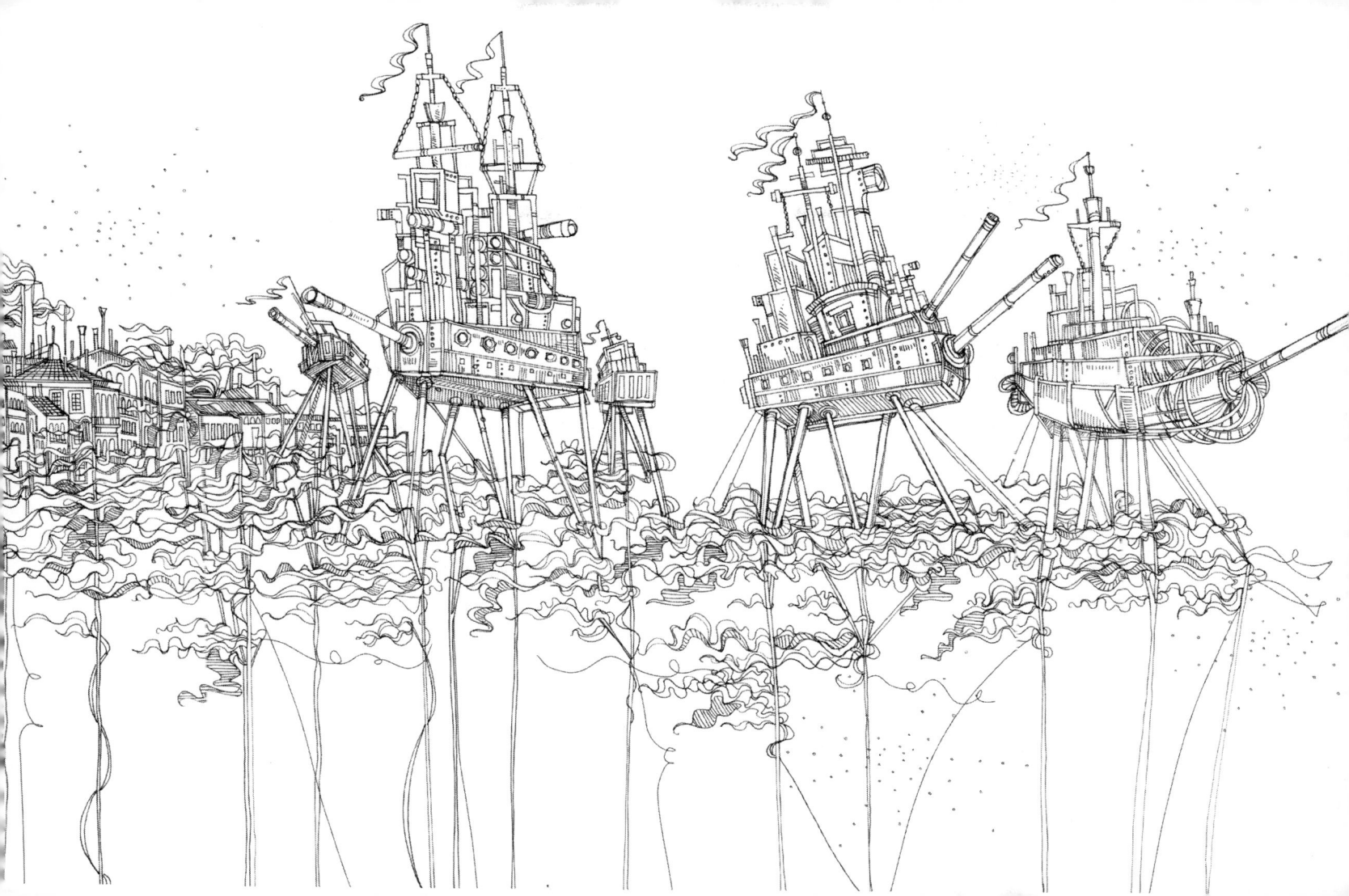

tourism, sustainability and the evolving stage.

Now, more than fifteen hundred years after her birth, millions upon millions have come to walk the magical remains of this fascinating empire. By the mid-nineteenth century, the amount of visitors travelling to Venice had already begun to outnumber her own residents. With the advent of tours and guidebooks, their invasion swelled to the point of usurping the free ledges and steps that pigeons used to overrun.

Presently, over twenty million tourists visit Venice in a year; most come just for a day. They travel in the bellies of large air crafts and towering cruise ships to float down her waters, proclaim love in a gondola, and surge like fish through her labyrinth. They come to see the radiance of her gilded domes, indulge in tasty gelato, buy some postcards or alluring tokens, and snap up a pizza. Visitors throng to picturesque archways or corners and capture the exact same, stunning image from hundreds of thousands of different cameras before they are off again for some other amusement. It's an unending photo shoot. A one-dimensional curiosity. But she is not there. Instead, they capture a relic who has walked out of the grave.

Throughout her history, Venice seized everything within her grasp to keep herself alive and thriving. And now, the city acts like a grand stage that draws in revolving actors from the furthest reaches of the world to perform the exact same script every day. Although the player's faces change, they have become as much a part of her modern incarnation; they pump a fleeting sense of life through her veins and keep her heart faintly beating.

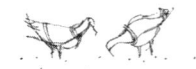

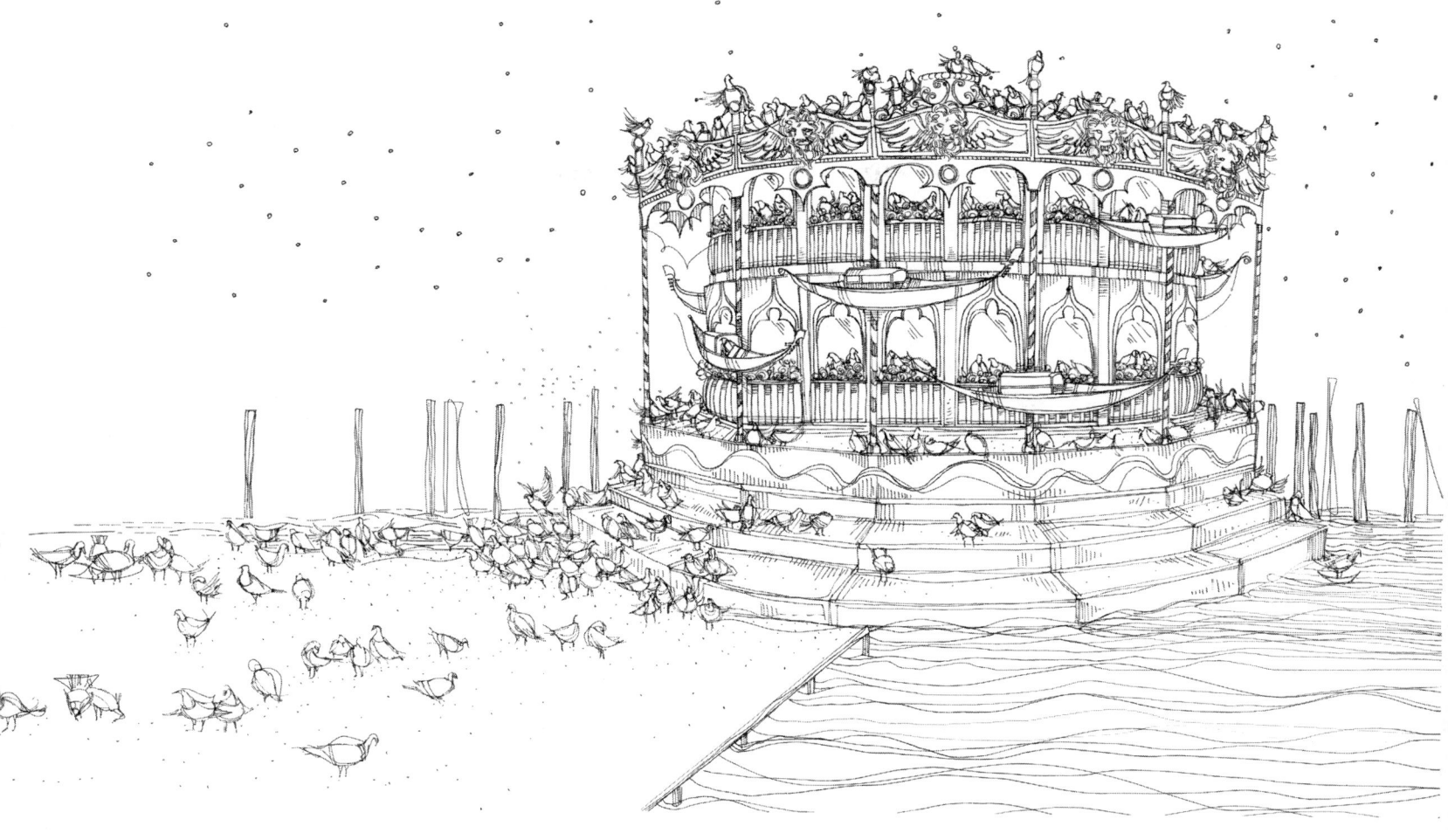

surrounding waters & flooding.

Although modernization increased Venice's carrying capacity, growing tourism has placed more stress on her fragile joints. This spectacular city still sits on an ancient, buried forest of logs, which is scarcely protected from the harsh, open sea by a few sand bars and sea walls. Remnants of rivers continue to lethargically grind down mountainous rock on the mainland and deposit silt on the lagoon floor, raising the water levels around her.

Furthermore, Venice has sunk deeper into the sea floor because her surface-dwellers and industries near Mestre squeezed and drained her aquifers below. This descent has left her more exposed to high tides, or *acqua alta*, especially after heavy rains or when the forceful, warm, *sirocco* winds blow down from Africa and kick up the lagoon's waves. When Venice was founded, the sea was almost five meters lower than its present level. As a matter of fact, had not humans intervened, the lagoon would have naturally filled in as much as five hundred years ago.

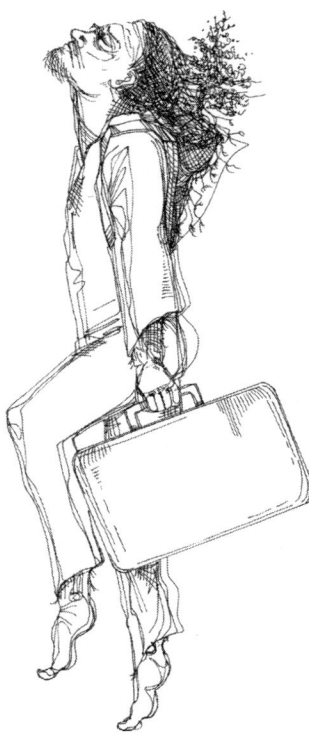

From her early beginnings, Venice was placed in an artificial, ecological state; Venetians carefully diverted her feeding rivers, dug up saltworks, and shored up her banks. Yet, her currents and tides had to be kept in balance they cleaned and scoured the city, carried wastes out to the sea, and renewed her murky waters harbouring below the city.

Throughout our modern era, many of Venice's canals have been recklessly filled in to make walkways. Lagoon entrances were dredged deeper for oil tankers, and her feeding rivers have been significantly diverted. Industry on the nearby coasts have also spewed out pollutants into her basin.

Although *acqua alta* have been noted as early as the thirteenth century, floods have become more frequent. In 1900 C.E., the city experienced high tides approximately ten times in a year; now she is menaced up to sixty times a year.

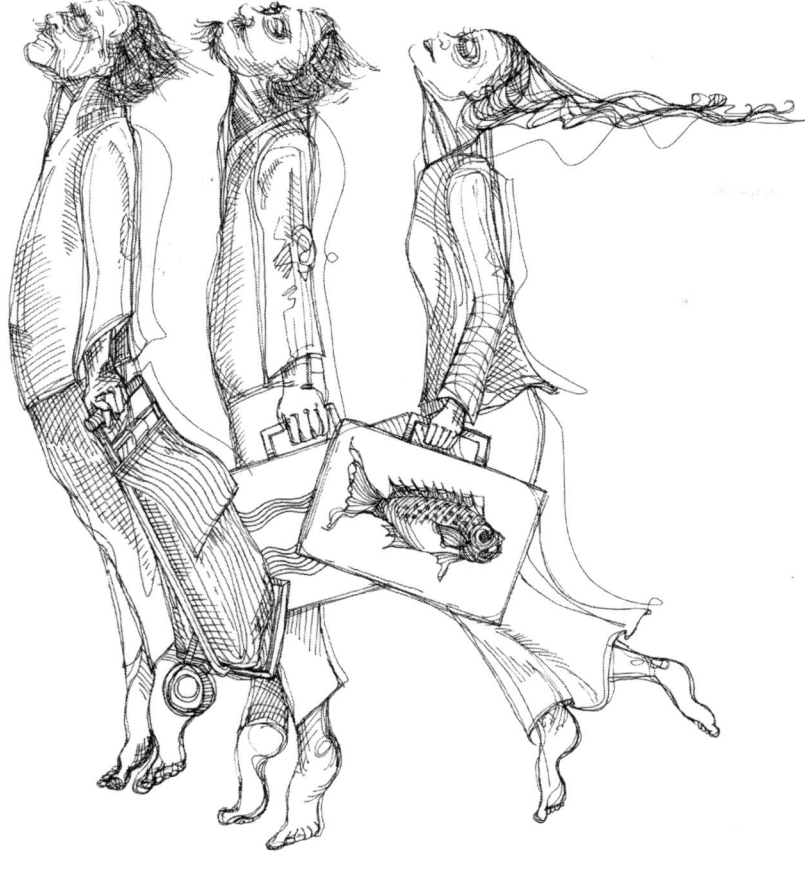

When sirens warn of *acqua alta* the city experiences a taste of her inevitable demise. In 1966 C.E., the afternoon tide rose almost two meters higher than average, and for a moment, swallowed the city whole. Sirens rang all evening as water relentlessly poured into every home and shop, devastating her exhausted habitat.

And yet, her inhabitants have come to adapt even to these uncertain conditions. Protective steel doors slid down, furnishings and merchandise are raised off the floor, water is patiently pumped out of buildings, and thigh-high rain boots are slipped on as Venetians wade through their daily lives. For her more hurried travellers, elevated boardwalks, or *passerelle*, on top of metal legs, are set out to keep feet and luggage dry. Tourists have even stepped out of their sopping shoes and stripped down for an unusual swim in the *Piazza San Marco*. All throughout the city, the tide comes and then goes, adumbrates the storm to come, and life goes on.

the mose project: parting from the sea.

Over a thousand years ago, after the Venetian fleet had returned from successfully conquering the majority of the Mediterranean, *Doge* Pietro Orseolo II began a tradition which formally committed the fate of Venetians to their surrounding waters. From his seven-storey high, golden gondola, called the *Bucintoro*, just past the Lido's sand bars, where the waters of the lagoon meet the edge of the Adriatic, the *doge* ceremoniously threw a golden ring into the sea to honour Venice's intimate relationship to her surrounding waters. *La Sensa* has continued every subsequent spring. But now, in order to evolve with the reality of their dynamic relationship, a new offering has been proposed by Venetians to the sea.

In the 1980's C.E., engineers began planning and devising a strategy to protect Venice from further destructive flooding. Just as its fabled namesake once parted the tides of Red Sea, the *MOSE* Project, *(MOdulo Sperimentale Elettromeccanico,* or "Experimental Electromechanical Module") attempts to tame the rising tides entering the lagoon.

The giant initiative involves the construction of a seventy-eight large, steel gates, strategically placed at the bottom of the sea, at three narrow passages in the lagoon's inlets of Lido, Malamocco and Chioggia. The mobile gates would be bolted down flat on the sea floor, then pumped with air in order to rise up and form a massive, protective shield against any surging high tides.

Criticism have arisen over this project's exorbitant price, constant delays, and a controversial slew of suspected political kickbacks. Fears have also been voiced concerning its possible ecological impacts on the lagoon's natural tidal flux and threatened avian habitats. Still, the *MOSE* Project continues to proceed slowly, passing its initial tests. It is far from a golden ring, but just as their ancestors toiled to forge an unlikely habitat, Venetians continue to persevere their existence in the sea.

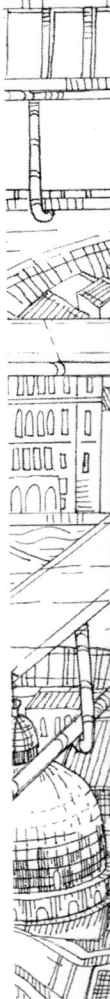

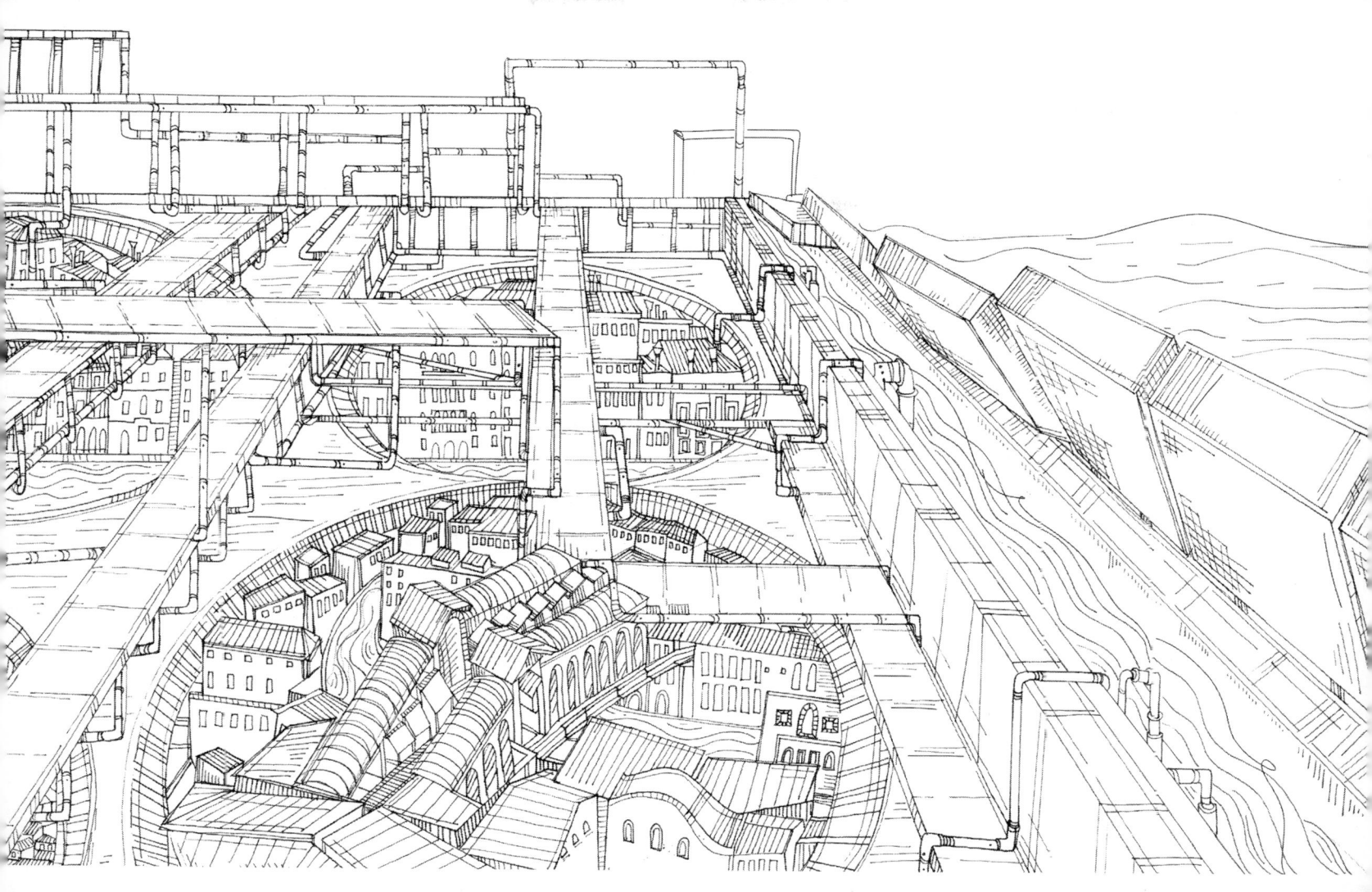

evolving technologies.

Other ideas using innovative technology and science have been proposed to help address Venice's tempestuous relation with water. New instruments and satellites are mapping different layers of the city, which can identify which areas are actually sinking and rising, down to the 50-meter scale. With more precise data, ecological and human impacts on this UNESCO world heritage site can be analyzed and addressed more effectively, if not too late. Simulations have also been run to test injecting seawater water underneath the city in order to increase the pore pressure between the grains of lagoon's sediment. After ten years of this continuous intervention the city may be potentially lifted 30 centimeters, complementing the MOSE project, if only to a small effect.

Synthetic biology and innovative building materials are also being designed which could reinforce Venice's decaying supports. One such research project utilizes metabolic materials called protocells, which are simple fatty bags with a chemical battery and potential promise. Protocells are currently being fine-tuned to deposit durable calcium carbonate on the city's underwater surfaces. In time, it is thought that they could grow a viable, reinforcing, limestone reef overtop the city's decaying wooden piles, and even sequester carbon dioxide in the process. Other applications of equally exciting technologies may help preserve and reimagine Venice, presenting a more hopeful fate for the city. Using all means available, Venetians continue on, always struggling to balance their niche in the protective and destructive waters which flow around them.

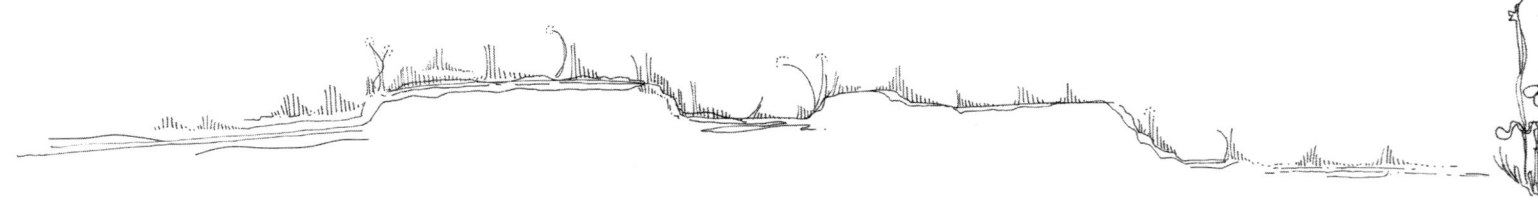

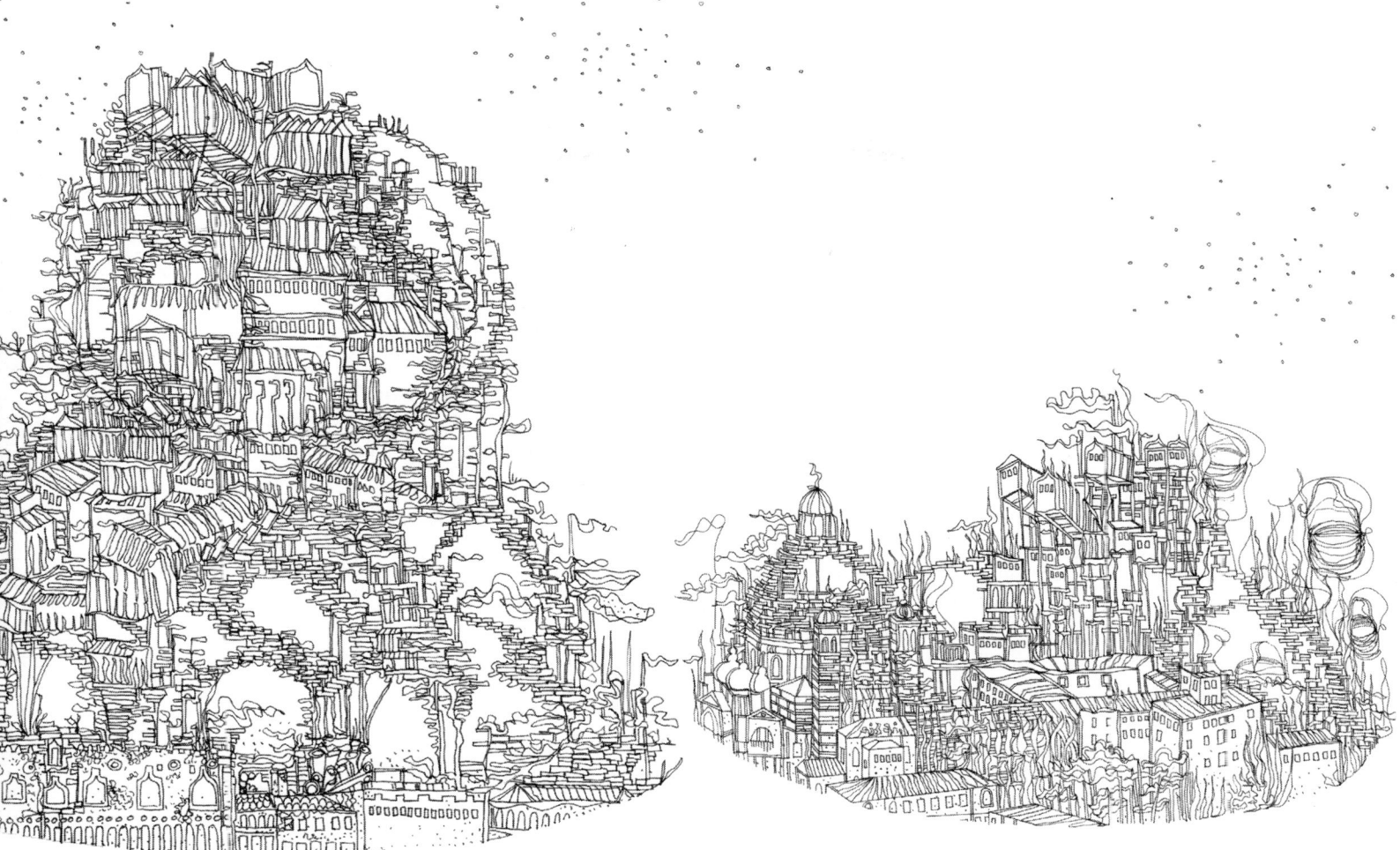

expanding archives.

Throughout the years, it has become more and more difficult for Venice to hold back the tide of change. As the global population continues to unsustainably extract and overconsume resources, and haphazardly manage its wastes, the Venetian microcosm has the opportunity to model how a city may adapt to brewing ecological imbalances.

Still, with less than sixty thousand residents, and tourists outnumbering locals on any given day, Venetian cultural identity weakens. Venice faces the danger of dissolving into a menagerie of foreign trinkets, even before succumbing to the powers of nature. And yet, because her demise is so beautifully framed, that all who set foot on her stones can consciously ignore her prognosis and fall madly in love with her as she is, again and again. It may be that the incessant habit of Venetians to record everything within their realm will lead to its ultimate preservation. The Republic was one of the most bureaucratic administrations of the past and it compiled one of the most extensive analogue archives.

The memories and functions of the lives and activities of Venetians and their trading partners throughout the Mediterranean have been preserved in tenaciously detailed wills, contracts, maps, stocks, shipping records, taxation documents, and state minutes, to name a few sources, over centuries.

Her dense accounts now lie in over eighty kilometers of shelf space in the *Archivo di Stato*, and are being digitalized and translated through several ambitious projects. Memories of the Republic will be kept safe from any degradation and available for the public to access freely. From all of this data, we can now imagine that this information can be used in the future to recreate her past. The Republic may be artificially rebuilt and placed in an augmented reality, combining her historical details with geographical space-time, emulating a possible picture of a picture of her fascinating past. Meanwhile, places like Las Vegas, in the United States, and Dalian, in China, have already cloned the city, if only, her physical shell.

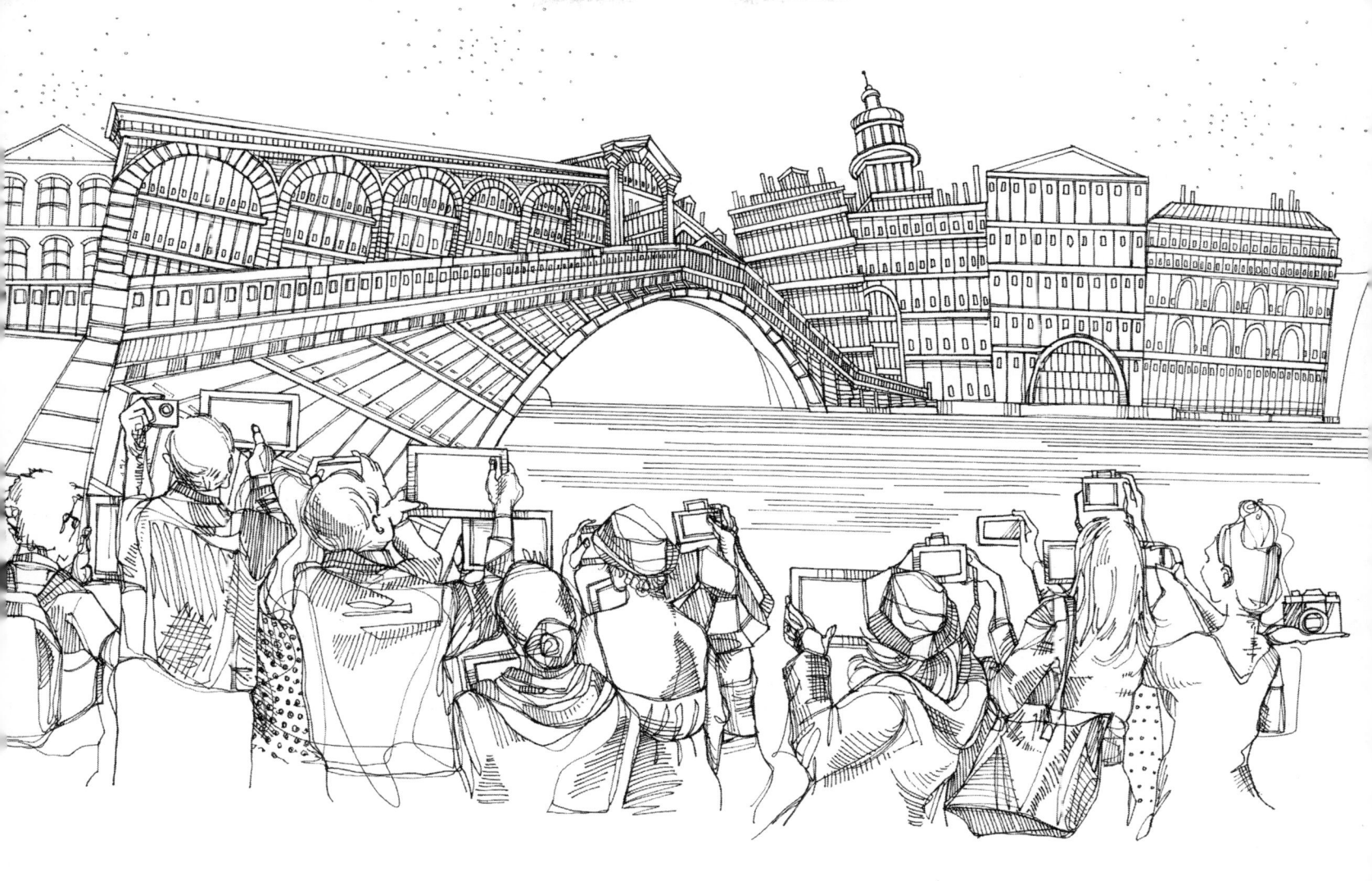

sempre dritto. ("always forward")

The inevitable end of the city of Venice reminds us that even the grandest of empires can be weathered into oblivion. Like mountains, all structures can be ground into a pile silt, by drop by drop of water.

It is possible that we can place ourselves into the Venetian narrative and propel her story. Together, we implore her to tenaciously survive in unexpected ways. But we must learn her story, and understand the heart of her fading spirit, for it calls use to be inventive, to push through adversity, to create beauty amongst the seemingly impossible; this is what it means to be *Venetian*.

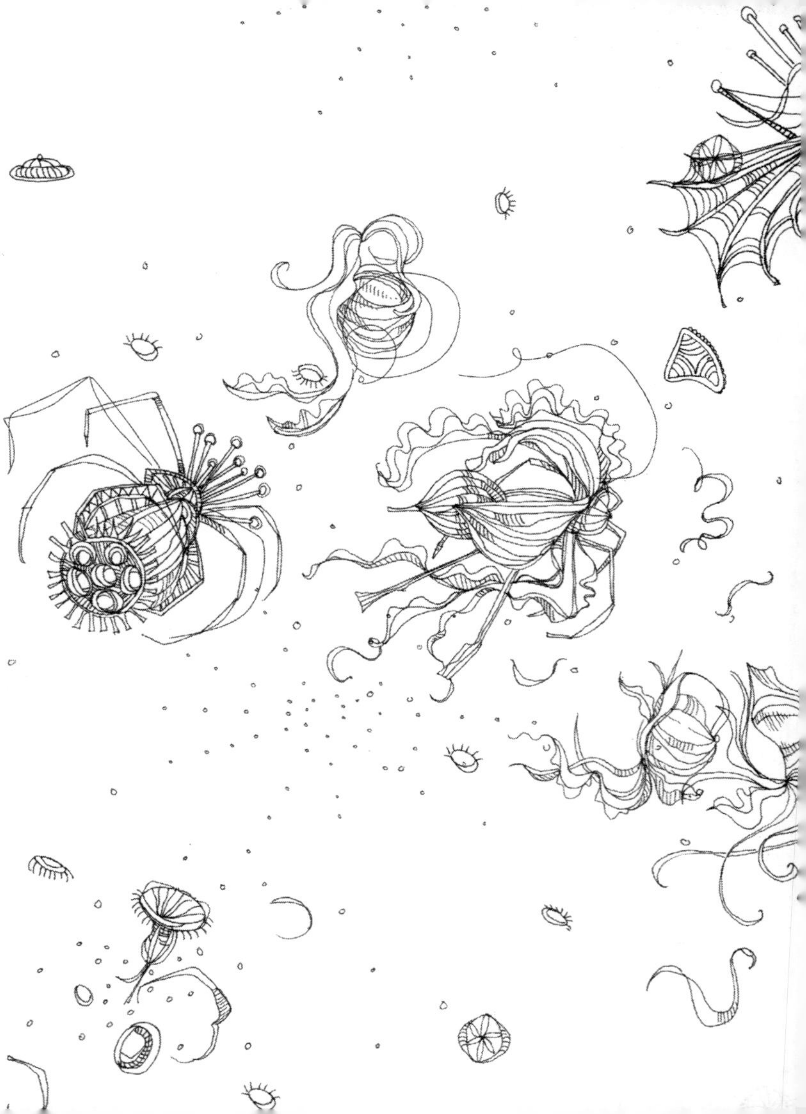

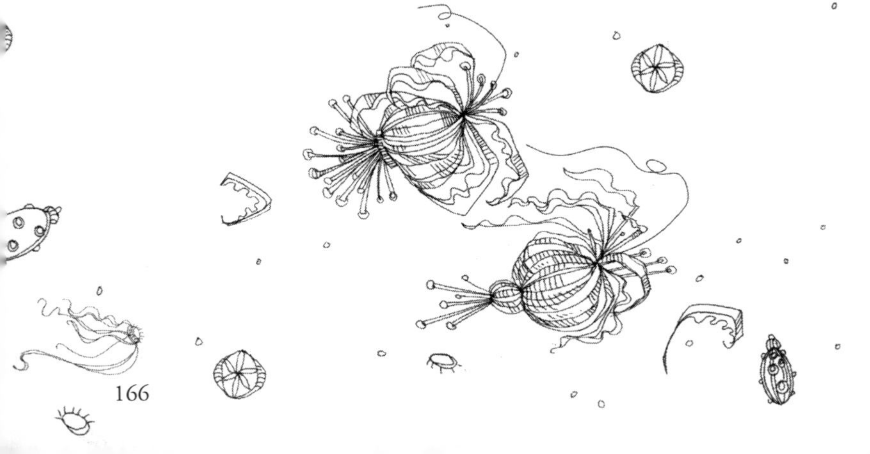

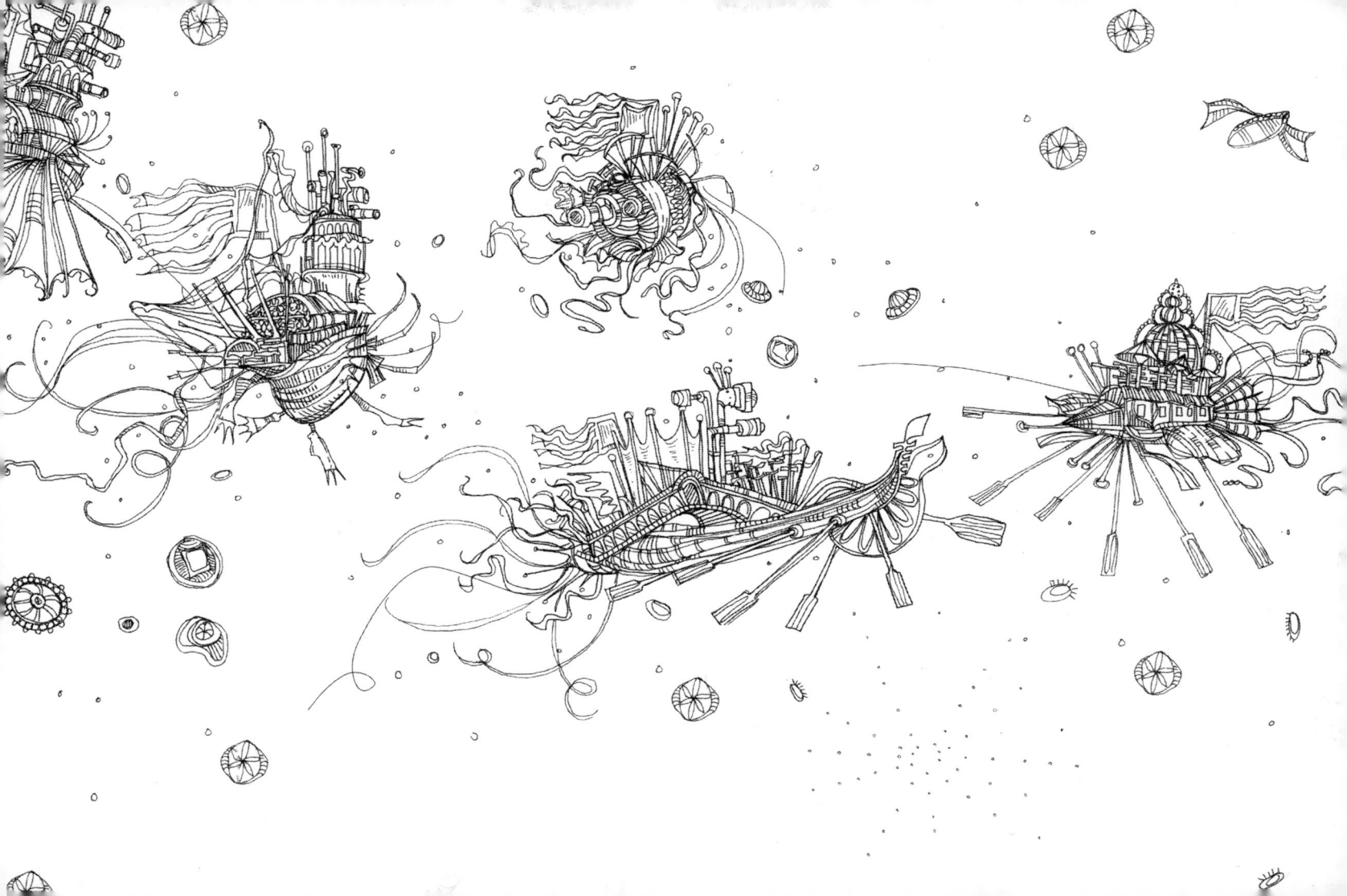

historical inspiration.

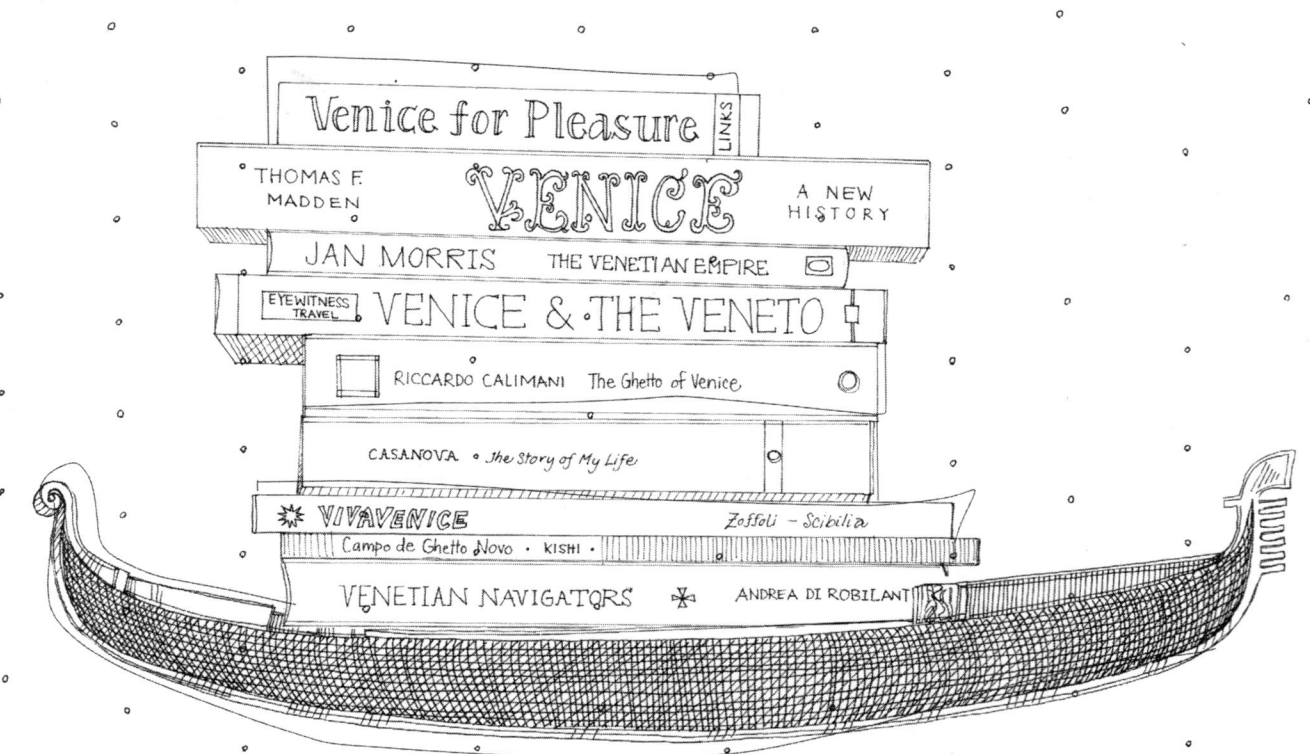

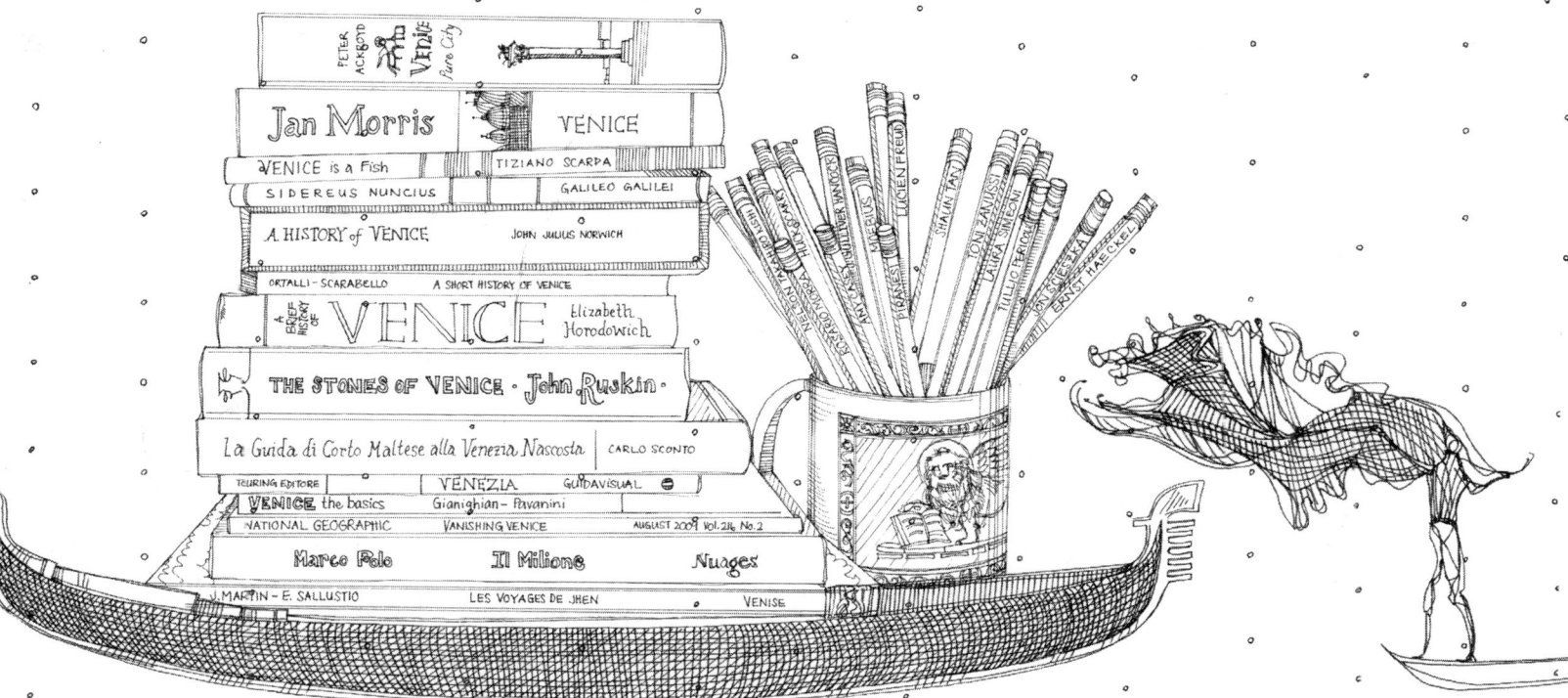

about the author.

Sarah Pierroz is an international educator, who has extensively travelled the world. She wrote and illustrated this story while teaching Visual Arts and Environmental Sciences at the United World College of the Adriatic, in Italy.

She fell madly in love with Venice and spent close to a decade exploring the Republic's ubiquitous remnants throughout the Mediterranean basin. Finding hidden stories of a space and a deeper connection with history inspires her to share.

Born in Canada, she studied the multi-disciplinary Arts & Sciences Programme at McMaster University, as well as the Artist in the Community Education Specialization at Queen's University.

She is currently based in South East Asia, casting her net wider, chasing another story .